INTERNATIONAL HEALTH

A North-South Debate

PAN AMERICAN HEALTH ORGANIZATION
Pan American Sanitary Bureau • Regional Office of the
WORLD HEALTH ORGANIZATION
525 Twenty-third Street, N.W.
Washington, D.C. 20037, U.S.A.

1992

PAHO Library Cataloguing in Publication Data

Pan American Health Organization
    International Health: A North-South Debate
    Washington, D.C.: PAHO, © 1992.
    xxxiii + 259 pages

    ISBN 92-75-12081-1

    I. Title
    1. PAHO   2. World health
    3. Public health—education   4. Technical cooperation
    NLM WA 540.1

ISBN 92-75-12081-1

© Pan American Health Organization, 1992

Foreword

Carlyle Guerra de Macedo

This book is based on the material presented and discussions held at the Seminar-Workshop on "International Health: A Field of Professional Study and Practice" held at Quebec, Canada, from March 18 to 20, 1991. That event brought together a group of public health specialists, sociologists, economists, ecologists, university professors from the United States of America, Canada, and certain countries in Latin America, and officials in international organizations and technical and financial cooperation agencies.

The meeting was convened by the Pan American Health Organization/World Health Organization, the Ministry of Health and Social Welfare of Canada, and the Ministry of Health and Social Services of Quebec to consider three basic subjects:

- Analyze the major challenges facing health in the Region of the Americas and their implications for training international health workers.
- Examine experiences in the training of personnel in the field of international health which are being carried out in the hemisphere.
- Establish bases for formulating the concept of international health and proposing guidelines for future work.

These objectives are recorded in the framework of a recognition of the importance of international action to achieve better health conditions for our populations.

The term "international health" has been and is customarily used to designate educational, assistance, technical, or financial programs and activities conducted by various governmental or nongovernmental bodies, agencies, and institutions. In the face of this variety of actors and actions, we should ask: Why international health? What does international health mean? and What are its basic practices? The best known of these practices is technical cooperation, and it is to it that the activities of the Pan American Health Organization have been oriented since its creation in 1902; it is thus the oldest intergovernmental institution in the field of international health.

In carrying out its work of technical cooperation with the countries and in the context of activities to help develop leadership in the health field in the region, the Pan American Health Organization began to develop an International Health Training Program in 1985 which is part of a special presentation in this book. Through this program it has been possible to stimulate reflection and analysis in the field of international health, a field whose importance grows daily in an ever more internationalized world in which a region in which international action and joint efforts between countries become more necessary.

This effort by the Organization occurs in a context of a scenario characterized by a growing interest in the field of international health in the developed countries. That interest is manifested by the organization of international health units, especially in universities, the execution of educational and research experiments in developing countries, and the increase in postgraduate courses, particularly in schools of public health, a situation which is also the subject of another presentation in this publication.

Various seminars and publications about the subject take the foregoing into account, especially in the United States of America, a situation which contrasts with the absence of educational experiments and reflection on the subject in schools of public health in Latin America despite the development of an abundant Latin American theoretical production in the field of social sciences applied to health dealing with topics related to this field.

Progress in analysis of the subject within the Organization and the interest shown by some Latin American schools of public health, particularly in Mexico and Brazil, were a stimulus toward organizing this meeting. In addition, the decision to convene this event received broad support from the Government of Canada through its Ministry of Health and Social Welfare and the Ministry of Health and Social Services of Quebec, agencies which since the creation of the international health program have provided major collaboration and stimulus in its development.

The meeting offered an opportunity for fruitful exchange between representatives of the North and South in the region, which is set out in both the content of the papers as well as the analytic summary drawn up from the basic statements in the presentations and the discussions held about each topic.

The studies presented are grouped in two parts. The first contains those related to the major health challenges in the Americas and their impact on international health, and the second groups those aimed more specifically at analysis of the concept and practice of international health, among which those dealing with educational experiences occupy an important place.

We hope that the contents of this book will not only help stimulate collective reflection and a productive exchange among health workers in the region about the field of international health, but also increase the execution of activities which through collaboration and joint action between the countries will tend to ensure a better future for health in the Americas.

Contents

The Editors, Contributors, and Participants

The editing and publication of *International Health: A North-South Debate* is an initiative of the Division of Human Resources Development of the Pan American Health Organization.

The Human Manpower Development Program's mission is to collaborate with the governments of the Region of the Americas in strengthening their capacities for coordinating, planning, training, and using human resources to improve the health levels of their populations.

The editing team consisted of José Roberto Ferreira, Charles Godue, and María Isabel Rodríguez.

The papers which appear in this book are versions revised by the authors of the principal presentations during the conference. The authors' views are their own and not necessarily those of the Pan American Health Organization or the institutions with which they are affiliated, and they are responsible for the accuracy of the information, which is as of early 1991, in their papers. Those who took part in the conference or contributed to the publication of this volume, together with the positions they occupied at the time of the Conference in March 1991, are:

Gilles Arès, a Canadian political scientist, is a consultant to the Ministry of Transportion of Quebec at Quebec.

Paul F. Basch, an American physician, is Professor of International Health, Department of Health Research and Policy, Stanford University, Stanford, California.

E. Richard Brown, an American sociologist, is Associate Professor in the School of Public Health at the University of California, Los Angeles.

Paulo Marchiori Buss, a Brazilian physician, is Director of the School of Public Health at Rio de Janeiro.

Eduardo S. Bustelo, an Argentinian economist, is Director of the United Nations Children's Fund (UNICEF) in Argentina at Buenos Aires.

Fernando Chacón, a Mexican public health specialist, is Coordinator of the International Studies Unit in Public Health, National Institute of Public Health, Cuernavaca.

André Pierre Contandriopoulos, a Canadian economist, is Director of the Interdisciplinary Health Research Group and a Professor in the Departments of Health Administration and Social and Preventive Medicine at the University of Montreal.

Octavio de Caso, a Mexican physician, is Director of Promotion and Development in the Mexican Foundation for Health at Mexico City.

Gilles Dussault, a Canadian sociologist, is Acting Director of the Department of Health Administration at the University of Montreal.

Ray Elling, an American sociologist, is Professor in the Department of Community Medicine at the University of Connecticut Health Center, Farmington.

José Roberto Ferreira, a Brazilian physician, is Coordinator of the Health Manpower Development Program in the Pan American Health Organization, Washington, D.C.

Julio Frenk, a Mexican physician, is Director General of the National Institute of Public Health at Cuernavaca.

Alfredo Gastal, a Brazilian economist, is Director of the Environment and Human Settlements Division in the Economic Commission for Latin America and the Caribbean (ECLAC), Santiago, Chile.

Jacques E. Girard, a Canadian physician, is Professor of Community Health in the Faculty of Medicine, Laval University, Quebec.

Charles Godue, a Canadian physician, is Associate Director of the Department of Community Health, Maisonneuve Rosemont Hospital, Montreal.

Eric Goon, a Malaysian physician, is Director of the Division of Development of Human Resources for Health in the World Health Organization, Geneva.

Lise Gravel, a Canadian community health specialist, is Advisor on International Cooperation in the Directorate General of Planning and Evaluation, Ministry of Health and Social Services, Quebec.

Carlyle Guerra de Macedo, a Brazilian physician, is Director of the Pan American Health Organization, Washington, D.C.

Polly F. Harrison, an American anthropologist, is Director of the Division of International Health, Institute of Medicine, Washington, D.C.

Margaret Hilson, a Canadian public health nurse, is Assistant Executive Director, Canadian Public Health Association, Ottawa.

Margarita Hurtado, a Colombian biologist, is resident of the Training Program in International Health, Pan American Health Organization, Washington, D.C.

Robert F. Knouss, an American physician, is Deputy Director of the Pan American Health Organization, Washington, D.C.

Paul-A. Lamarche, a Canadian sociologist, is Associate Deputy Minister in the Ministry of Health and Social Services, Quebec.

Frédéric Lesemann, a Canadian sociologist, is Professor in the School of Social Services at the University of Montreal.

Miguel Malo, an Ecuadorian physician, is resident of the Training Program in International Health, Pan American Health Organization, Washington, D.C.

Patricio Márquez, an Ecuadorian sociologist, is a specialist in the Division of Population, Health, and Nutrition at the World Bank, Washington, D.C.

Maurice McGregor, a Canadian physician, is Chairman of the Health Technology Evaluation Council, Quebec.

Jean-Paul Menu, a French physician, is Chief Medical Officer for Human Resources Management, World Health Organization, Geneva.

Laura Nervi, an Argentinian anthropologist, is consultant to the Pan American Health Organization, Washington, D.C.

Vic Neufeld, a Canadian physician, is Director of the International Health Center at McMaster University, Hamilton, Ontario.

Ulysses B. Panisset, a Brazilian physician, is a consultant in the Health Policy Program at the Pan American Health Organization, Washington, D.C.

Norbert Préfontaine, a Canadian, is Assistant Deputy Minister, Intergovernmental and International Affairs Branch, Department of National Health and Welfare, Ottawa.

Eleutério Rodrigues Neto, a Brazilian physician, is Professor at the University of Brasília, researcher at the Public Health Studies Unit (NESP), University of Brasília, and Legal Advisor to the Chamber of Deputies, Brasília.

María Isabel Rodríguez, a Salvadorean physician, is Coordinator of the Training Program in International Health, Pan American Health Organization, Washington, D.C.

Mario Rovere, an Argentinian physician, is a Regional Advisor in the Health Manpower Development Program, Pan American Health Organization, Lima, Peru.

Steven Simon, a Canadian physician, is Director of the Health and Population Directorate, Canadian International Development Agency, Ottawa.

José María Salazar Buchelli, a Colombian physician, is Chief of External Affairs Coordination, Pan American Health Organization, Washington, D.C.

Milton Terris, an American physician, is Editor of the *Journal of Public Health Policy*, South Burlington, Vermont, USA.

Carlos Vidal, a Peruvian physician, is a former Minister of Health, Lima, Peru.

Acknowledgments

The idea of publishing *International Health: A North-South Debate* originated after the conference entitled "International Health: A Field of Professional Study and Practice," which was held by the Pan American Health Organization in collaboration with the Ministry of Health and Social Welfare of Canada and the Ministry of Health and Social Services of Quebec from March 18 to 20, 1991, at Quebec.

The Pan American Health Organization wishes to thank the Governments of Quebec and Canada as well as their respective ministries for their hospitality and indispensable support in holding the conference. We especially wish to thank Lise Gravel, of the Ministry of Health and Social Services of Quebec, for her dynamism and efficiency in organizing the meeting.

The editors also wish to thank the experts who took part in the meeting and ensured its success. They are Eduardo S. Bustelo, of Argentina; Paulo Machiori Buss and Eleutério Rodrigues Neto, of Brazil; Lise Gravel and Margaret Hilson as well as Gilles Arès, André Pierre Contandriopoulos, Paul-A. Lamarche, Frédéric Lesemann, Maurice McGregor, Vic Neufeld, and Norbert Préfontaine of Canada; Alfredo Gastal, of Chile; Polly F. Harrison and Paul Basch, E. Richard Brown, Ray Elling, and Milton Terris, of the United States; Julio Frenk, of Mexico; Carlos Vidal, of Peru; Eric Goon and Jean-Paul Menu, of the World Health Organization, Geneva, and finally, our Director, Carlyle Guerra de Macedo; our colleagues, Robert F. Knouss, Ulysses B. Panisset, Mario Rovere, and José María Salazar Buchelli, as well as our Residents of the Training Program in International Health, Margarita Hurtado and Miguel Malo, of the Pan American Health Organization.

We wish to express our recognition to Gilles Dussault, Jacques Girard, and Steven Simon, of Canada; Fernando Chacón and Octavio de Caso, of Mexico, and Patricio Márquez, of the World Bank, for their participation in the discussion as observers.

Finally, for logistical support in preparing this book, our warm thanks to Sylvia Chavarry and Olga Ringgold for secretarial work; to Eleana Gómez and Gustavo Strittmatter, for their support in its translation and publication, and to Laura Nervi for her outstanding synthesis of the meeting.

The Editors

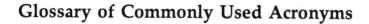

Glossary of Commonly Used Acronyms

CEPAL	Comisión Económica para América Latina (changed to Comisión Económica para América Latina y el Caribe de las Naciones Unidas; = ECLAC)
CIEPP	Centro Interdisciplinario para el Estudio de Políticas Públicas (Interdisciplinary Center for Research in Public Policy), Buenos Aires
ECLAC	Economic Commission for Latin America and the Caribbean (United Nations)
FLACSO	Facultad Latinoamericana de Ciencias Sociales (Latin American School of Social Sciences), Santiago and Mexico City
GATT	General Agreement on Tariffs and Trade
IMF	International Monetary Fund
NESP	Núcleo de Estudos em Saúde Pública (Public Health Studies Unit), University of Brasília
NGO	nongovernmental organization
OECD	Organization for Economic Cooperation and Development
PAHO	Pan American Health Organization
PNUD	Programa de las Naciones Unidas para el Desarrollo (United Nations Development Program)
PREALC	Programa Regional de Empleo para América Latina y el Caribe (Regional Program on Employment for Latin America and the Caribbean; a component of the International Labor Organization), Santiago
SELA	Sistema Económico Latinoamericana (Latin American Economic System), Caracas
TCDC	Technical cooperation among developing countries
UNDP	United Nations Development Program
UNICEF	United Nations Children's Fund
WHO	World Health Organization

Preface

Norbert Préfontaine

In March of 1991, I had the pleasure of addressing a WHO/PAHO seminar on international health. At that time, I suggested the need to define what international health is and who its practitioners could or should be. I think those questions remain as relevant today as they were then.

Just what, then, is international health? Is it a clearly distinct discipline? A specialty like cardiology or public health? Are there international health providers, international health consumers? Or is "international health" more a descriptive word to qualify the area in which those in the health field at the international level work?

In order to determine the necessary qualities of an international health worker, we might perhaps analyze in greater depth exactly what an intentional health worker does at the present time and identify the skills he or she must possess to operate efficiently.

I would not be surprised to have it suggested that the skills required t the international level are identical to those required for health workers at the national level. The major concerns of international health are national and multinational problems rather than international ones. In actual fact, a problem present in a number of countries is a multinational problem and not necessarily an international one.

Today more than ever we consider health a multisectorial field. We therefore have need, at the national level, of people with backgrounds in anthropology, sociology, political science, epidemiology, marketing, administration, communication, law—in other words, we need "universalists" as much as we do technicians.

In my opinion, international health also has as much need of generalists as it does of specialists with the acquired baggage of what we might call "international health sciences" (a specialty for which I personally would have great difficulty defining clearly enough to devise a master's degree program).

Friends to whom I have spoken about this have told me that the expression "international health" covers such things as diseases transmitted by human and animal migrations, environmental pollution (particularly of air and water)—in other words, phenomena which know no boundaries. I would doubt, however, that those seeking to have international health recognized as a field of occupational endeavor would be satisfied with such a narrow definition. Creation of a master's degree or doctorate in international health will require that the essential elements of the discipline be defined.

We are still a long way from that process. This report may help us determine how we do so and, more importantly, whether we should do so.

Overview of the Quebec Meeting

José Roberto Ferreira, Charles Godue,
Laura Nervi, and María Isabel Rodríguez

The meeting at Quebec from March 18 to 20, 1991, called "International Health: A Field of Professional Study and Practice" made clear the pertinence of a meeting whose subject was an analysis of the status of thinking in the field of international health.

As the sessions revealed, that pertinence was emphasized from three viewpoints. The first was represented by those participants who held that the meeting could create a landmark by helping advance from the old to the new international health, from the colonial or neocolonial idea which has reigned until now to an independent-cooperative model. The second viewpoint was represented by those who thought that beyond a break, the meeting established the status of the question in the field and to what point it had advanced, and who were concerned about the impact it might have on formulating new approaches to the subject. Finally, some participants stressed the relationship between public health and international health, and noted that the meeting disclosed certain limitations on explanations provided exclusively by the health sector.

With the idea of recovering some of the central points in the discussion, some of the items of collective reflection are dealt with quite schematically in the first section below, while aspects considered central to defining a field of study and practice are taken up in the second. Finally, a few proposals for developing the field of international health as to the production of information and training of human resources are enumerated in the third section.

Recapitulation: Toward the construction of an alternative to the classic international health approach

On the basis of the discussions which took place during the meeting, it is possible to identify the existence of at least three approaches to the question of international health according to the boundaries of their subjects of study. Indeed, this was the aspect dealt with most extensively during the discussions.

International health approached from the viewpoint of delimiting its subject matter does not exhaust all the aspects which various authors have taken into consideration in defining the field. The approaches which are implicit in an equal number of meanings of the idea of international health, using different variables, have been the subject of a survey which is set out in one of the studies published here. Such approaches involve other ways of defining priorities, theoretical frameworks, and areas of application.[3]

The first of the three approaches identified during the meeting, which might be called the "classical approach," construes its subject of study and intervention as health in the underdeveloped countries and, in some instances, adds minorities and marginal groups in the central countries to this delimitation. This approach basically occurs in most of the international health programs offered by schools of public health in the United States.

The second approach tries to go beyond the classical approach by highlighting the need to construct a "new international health" whose subject would not be defined by delimitation based on the level of development achieved by countries but by recognition that there are national and international arenas. International health would be the correlate of public health on the plane of the ... "phenomena, links, actions, and interactions in the health-disease process that occur among the members, and in the territories of the international community."[2]

Finally, the third approach joins the international dimensions of health with health as an international matter. It is differentiated from the first in that it does not limit its subject to the underdeveloped countries; on the contrary, it characterizes a view of that kind as ethnocentric. And it is differentiated from the second by not giving priority to the national-international relationship in its delimitation but rather to the structure, processes, and relationships of world power which in turn and to a different extent and in different ways affect the configuration of the health-disease process and the care systems within each national unit.

The classical approach. The discussions during the meeting revealed the structural features of the model underlying the classical approach to international health. There was basic agreement as to the characteristics of those features.

The features in question refer to both the definition of the subject of study and the practices stemming from it.

In trying to present the characteristics of the classic model schematically, as discussed during the meeting, the ideological nature of the definition of the subject of study which, based on an ethnocentric concept, defines the subject of international health in relation to the "others" is seen. This definition of the "other" involves an attempt to understand what is different by focusing on an implicit "we." The "other" may be peripheral countries or minorities in the central countries. Public health is limited to explaining and intervening in the health question of the central countries, sometimes by excluding minorities. On the basis of this concept, the subject of public health is thus defined on the basis of this implicit "we," while that of international health is constructed in relation to the cultural or economic "other."

This definition is not based on a relational analysis, i.e., on an approach that explains the emergence of a state of development (for example, technologic underdevelopment) through observation of those general processes which produce states of technologic overdevelopment on the one hand, associated with situations of technologic underdevelopment on the other.

Indeed, in this approach each category (underdeveloped countries or minorities) appears as a total system, to explain which it is only necessary to refer to the internal functions and relationships of the system.

In this way, the asymmetry of power which occurs on a global scale is hidden, and thus the fact that this may to a large extent explain the conditions under which the countries on the periphery are evolving.

In the same way, the fact that the asymmetrical relationships of the different social groups within a national unit is often omitted, which may explain the structures and processes on which the subordinate social groups in the central countries are articulated.

As discussed during the meeting, one of the consequences of this definition is that the subject of study is made uniform. The peripheral countries appear to be subjects of uniform actions. The classic approach has in many cases operated on the assumption that such countries are homogeneous among and within themselves.

The foregoing has been expressed in the activities carried out on the basis of this viewpoint in homogeneous and decontextualized responses imposed on heterogeneous realities, both from the cultural and economic viewpoints, of the peripheral countries.

At the same time, the assistance concept implicit in the classic approach was noted. It determines the set of activities that are undertaken on the basis of this viewpoint and that reduces a counterpart to an uncritical internalizer of models and technologies whose priority and pertinence were decided extranationally and from a unilateral perspective. Likewise, the importance of the prevalence of this assistance concept in the treatment provided to social groups defined as minorities became clear.

This assistance concept has impeded the execution of activities aimed at strengthening the scientific and technologic capacity of underdeveloped countries.

Some categories that could shape an alternative view of international health. Points of agreement in relation to the critique of the classic approach were not the only matters presented during the meeting. Certain categories could also be identified which were pointed out by participants supporting different approaches which could shape an alternative view in the subject of international health.

In other words, there was a consensus on two points: first, on the recognition of the limitations of the so-called classic approaches, and second, on the need to construct new approaches in a process already initiated by various groups in the region.

The characteristics proposed for working out this new approach include the aspects of delimiting the subject of study from adequate theoretical and methodologic frameworks as well as those aspects dealing with the mechanisms on the basis of which the principles of international health can be implemented.

The need was pointed out for constructing independent approaches which do not uncritically reproduce the dominant concept of international health in the developed countries. This construction should include the contributions of investigators in such countries who share the need to achieve a cooperative approach.

The importance of not establishing a false dichotomy between the northern and southern positions was stressed, but rather of making an effort to develop, in view of the scant reflection in this field in Latin America, an alternative of Latin American thought as well as self-reflection for the set of actors involved in matters of international health in the developed world.

With respect to delimiting the subject of study, it was understood that international health should not be limited to the field of underdeveloped countries. It was noted that there are common themes in the regional health question which warrant common reflection, basically at the level of the powerful spurs which influence the health systems in most of the countries above and beyond the north-south relationship and which are crystallized in problems of financing the system; of medicalization; of asymmetry in the relationships between the different professional categories working in the sector; of the limitations of the proposals which are predicated on volunteers, from whom it is expected that they will make up for the inadequacies of the system; the introduction of indiscriminate technologies; attempts to solve through biomedical criteria the social problems arising from socioeconomic determinants, environmental risks, and the atomization of the health system.

As was emphasized in the meeting, the field of international health requires an interdisciplinary approach. This involves the concurrence of both those disciplines which focus the analysis on the international arena and the contribution of public health and the social sciences.

At the same time, the intersectoral nature of the problems of international health was noted. In for dealing with them, both the sectors directly linked to health care and those related to their conditioners and determinants should play a part.

Considered central in constructing an alternative approach was the historical, national, and regional contextualization of the activities established in order to preclude standardizing normative actions by the countries, with a lack of information about national processes. Such contextualization would be based on recognition of the cultural and economic heterogeneity among and in each of the countries.

The essential objective of international cooperation in health adjusted to this new approach would be to strengthen the self-capacity of the countries intervening in the process of cooperation in a conception according to which international health activities would be used as an instrument of diplomacy and solidarity and not as a mechanism of domination.

In turn, stress was put on the need to strengthen technical cooperation among countries, which means a process of interaction which is not unidirectional in nature and which is conducted not only in the way in which it has been classically, i.e., from the technologically developed countries toward the underdeveloped ones. In fact, the need was also considered of stimulating cooperation between developing countries, between developed countries, and from the former toward the latter, highlighting the subjects of financing, organization, and development of medical care services, human resources development, social participation in health, and the environment.

Two approaches to drawing up alternative models in international health. Basically, two proposals were put forward during the meeting to deal with the field of international health in order to overcome the limitations of the classical approaches. The first is known as "new international health,"[2] in contrast to that called "traditional international health." The second refers to two dimensions of analysis: on the one hand are the questions which, from the international sphere, unduly influence the health-disease process and the health care systems obtaining at the national level (international dimensions of health); on the other, there is the question of health as an international matter.

These two proposals[4,7] are developed by their authors in this book and reflect the presentations made during the meeting.

The first approach starts from the idea that traditional international health focuses on health problems which affect the developing countries, while the new international health extends to health problems which affect all countries.

Traditional international health could be characterized by an approach based on a view of developing countries which assumes them to be homogeneous, while the new international health takes into account the diversity between and within the developing countries. Traditional international health flows through unilateral measures from the center to the periphery, while the new international health would stimulate bilateral and multilateral measures. Traditional international health would be based on the concept of aid in providing health services, while the new international health would define the relationship according to the concept and practice of cooperation in a gamut which would include health teaching, research, and services. The approach of traditional international health would be based on the concept of dependence, while that of new international health would be carried out through the concept of interdependence. In turn, there is probably a difference of emphasis between traditional and new international health: while the former deals with the communicable diseases, the latter would operate on the basis of the epidemiologic transition. Finally, while traditional international health would be based on primitive health services, new international health would operate on and for the transition of the health services.[2]

In the latter approach, international health is defined as a field of public health and its interdisciplinary nature is stressed. Between the one and the other the difference would be in the spheres of action. While public health would constitute a field of research and of action in health activities defined by population level and framed within the political and administrative boundaries of the countries, international health would take into account questions that transcend a country's borders by using the tools of public health and information contributed by other disciplines.

The second approach rests on two substantive factors: consideration of international health as a division of the vast field of international relations which are thought of as a system of power relationships and, in the second place, international health as a field of health, thought of on the basis of its internationalization as part of economic transnationalization.[5]

These two elements are articulated to delimit a field expressed as follows:

> The first of these identifies a certain segment of the sphere of international relations—conceived as a superstructure containing political, economic, military elements which governs the relations between nations—which has been called "health as an issue in international relations" (HIIR). The aim here is to analyze health-related regulations, rules, practices, and customs in the international arena and the flows of funds, goods, and services that circulate from one part of the planet to another, and to show how certain health actions have been turned into political actions (closing of frontiers), economic actions (quarantines), and military actions (blockades of medicines and medical inputs).
>
> The other analytical approach developed in Latin America, using the viewpoint of national health systems, seeks to reveal international phenomena or processes that can help our understanding of the structure and operation of these systems and the dynamics of their reproduction and transformation. We have called this second line of inquiry the "international dimensions of health" (IDH) and it is on this area that this paper focuses.[7]

From this approach an attempt would be made to reveal dimensions which are systematically concealed in most investigations of the health sector and which are, for example, related to the marked and growing dependence which national health systems have toward the transnationalized medical-industrial complex.

From this perspective it is emphasized that the concept of interdependence, used to take into account relationships between countries of different technologic, economic, and military development hides the asymmetry of such relationships. "It is obvious that a technologically advanced nation needs the markets, resources, labor, and materials of other nations in order to guarantee its development. In this sense there exists some level of interdependence, but the quality of the two dependencies is distinct."[4]

Elements for defining a field

One of the advances at the meeting was the articulated formulation of a set of questions about international health. Some of these questions are strategic in nature, while others are theoretical and methodologic, and still others deal with practices. All of them refer to points which appeared to be central in the discussions and implicitly or explicitly express that need several times to construct explanatory models which lead from international health to the search in which various groups in the region are engaged which, from different disciplines, deal with the health-disease process and care systems.

From this set of questions arise those which deal specifically with international health as a subject of consideration and whose point of departure is, What is meant by the concept of international health? It continues with the following: When international health is spoken of, is one referring to an explanatory model, a discipline, an intellectual field, a problem area within public health, or a subject for consideration?

And, in any case, What is the strategic usefulness of arguing about legitimacy in a field appropriated by a concept termed ethnocentric by most of the meeting's participants?

And then: If up to now international health has had to do with health in the developing countries defined according to the views of certain interests in the central countries, what meaning does the subject of international health have when seen from the perspective of the peripheral countries? And in such a case, Is it pertinent to work out a view of international health which can explain the problems we have to confront in the region and are therefore important in the North and South?

What is the body of knowledge, specific skills, and field of application of international health?

These and other questions should be dealt with in order to define the nature of the question. Some of them are also found in the studies presented here.

Why international health? Without other intent than to initiate a problematization and, in any case, a contextualization of the foregoing questions, it is understood that it is important to observe that, in the concern of the teams which are trying to develop international health as a subject of reflection, two observations converge, the first sociohistorical and the second theoretical.

In the first, reference is made to the intensification of economic and political processes at the global level during the past decade, with repercussions in the health field, which have resulted in the adoption in the region of economic adjustment measures which lessen the ability of health systems to care for the health of the population at the same time poverty increases and health conditions worsen.

As noted in one of the studies presented herein, at the beginning of the 1990s the Latin American economies had experienced a serious economic regression which accentuated their basic characteristics of high inflation, external indebtedness, and inequalities in income distribution, which are among the highest in the world.[1]

Latin America's economic regression, as another of the studies notes, imposed to a large extent by concealment of the geopolitical nature of external debt, occurs in a world which has undergone changes during the past decade characterized by the development of the multipolarity of world power centers, a period of instability in the industrialized countries characterized by chronic inflation, reduction in their rates of growth and disequilibriums in balances of payments, inclusion of the peripheral countries in the new world order under conditions of asymmetry characterized in the economic sphere by the internationalization of their national markets, external indebtedness, and strengthened relationships of economic and political interdependence stimulated by the expansion of financial markets, the interests of transnational companies, and the opening of economic borders caused by decontrol of exchange rates.[5]

The industrialized countries take part in this economic international-ization by forming internal alliances among economic interests, coopera-tion agencies, and the state. For that purpose, they also redefine the role of the state and adapt their national policies on the basis of the new stage and, in turn, formulate through it the rules which stimulate trade exchanges and different bilateral and multilateral forms of cooperation.

Meanwhile, the periphery is involved in this process with nation-states weakened by those who impose integration rules on them which are often contrary to national interests because of the external indebted-ness and relationships of subordination with the centers of power.

In Latin America there is discussion about the need for regional integration as a way to deal with such subordination. It is recognized that the health sector can contribute thereto by drawing up joint policies designed and implemented through different mechanisms of technical and financial cooperation among countries.

To support the elaboration of such joint policies, whether govern-mental or not, as well as to take account of the socioeconomic and health conditions in which they will be formulated, a level of explanation is required which can be seated in the field of international health, as will be defined below.

The foregoing does not mean that that level of explanation required cannot be found through another kind of approach, but that the concept of international health necessarily refers to the consideration of the sociohistorical and health conditions mentioned above with an implicit unity of analysis which is the global social system.

So much for the sociohistorical approach to to international health, a characterization of which is set out in the first part of this book.

The second observation to which we refer is theoretical in nature and based on the notion that explanatory models which try to take into account the economic, political, and health-system processes which Latin America is experiencing are passing through a crisis or stagnation which began about 15 years ago and corresponds to that of the model of Latin American development promoted since the 1950s.

Public health and the social sciences, as well as social sciences applied to health, are constructing new approaches, including a reconstruction of their epistemologic, theoretical, and thematic bases which go beyond those which today seem mechanistic explanations with slight power of explanation and prediction.

Equally, in the social sciences and in public health, present ability to intervene and the lack of effectiveness of activities undertaken which are not based on normative and ahistorical principles is questioned.

The concerns of the teams trying to develop the field of international health thus occur in a movement which attempts to build new analytic frameworks by recovering the knowledge produced in a set of areas and disciplines of which it forms part. Such analytic frameworks will in turn support the shaping of intervention alternatives in accordance with the explanations obtained.

Elements for defining a concept of international health. Approaches can be found in the literature on international health which present it as a discipline, others which describe it as an approach or an explanatory model, and still others which define it as a field. Some of these approaches are illustrated in the studies presented herein, while others have served as a basis for preparing some of the papers discussed at the meeting.

In the published literature on international health which defines it as a field are authors who limit that field to a set of activities of international technical and financial cooperation in health and those who define it as a field of professional knowledge and practice.

In the perspective proposed here, international health is not a discipline in the sense of being a particular body of knowledge and methodology, nor is public health a discipline. International health is shaped from the knowledge produced by different disciplines which converges in an area of specific problematization.

According to the direction which we have opted to examine, the concept of international health refers to two levels, which it is well to limit: the first is international health as an approach and the second is a field of study and practice. In this view, the two levels are not exclusive; on the contrary, it is understood that they help delimit a field from a particular approach.

The approach in international health attempts to make reference to a dimension of analysis of the health-disease process and the care systems which involves explicit consideration or not of a set of global determinations and which deal not only with economic and political processes but also health ones. In this approach, the category of totality is both a theoretical and methodologic requirement in constructing the subjects of study.

Going beyond some reductionist approaches to public health involves not only switching from a sectorial to a multisectorial viewpoint, or from an institutional one to a relational approach with an axis set in social groups, but also transition to consideration of the world social system as a unit of reproduction in power relationships, which in varying degree influence the configuration of the morbidity and mortality profile as well as the structure, execution, and response capacity of health systems.

Explaining the health-disease process and care systems in most cases involves bearing in mind the global operation of the capitalist system, the international division of work between the central capitalist countries and the periphery, and the asymmetry in power relationships which spring from that structure.

In the second place, an attempt is made through the concept of international health to limit a field of professional study and practice by adopting an alternative to the traditional definition, according to which international health is the study of health in the underdeveloped countries.

In this alternative view, the term "international health" is used to designate a field of research and intervention embracing the international dimensions of the health-disease process and care systems. This refers to a level of analysis which includes focusing on external economic, political, and health determinants as well as reciprocal determination of the health of populations.

To take account of the problems identified in this field, the articulation of knowledge produced in different disciplines is required.

The processes of intervention in international health include, among other dimensions, international technical and financial cooperation in health and analysis of the assumptions and mechanisms on the basis of which such cooperation is defined.

An approach to these characteristics may reveal other levels of explanation than those public health customarily offers by promoting the production of information about international arenas and the external processes which influence national health systems.

International health and commitment. One of the emphases of the meeting was on the idea that talking of international health also involves recognizing a dimension of political activity which defines at the service of which strategic project will be the information produced and the practices derived from it. This was again noted basically because international health is defined as a field of intervention as well as a field of professional study and practice.

If the activities of one country can be used as both a tool of diplomacy and cooperation and of domination, then an independent approach in international health has a role to play in supporting the strengthening of solidarity among people.

This commitment also involves the production of information about strategic problem areas which support both the development of health awareness at the level of social groups and the unlinking of processes aimed at redefining the peripheral countries' subordinate relationships with the central ones.

At the level of human resources training, in addition to academic aspects related to the training of investigators in various disciplines oriented toward scientific production, it is important to consider the spheres of international action in which a sizable part of the practices in the subject which concerns us are carried out and the commitment of the subjects toward cooperation.

As the study which refers to PAHO's international health program noted,

> An individual's involvement in a cooperation exercise is in itself no guarantee that he or she will be transformed or develop a commitment. Uncritical involvement, in which the individual merely figures out how to be a "successful manager" but acquires no real commitment to the countries, would be truly frustrating. We consider that the dynamics of the process, group reflection, and the effort of an individual aware of his or her responsibility as a social being are essential to proper interaction of the participants with the different areas of work of the institution and will help improve his or her future placement in the field.
>
> The program has been very clear that its aim is not to train individuals to enter the market of competition, or what Taussig calls the scramble for grants. On the contrary, we are agreed that the individual must not just know the financing institutions and their policies and how to formulate a project, but above all else must know the impact and implications of aid, the best time to grant it, the responsibility to oversee its utilization, and the part played by the institutions. We would not want our residents to enter the labor market of experts who parade through the countries with no commit-

ment and completely uninvolved with the country and the groups they are supposed and paid to help. This is why we repeat that the most important part of this articulation into the work of international health is technical excellence which includes involved commitment.[6]

Some proposals

It should be pointed out that the contributions made during the meeting focused basically on the aspects noted above, without for reasons of time being able to deal in depth with proposals for carrying out lines of work at the different levels.

The proposals which are set out here were in part drawn from those made by the participants during the discussions and can be organized in two categories: the first are those which have to do with the production of knowledge; the second deal with aspects of training human resources in the field.

Production of knowledge. It is understood that it is necessary to conduct knowledge production at three main levels: (a) in each of the problem areas which appear to be the most noteworthy in the field of international health; (b) in the aspects of conception, transmission of knowledge, and practice in international health, and (c) of the processes and mechanisms of international technical and financial cooperation in health.

(a) The problem areas initially identified were: (1) the health-disease process: the international determinants of environmental health (including the environment and occupational health); (2) the health-disease process: profiles of morbidity and mortality, opening of borders, and communicable diseases; (3) processes of health care: the medical-industrial complex, the medical model, and dissemination of service models on an international scale; (4) processes of health care: comparative national health systems; (5) processes of health care: comparative informal health care systems; (6) the health-disease process and international policies on controlling birth rates, communicable diseases, and developing national health services.

(b) A second aspect to take into account is production of information based on the field of international health taken as a subject of reflection, i.e., those aspects having to do with the study of the conception, transmission of knowledge, and practice in international health. The objectives would be to (1) reconstruct the emergence and development of the concept of international health and analyze the historical processes which affected it; (2) continue research on the teaching of international health in schools of public health in the United States by determining the times of structuring of the units and their determinants, as well as the amounts and origins of the financing obtained; (3) making a survey of the academic institutions in Latin America which work in fields which, because of their content, are interested in the field of international health, not limiting this to the programs of schools of public health, and (4) studying the state of thought in international health, which means the updating of information in each of the identified problem areas.

(c) Finally, it was thought that information must be produced about the processes and mechanisms of international technical and financial cooperation in health. The main aspects are (1) international cooperation in health: international economic and political determinants in the processes of cooperation; (2) international cooperation in health: the actors and arenas in the processes of international cooperation; nations and agencies, banks and cooperation agencies; strategies; and (3) international cooperation in health: international policies regarding health and how they are implemented.

Training human resources in the field of international health. The characteristics of the training of human resources in the field of international health are determined both by the approaches training institutions employ and the spheres of recruitment of qualified staff.

To analyze the interests of the training institutions, the objectives which are pursued in the field of international health in each institution, and the national needs according to which they operate to definitively design the nature of training in this field as well as the arenas of professional practice, a process of regional discussion must be undertaken which deals with matters such as (1) the scope of training in international health: area of specialization or supplementary training programs for public health workers, social scientists, or specialists in international affairs; (2) scope of training in international health: public health-international health articulation, analyzed at both the theoretical and methodologic levels, of the delimitation of their subjects of study and intervention, as well as matters dealing with prevailing or anticipated professionalization in each area; (3) scope of training in international health: training institutions and limitations or not on training in schools of public health; (4) scope of training in international health: definition of curricula linked to the production of information in the field, and (5) scope of training in international health: programs of training for international cooperation in health.

Final thoughts

We have so far presented an outline of the contributions made during the discussions at the Quebec meeting and certain proposals worked out on the basis of analyzing the reports and discussions.

The significance the meeting may have will depend on the ability of those who took part in it to move forward and deepen the orientations which were profiled and, in turn, promote the production of information, training of human resources, and action in the field of international health in relevant spheres in accordance with a concept which goes beyond the limitations of the classical models and appropriately establishes the actors linked to the commitment to health and solidarity among peoples.

The Quebec meeting represents progress in this direction because explicitly and almost unanimously it showed the need to strengthen North-South communication through joint construction of alternatives both in developing approaches which can take account of the problems international health should deal with and in reworking its practices.

In this vein the participants from the North contributed a critical view of the principles which have predominated in the knowledge and practices in this field by recognizing the common problems North and South face in health questions and the importance of joining forces to deal with them.

In turn, the participants from the South agreed on the so far limited contribution by their part of the world in making international health a subject of reflection, even though they recognized themselves as part of it with respect to practices, the best defined of which until now has been international technical and financial cooperation in health.

The time for dealing critically and jointly with common problems or those which are explicable only on the basis of consideration of the South's subordinate articulation toward the North is determined by the importance of the changes which are occurring in the world at the end of the century and which involve all dimensions of the social world of life according to the principle of restructuring the order of power at the international level based on the reordering of economic relations.

The New World Order creates new challenges and consolidates old inequities which, especially in health, cannot be approached using explanatory models which have ruled until now. It is important to note that to the deep crisis in the economic, political, and social spheres at the world level must be added another crisis, that of the theoretical and intervention models produced to deal with social processes and, in them, the health-disease process in particular. Today one speaks of the crisis of paradigms, of the crisis of mechanist explanations, of the crisis in the explanatory capacity of biological, historical and structural, and cultural models, as well as in explanations based on subjects as isolated social individuals. And one also speaks of the crisis in public health, with respect to both its explanatory and operational capacity in relation to activities conducted in the sector with regard to the health-disease process.

The explanations appearing in the field of international health cannot elude the double challenge in turn resulting from confronting the determinants which arise from the economic, political, and social processes of the century's end crisis with the crisis in the theoretical and methodologic as well as operational models which have attempted to take those processes into account.

Constructing the "independent-cooperative model" which was discussed with emphasis at the Quebec meeting also involves concretely rethinking the role of agencies, universities, institutions promoting international technical and financial cooperation in health, and bilateral and multilateral bodies in the field of international health. Basically, it involves the participation of social movements and the organizations representing them in crystallizing a commitment which will enable supporting the questions of equity, efficacy, and democratization in health, which in the end are the matters for which people in both the North and South are militating and to which those interests whose power comes from the marketing of medical care, medicalization of life, and social injustice in both hemispheres are opposed.

References

1. Bustelo, E. La producción del estado de malestar: Ajuste y política social en América Latina. Conference document, 20 pages, Quebec, 1991.

2. Frenk, J., and F. Chacón. Educación, investigación y acción en salud internacional. Conference document, 14 pages, Quebec, 1991.

3. Godue, C. La salud internacional: Un concepto en formación. Conference document, 29 pages, Quebec, 1991.

4. Panisset, U. Reflexiones sobre salud como asunto internacional. Conference document, 27 pages, Quebec, 1991.

5.   Rodrigues Neto, E., I. Ferreira Brito, and A. Almeida Souza.   Saúde international e integração latinoamericana. Conference document, 12 pages, Quebec, 1991.

6.   Rodríguez, M. El programa de salud internacional de la OPS. Conference document, 19 pages, Quebec, 1991.

7.   Rovere, M.   Dimensiones   internacionales   de   la   salud.   Conference document, 15 pages, Quebec, 1991.

PART ONE

THE GREAT CHALLENGES
TO HEALTH
IN THE AMERICAS

The Great Challenges of the Nineties and their Impact on International Health

Carlyle Guerra de Macedo

The challenges facing the health sector in Latin America are inseparable from the other great challenges confronting the region at the end of this century, the greatest of which is the challenge of development. I do not mean just growth, but rather the quality of the development, the model itself. Some development models have promoted high rates of growth that were regarded as economic miracles, but the "development" they generated was not enough to solve the central problem of organized societies, states, and economic systems, which is the welfare of the people. To cite just one example of this failure, during the Seventies—10 years before the onset of the current crisis—the absolute number of the poor rose by almost 40 million people at a time when practically every Latin American economy was growing at a fairly rapid rate.

The problems we face in maladjustments, economic disequilibrium and, above all, the ineffectualness of our economies in their responses to the problems of the lives and welfare of our peoples, are not primarily an outcome of the crisis, nor did they begin in the "lost decade." They are far more deep-seated, structural problems, which are part and parcel of the development model we have been applying all along in our societies.

Eduardo Bustelo's presentation eloquently describes the undesirable features of current developments. He shows that there is no going back to the development models of the past. To respond to the challenge of development for Latin America we need a new model with certain characteristics that are of fundamental importance for health. I will cite six of them, which I want to emphasize even at the risk of oversimplification.

Firstly, development requires growth, production and productivity. The first challenge is to create the conditions in which that production can take place efficiently and with rising productivity. Hence institutional conditions must be created for solving the problems of economic disequilibria, inflation, debt service, capital flight, fiscal deficits, and reduced capabilities for savings and investment, which compromise the future for all of us.

Secondly, increasing production is, in and of itself, insufficient. Its effects must carry over into social welfare and equity, which will not be

1

achieved automatically by the free play of market forces, especially in the complex social setting and economic conditions of Latin America. The magic of the market, even if sufficient to increase production with the stimulus of private enterprise and creativity, cannot solve the problems of equity and welfare. These must be an explicit object of political will and of specific and effective decisions.

The third requirement for the new development model is the existence of governments that ensure liberty and democracy. Dr. Bustelo says in his paper that "with or without democracy, capitalism there will be," and I think that is so. There will be no new development if by democracy we mean a process that does no more than periodically elect governments, important though that is. Democracy must be identified with a model of life in which the entire population participates daily in decisions affecting it. In times past it was theorized in our region that the development of our countries might be more effectively promoted by the so-called rational decisions of technocracies supported by de facto governments. In some cases this arrangement was able to promote economic growth, but not the real growth that is based on participation by all.

The fourth requirement is that we not act in isolation from the rest of the world. Development must be brought about in the countries of Latin America and in the region as a whole by making them better and more effective participants in the world economy. That economy has become so internationalized and globalized that no country has the political and economic power to pursue its own development single-handedly. To surmount that limitation Latin American development must be based on a ceaseless search for regional integration, which is no longer a mere ideal or slogan handed down from our founding fathers, but a necessity for survival.

Fifth, a development model that merely exploits conditions of the moment is of no use to us. The development we must build has to provide continuity and permanence. In addition to institutional conditions, there must be social peace and knowledge of science and technology, and the capability to put them to use. The new model demands a new culture, a shift toward values that sustain social participation, and protection of the environment. Natural resources must be among the resources we rely on to promote our development, and we must ensure that they remain renewable. We are therefore under an obligation to protect them so that our development will endure, and to safeguard the future of the generations to come. Protection of the environment is an integral component of the development process and of health.

Sixth, there is the central problem of defining the part played by the state in providing the conditions for development and the welfare of its people. It is a source of concern to me that, now that the ideological conflict between East and West has ended, privatization is being put forward as the magical solution to every problem. There is the idea that the state is to blame for all our troubles. In Latin America this brings a very great danger, not because the state should not remove itself from the minor functions of the production of goods—which it is not cut out for and can be done much more effectively and efficiently by private enterprise—but because to ensure the welfare of all and bring about the development we all want, we do need more from a state, but from a state different from what we have known. A state that does more, with a greater capability for making decisions, and has a degree of autonomy from interest groups, above all from the interests of capital, and thus will ensure social stability and peace and at the same time promote and guide needed changes.

These features of the state are of special importance for health given the nature of health as a good and the services it requires. Health and development, as historical and social structures, are essentially the result of decisions and a political process that include the participation of all actors in society. The most important of the institutional changes is the democratization of power and therewith of the power to decide.

In this setting I would like to refer to the specific challenges confronting health. The first of them is the proper placement of this sector in the Latin American development processes needed, not just as an end in itself but as an integral component of those processes.

Health work in the Americas continues to face the problems created by extreme inequalities and the marginalization of broad sectors of our population: something like a third of the Latin American population remains barred from regular access to essential minimum health services.

Even so the health sector has still managed some important contributions, such as—in the midst of the crisis—a decline in mortality. If the Latin American mortality rates of 1981—the year before the onset of the current crisis—had held constant, there would have been 700,000 more deaths in 1990 than there actually were. That those deaths did not happen cannot be credited to improvements in living conditions, or to an enhanced welfare of the population, for during those 10 years per capita income dropped almost 10% and, moreover, became much more concentrated than ever before. Today about 190 million people live in poverty, and almost half of them are destitute.

From the empirical studies we are making and the information we are acquiring we learn that the health sector of Latin America has exhibited a strong ability to adjust, and especially to fix on the main problems. The main explanation for this remarkable reduction in mortality is a rising level of information available to families, and especially to mothers, including information on the use of the few available services in their survival strategies. This is a contribution of the health sector to the development process. Health has an extraordinary potential for contributing to the generation of a psychosocial environment favorable to production activities and to implementing the development we need to counteract the hopelessness and disbelief induced by adjustment policies and the experience of regressive economic models and policies long ago imposed in most of our countries. Health can help bring about the needed development in each of those characteristics I have mentioned.

In the next ten years the Latin American health sector will see a profound change in the problems, the risks and their determinants, and the coexistence of old and new. Inequalities within countries cause the old to persist side by side with the new: new, more complex problems, which are more demanding and more costly to deal with. The population is still growing despite a decline in fertility, and is aging and becoming increasingly urbanized, more and better informed, and so more demanding. The need to address these challenges makes it increasingly important to reorganize the health systems in practically all the countries of the region to enable them to deal with the specific epidemiological characteristics and particular conditions of normal development. The first order of business is to devise new models of care, and to establish new health practices that are also life practices.

The most important factors for building the kind of system we need are proper use of science and technology, and decentralization. One of the characteristics of the historical tradition of all administration in our societies, accounting for the extraordinary inefficiency of present systems, is overcentralization. Decentralization must be not merely a pretext for transferring responsibility without resources and for relieving the state of its responsibilities in the health field, but a process for bringing services to the populations they are intended to serve, and to establish mutual responsibility between services and communities. The fact is that in Latin America no one is made responsible for the death of a child, a mother, an old person, a man or a woman for lack of a drop of vaccine or rehydration salts, or in bringing a new human being into the world.

Even where we have been successful, the greatest of the specific challenges to health is the idea of change itself. Milton Terris has said that there is much that can be done in Latin America. It is all a matter of will, of capacity for leadership, of organization and promotion, of presenting the problems of health in the political sphere as part of development. The challenges to health and development at the end of this century have profound implications for international health. The purpose of international health does not derive solely from health itself, that is, from the problems or the risks, but rather from the overlap between health and development. Health is part of the development process; it implies the concern that arises, with the internationalization of economies, in the sphere of international activities and relationships, of which health is daily a more important part. At the same time, the internationalization of health problems is a fact of life: it is expressed in the risks and the problems, and in the inputs and factors we use to organize systems and provide services. This is also the case in the transfer of knowledge and technology, of patterns of organization, of values, ideas and practices. In each of these areas international action is becoming necessary as a complement to what is being done in each country. For the Pan American Health Organization, this means the challenge of change also in how cooperation is to be carried on, which is our business.

The Rise of the Ill-fare State: Adjustment and Social Policy in Latin America

Eduardo S. Bustelo

"The Saracens came and beat us to a pulp, for God sides with the bad when they outnumber the good." (From the *Refranero Español*, or "Book of Spanish Proverbs")

Introduction

This paper is intended to provide some recent basic information to document the regressive effects of external indebtedness and to put forward some considerations on what is referred to as the Ill-fare State, which adjustment policies are producing in the region, as against the classical Welfare State. It also presents some points that appear to be ineluctable in the debate which is still open on the relationship between growth and equity in Latin America.

The exposition opens with a review of the leading economic and social indicators at the beginning of the Nineties. There follows a summary of the adjustment paradigms introduced and an analysis of some of their problems and results. Thirdly, as an effect of successive adjustments that have achieved neither the desired macroeconomic equilibria nor economic growth, the paper considers the generation of the Ill-fare State by the breakup of the incipient Welfare State existing in the region. This disarticulation has brought with it a significant reduction in the quantity and quality of the social services provided by the public sector and the exclusion from them of an even greater segment of the population, which has been relegated to the low-productivity informal subsistence economy. The intent is not to deny the need for the adjustment or that it must also apply to the social sectors, where sizable financial allocations to combat poverty and want have not prevented these evils from spreading, to say nothing of eliminating them, which they were intended to do. The problem is not adjustment, but what adjustment and for whom. Fourthly, the final section of the paper presents some ideas about a mixed welfare economy which would restore the potential of the public sector and the market in an exercise of collective macro-regulation that would make possible the investments needed to finance growth with greater social integration.

Latin America in the Eighties

As the Nineties began the national economies of Latin America retained their three basic features: the highest inflation in the world, the highest indebtedness in the world, and some of the most unequal income distributions in the world.

External indebtedness remains the factor that most severely limits the region's growth. Latin America is still a net exporter of capital to the developed world: between 1983 and 1990 the net transfer of resources out of the region exceeded US$200 billion (Table 1). The flows of foreign investment into the region have not been restored and, yet more traumatic, in recent years Latin America has suffered a negative overall transfer of resources of between US$2 and US$3 billion a year to multilateral financing agencies such as the International Monetary Fund, the World Bank, and even the Inter-American Development Bank.[17]

The transfer of resources caused by external debt and implemented adjustment policies have significantly weakened the dynamics of the region's growth. Gross domestic product (GDP), which in the period 1950-80 grew at a rate of 5.5% a year, grew only 1.2% a year during the Eighties. As a result, per capita GDP dropped 9.6% between 1981 and 1990 (Table 1). This was accompanied by a plunge in real wages, which reduced the average income of the urban informal sector by 42% and the urban minimum wage by 24% (Table 2). This is made particularly significant by the fact that 74% of the economically active population in Latin America is urban. Moreover, after a historic drop during the period from 1950 to 1980, underutilization of the labor force (open unemployment plus underemployment) in the region rose during the Eighties from 40% to 42%. And this, in turn, is associated with a shift in the labor market to low-productivity jobs (or an increase in the urban informal sector from 24% in 1980 to 30% in 1990) together with a heightening of job insecurity.

With these indicators it is no wonder that poverty in Latin America increased during the Eighties. In fact, poverty and destitution have increased absolutely and relatively in both urban and rural areas (Table 3). With fertility still very high, the population age groups of greatest weight in poverty are children and young people.[1] The most striking feature in the crisis of the Eighties, however, is that the drop in real wages, loss of quality jobs, and increasing underutilization of labor have given rise to a "new poor." The "new poor" are workers of the middle sectors who had managed to extricate themselves from structural poverty and gain access to a broader market for goods and services, including apparel, household electrical appliances, housing, and education and health services. These "new poor" suffered a loss of wages amounting to 4 points of GDP in the period 1980-1989.[12] All workers combined lost a volume of wages measured at 6 points of GDP (Table 4) while the sectors living in structural poverty lost a mere 2 points of GDP (Table 5). This means that much of the crisis fell on the backs of the urban middle class.

The situation created by the emergence of the "new poor" is of particular importance in Latin America. During the Sixties and part of the Seventies the region made significant advances in health (a decline in maternal and child mortality) and education (increasing primary and secondary school attendance and declining illiteracy), thanks to the growth of the middle-income sectors. These middle-income earners are, after all, those who provided—and still provide—support for the long, difficult, and still incomplete process of democratization in the region. In creating societies that are more dualized and freezing the mechanisms of social mobility, the present socioeconomic crisis will pose a very great challenge to the consolidation of democratic processes by making it necessary to process increasingly complex demands with diminishing resources. It must be noted that this situation arose in a setting in which several countries in the region already had some of the greatest inequalities of income distribution in the world,[8,15] which probably worsened during the decade, as shown by the data on functional income distribution (Table 4).

The adjustment processes have been accompanied by high inflation. In 1990, in almost no country of Latin America or the Caribbean was inflation lower than 25% a year, and the consumer price index for the entire region, weighted for population size, soared almost 1,500% a year (Table 1). And this inflationary trend could become yet more pronounced if petroleum prices rise in the wake of the Gulf crisis.

Owing to high inflation rates, most of the countries in the region have implemented extremely harsh adjustment packages to control the fiscal deficit. As a combined effect of inflation and the harshness of the adjustment, the rate of capital formation declined from 22.7% of GDP in 1980 to 16.4% in 1989.[18] The drop in public and private investment, capital transfers to the developed countries as debt service payments, and negative terms of trade pose serious threats to the formation of savings, and therewith to the prospects for a resumption of growth in the region.

In sum, during the Eighties Latin America experienced a severe setback in the form of a sharp economic relapse characterized by increased its external indebtedness, accelerated inflation, and accentuated social inequalities.

Table 1

Latin America and the Caribbean: Economic Indicators

	1983	1984	1985	1986	1987	1988	1989	1990	Variations 1981-90
Gross domestic product at market prices (1980 = 100)	96.4	99.7	103.2	107.0	110.3	111.3	113.0	112.4	
Population (millions)	381.8	390.3	398.8	407.4	416.1	424.9	433.7	442.6	
Per capita gross domestic product (1980 = 100)	90.0	91.0	92.2	93.6	94.5	93.3	92.8	90.4	
Growth rate									
Gross domestic product	-2.7	3.5	3.5	3.7	3.1	0.9	1.5	-0.5	12.4
Per capita gross domestic product	-4.8	1.2	1.2	1.5	0.9	-1.2	-0.6	-2.6	-9.6
Consumer prices	130.5	184.7	274.1	64.5	198.5	778.8	1161.0	1491.5	
Trade price ratio	1.3	6.6	-4.4	-10.3	-0.8	-1.1	3.3	-1.2	-20.6
Billions of dollars									
Gross aggregate external debt	356.7	373.5	383.5	399.4	426.0	417.9	417.5	422.6	
Net transfer of resources	-31.6	-26.9	-32.3	-22.8	-16.3	-28.8	-27.3	-18.9	

Source: United Nations Economic Commission for Latin America and the Caribbean (ECLAC). *Transformación productiva con equidad: La tarea prioritaria en América Latina y el Caribe en los años noventa.* Document LC/G 1601-P. Santiago, Chile, ECLAC, March 1990. United Nations Publication S.90.II.G.6.

Table 2
Latin America: Real average wages and income by branches of economic activity and segment of the labor market, 1980-89*
(Percentages)

	Annual growth rate				1989 Index
	1980-83	1983-86	1986-89	1980-89	1980=100
Branch of economic activity					
Agriculture (**)	-4.3	0.4	-3.3	-2.4	80.0
Manufacturing	-1.8	0.6	-0.6	-0.6	95.0
Construction	-2.1	2.7	2.5	0.8	93.0
Segment of labor market					
Private formal sector					
Medium and large enterprises	-4.5	4.8	-2.4	-0.8	93.0
Small enterprises	-3.1	-3.4	-5.1	-3.9	70.0
Public sector	-6.4	-1.9	-3.5	-3.9	70.0
Informal sector	-10.3	-0.3	-6.5	-5.9	58.0
Minimum wages					
Minimum urban wages	-3.4	-2.0	-3.7	-3.0	76.0

Source: Regional Program on Employment for Latin America and the Caribbean (PREALC) (International Labor Organization). Empleo y equidad: Desafío de los '90. Document 354. Santiago, Chile, PREALC, 1990.

(*) The average incomes are in the informal sector.
(**) Change of agricultural minimum wages in most of the countries.

Table 3
Latin America: Poverty in the Population

	1980				1989			
	Poverty		Indigence		Poverty		Indigence	
	thousands	%	thousands	%	thousands	%	thousands	%
Total	135,900	41	62,400	19	183,200	44	87,700	21
Urban	62,900	30	22,000	11	103,700	36	39,400	14
Rural	73,000	60	39,900	33	79,500	61	48,300	37

Source: United Nations Economic Commission for Latin America and the Caribbean (ECLAC)-United Nations Development Program (UNDP). Magnitud de la pobreza en América Latina en los años '80. Document LC/L 533. Santiago, Chile, ECLAC, 1990.

Table 4

Latin America: Gross Domestic Product and Functional Income Distribution, 1980-89

(Percentages)

	Composition				Annual Growth Rate
	1980	1983	1986	1989	1980-89
Gross national income at market prices	97	92	91	91	0.2
Returns to labor (*)	44	41	40	38	0.6
Gross returns to capital	53	51	51	53	1.2
Functional distribution of income (**)					
Returns to labor	45	45	44	42	
Gross returns to capital	55	55	56	58	

Source: Regional Program on Employment for Latin America and the Caribbean (PREALC) (International Labor Organization). Empleo y equidad: Desafío de los '90. Document 354. Santiago, Chile, PREALC, 1990.

(*) Estimate based on data from ECLAC National Accounts. The gross returns to capital were calculated as the remaining balance.

(**) Corresponds to distribution of Gross National Income at market prices.

Table 5

Latin America: Estimate of Poverty and Indigence Gaps, 1980-89

Component	1980	1989	Increment 1980-89
Poverty gap[a]	3.2	5.2	2.0
Extent of poverty[b]	40	44	4.0
Intensity of poverty[c]	32	47	15.0
Poverty line/average income	33	33	-
Indigence gap	3.2	1.1	0.5
Extent of indigence	19	21	2.0
Intensity of indigence	27	40	13.0
Indigence line/average income	17	17	-

Source: Regional Program on Employment for Latin America and the Caribbean (PREALC) (International Labor Organization). Empleo y equidad: Desafío de los '90. Document 354. Santiago, Chile, PREALC, 1990. Based on United Nations Economic Commission for Latin America and the Caribbean (ECLAC)-United Nations Development Program (UNDP). Magnitud de la pobreza en América Latina en los años '80. Document LC/L 533. Santiago, Chile, ECLAC, 1990.

a   Income insufficiency or gap relative to the poverty or indigence line. This gap is measured as a percentage of gross domestic product (GDP). In this calculation average personal income amounts to 75% of per capita GDP.

b   Percentage of persons in a state of poverty or indigence.

c   Insufficiency of the average income as percentage of the income at the poverty or indigence line.

Adjustment fatigue

During the Eighties a wide variety of general adjustment packages were implemented, all following the same paradigm though with different modalities.

At first the adjustment was geared to external indebtedness. The idea was to achieve balance-of-payments equilibrium by generating a trade surplus, expanding exports of tradable goods, reducing imports, and controlling the remaining macroeconomic variables, especially aggregate demand and its concomitant, fiscal deficit.

The hypotheses underlying this approach assumed an expansion of international trade with the industrialized countries, recovery of their growth rates, and interest rates in decline on the international capital market. With prices stabilized and a surplus generated to service external debt, investment would quickly recover and the flow of external capital would resume. The adjustment would hence be brief and, in general, its duration would be inversely proportional to its severity.

Neither did the international scenario evolve as expected nor were the measures taken effective. The result was that investment did not recover and, in consequence, the economies did not grow and the hoped-for price stabilization did not materialize. There are many reasons to account for what happened—several of them exogenous, as has been mentioned—but one important one appears to have been the ongoing trade surplus. While a reduction of imports and an increase in exports can solve the problem of foreign exchange for the payment of service on external debt, it does not solve the problem of acquiring possession of that foreign exchange. The public sector had to generate the resources with which to buy from exporters the dollars with which to service the foreign debt. Thus, the trade surplus became linked to the problem of fiscal deficit, which was seen as at the heart of the crisis. It may be noted that external indebtedness alone accounted for almost 5 points of GDP, which became encysted in the fiscal deficit.

A new adjustment arrangement was therefore proposed, based on the fiscal deficit and its foreign and domestic components. Attempts were made to redress the imbalance in both the expenditures and income of the public sector. Several instruments were used to reduce expenditures: adjustment of public remunerations at below the rate of inflation; suspension of public investment; postponement of payments on domestic and foreign debt;* reduction of expenditures for social purposes; a rein

---

*The amount of the postponed payments on the service of Latin America's foreign debt was US$11 billion in 1990.[20]

on transfers to municipalities and provinces; reductions in force and forced retirement and pensioning off of public employees, etc. On the income side, several tax reforms failed to produce expected results because they did not materialize in the short run. In consequence, indirect taxes—especially those on general consumption, which are easy to collect—and increased rates for public services have been resorted to.

A preliminary assessment suggests that some initial gains were made in reducing expenditures, but none in increasing revenue. The region's tax systems are complex and sensitive to internal fluctuations, to changes in relative prices, and to the volumes and prices of foreign trade.[17] A fall in the prices of some crucial products in foreign trade significantly reduces tax receipts. Similarly, wage decreases, inflation, and recession operate procyclically. As a result, the fiscal deficit, after an initial fall, has run out of control. With indebtedness exhausted as a remedy both at home and abroad, there has been no choice but to resort to spurious financing, with the high inflation that entails.

As it became increasingly difficult to redress the fiscal deficit and inflationary pressures were mounting, more drastic adjustments began to be considered in association with substantive medium changes. In this approach, achieving the stability needed to resume growth would demand institutional changes on a considerable scale in the profile of supply and demand and in the proportions between the public and private components. Therewith began the explicit dismantling of the public sector apparatus in what I call the building of the Ill-fare State.

To palliate the socially exclusionary effects of the adjustments, a series of measures were implemented. The social policies introduced—especially social development funds—may have reached some of the sectors hurt by the adjustment, but did not offset the loss of wages or the reduction in the quantity and quality of basic social services, and they side-stepped the equity aspect in the financing of the fiscal deficit.[5]

Following one adjustment after another, the region is now in a state of fatigue.[10] Not only that: the life-span of the adjustment packages is becoming ever briefer (five or six months at most) because the disequilibria are being accelerated by the exponential behavior of one or another significant variable (the exchange rate, the interest rate, declining fiscal revenues, etc.). The measures introduced still fail of the expected results, however: the recession is dragging out, inflation is climbing, the fiscal deficit is rising, businessmen are still not investing, and the quality of life of workers is still not improving to partially offset the high social costs of the successive adjustments.

The Ill-fare State

The socioeconomic situation of Latin America during the Eighties, as described above, has brought out the limitations of the incipient Welfare State in the region.

In particular, many studies have noted the exclusion of a major sector of the population from the benefits of social policy and the allocative inefficiency of social expenditure.[4] From the standpoint of the poor, the Welfare State is nonexistent or only a weak, fragmented, and/or constricted presence. This is the reason for criticism of state involvement in social policy, and particularly of governmental provision of social services in health and education.

But questioning of the Welfare State and particularly of government as the source of rectification of income distribution through the system of net transfers that operates with social financing and expenditure turned into a policy of explicitly dismantling its institutional scaffolding. This, in turn, was accompanied by preaching against the inefficiency of government and its services and of the uselessness of paying taxes to finance them. This preaching was intended to lay a basis of social legitimacy for eliminating or curtailing the presence of government in the economy. The crisis of the Welfare State and its attempts at reform evolved into erection of the Ill-fare State. Though the paradigm of the Ill-fare State is not uniformly applicable to every country in Latin America, it has to be admitted that it is fairly common in adjustment processes.

The Ill-fare State has two basic and intimately interrelated dimensions: one psychosocial and the other institutional.

The psychosocial dimension arises in the emergence of a more dualized society in which the middle strata tend to disappear and prospects for upward mobility are frozen. Around the demonstrated absence of basic government social services for low-income earners there is built an argument of dogmatic individualism which leaves each person to his own fate, which strains the social fabric and networks of communal solidarity.

The psychosocial dimension—which, as can be seen, has a basis in reality—is a collective perception or state of mind, particularly among low-income earners and the "new poor," which has two manifestations.

Firstly, a state of hopelessness deriving from a situation of steady social retrogression in the sense of declining real income and employment opportunities. And for the "new poor," limited access to low-skill, low-productivity, and low-paying jobs.

Secondly, loss of faith, for the services of the public social sectors have almost never been accessible to low-income earners, and, in the case of the "new poor," because the services to which they have access are degraded and overloaded.

These feelings of hopelessness and loss of faith, which are mutually reinforcing, have produced a State of Ill-fare that has resulted in a widespread decline in expectations for improving the quality of life. On these perceptions there has arisen interactively the institutional dimension of the Ill-fare State, which consists chiefly of the breakup of the incipient Welfare State which once was expected to be consolidated in Latin America.

The breakup of the structure of the public social services comes about in the following terms:

1) Procyclic behavior: From the beginning of its expansion the Welfare State was conceived within a macroeconomic scheme as a countercyclical device in both its expenditures and its financing. Viewing social expenditures as "soft," in Latin America the adjustment process cut and pared them and left behind only minimal compensating mechanisms. On the financing side there was a large component of indirect taxes owing to, among other things, the presence of "rigid" elements such as subsidies to capital and direct levies on high incomes and wealth.[3] This made the financing state 80% procyclic, which in turn caused continual fiscal crises, to resolve which successive expenditure cuts were proposed.

2) Depletion of the budget: The consequence of the foregoing was a depletion of the budget available for the social sectors, beginning with outlays for investment and continuing with cuts in operating expenditures. The result of the former was that the services failed to expand, at least fast enough to keep up with population pressure, which caused the services to be saturated by excessive demand. Reduction of operating costs resulted in a lack of basic inputs such as school supplies, chalk, and building maintenance in schools, and basic drugs, cotton, syringes, etc., in the health sector. The latter was also accompanied by a dramatic drop in real wages, particularly of skilled personnel such as physicians and teachers, which among other things led to strikes, absenteeism, and a degradation of professionalism in occupations plagued by scarcities of critical resources and inputs. All this produced a general decline in the quality of services.[14]

Another reason for this budget depletion was a rationale based on power and profoundly retrogressive pressures. The services in the most remote locations and those for the poorest and least organized were the first to be cut—before the urban services for middle- and high-income sectors or for groups with a good level of trade union organization.[13]

3)   "Decentralization" of services: National governments transferred services (networks of hospitals and health stations, schools, etc.) to lesser jurisdictions (provinces and municipalities) in a completely deteriorated state and bereft of financing. And the provinces, laboring under greater fiscal restrictions than national governments, received these "services," either to close them down or to keep them functioning at a minimal level. In this way, national governments "freed" themselves of the services not so much in order to decentralize a system but to rid themselves of a problem.

4)   Total or partial privatization of services: Abolishing the gratuitousness of basic social services facilitated the exclusion of larger sectors of society from them. In some countries the services remained public in character, but service rates were introduced without any selective arrangement to keep them free of charge for the lowest income earners. In some countries the public social services were handed over to private entrepreneurs to introduce "private efficiency" into public administration.

5)   Ritualization of the social ministries: Being left with just administrative responsibility for current appropriations (more than 90% of which were for remunerations), the social ministries became middle-men for the funds of the Ministry of Economic Affairs and/or the Treasury which were bargained for between the dismantled trade unions and/or surviving corporate groups (physicians, laboratories, etc.). Having no funds to transfer to local levels, the functions of national ministries were reduced to ritual, and they lost the power to determine the final orientation of social policy. The social ministries were ministries without policies and/or with no way to implement them.

6)   Utilization of nongovernmental organizations and the family: There was a return to the family and to different nonprofit civilian organizations as deliverers of welfare. At first a very constructive move, this began with the dismantling of public, universal, and minimal basic social services in health and education and the state's explicit renuncia-tion of its responsibilities for providing them. Self-help systems were "favored" not because of their organizational and participative advantages but because they imposed no financial burden on the public sector. And there was no transfer of knowledge and practices to families and communities to enable them to deal with their own health and education problems.

7)   Narrow focus: Social expenditure had to be concentrated solely on the structurally poor. The "cyclically poor" were not a concern of social policy and would be reabsorbed when economic growth resumed. Avoidance of a type B error (inclusion of nonpoor) led to an error of type

A (exclusion of poor people). There was no focusing on the income of the public sector.

8) "Flexibilization" of employment relations: The idea was to reduce the fixed costs of enterprises in order to generate more employment. To this end an attempt was made to amend labor laws to make employment relations more flexible by giving employers wider discretion and reducing intervention by trade unions. They were allowed wider latitude for dismissals and for hiring without job security; mobility between posts, tasks and shifts, and the setting of work paces; and a drastic reduction of monetary benefits and labor costs. As a result, employment conditions have become more insecure.

To summarize, there was lack of concern in either word or action for defining a social policy that would interact with economic policy to countercyclically sustain the consumption of universal, basic social services which would reconcile equity with growth. Adjustments have been retrogressive in content and have depressed job creation and real wages and rendered employment unstable. An attempt has been made to reduce the fiscal deficit by dismantling the public welfare apparatus and its structure of subsidies and transfers, thereby creating the Ill-fare State, which institutionalizes the lack of any distributional concern. The picture is rounded out by the principle of "badness," in which the state has become the single source in society of all blame: the state generates deficits, causes inflation, does not provide services, is inefficient, fiscally voracious, and, finally, corrupt.

Toward a mixed welfare economy

There is in Latin America and the Caribbean only one alternative to the adjustment paradigm described in the preceding sections.[20] The proposal of the United Nations Economic Commission for Latin America and the Caribbean is actually a broader approach to development that includes adjustment and stabilization processes. This approach centers on the generation of growth by bringing the region into the world market through technological innovation and higher productivity in manufacturing. Exports are thus the engine of growth and generate the surplus to finance development. Proposals complementing this approach provide the social policies needed to reconcile equity with growth.[12,20]

Those approaches lie outside the scope of this paper. However, and in light of the region's painful experience, there are two crucial points that may not be left out of consideration, whichever modality of adjustment-stability-growth is ultimately chosen. One is fiscal equilibrium as a basis for economic stability, and the other the investment needed to finance growth.

After decades of intense distributional effort expressed mainly through inflations that "lubricated" the relationship of wages to relative prices over time, it now seems that we have arrived at the source of the whole problem: the fiscal deficit. This deficit is related, on the one side, to external debt, and, on the other side, to income distribution, while the public sector is able to "shape" that distribution by modifying the structure of the net transfers effected through public income and expenditures.

Regarding external debt, it must be explained that the social sectors that contracted it are not the social sectors that are paying it back. To the extent that the payment of external debt is not at least proportionally distributed among the social sectors that contracted it, to that extent there is a component of explicit regressivity. This reasoning holds true even when we distinguish between public and private debt, for in several countries the latter has been nationalized or was contracted under real guarantees provided by the public sector. To meet payments on the foreign debt, a trade surplus has to be generated because of the negativity of the transfers with the rest of the world.

With exports relatively inflexible and the terms of trade negative, external adjustment is effected by depressing imports through devaluations which entail higher prices, falling wages, a contraction of consumption, and a loss of economic dynamism.[2]

On the one hand, then, external debt is associated with the fiscal deficit in that the public sector has to buy foreign exchange to pay it and, on the other hand, it compels a ratio of returns on domestic factors favorable to foreign transfers of tradable goods and devaluations which presuppose a combination of unemployment and falling real wages. In turn, fiscal equilibrium is associated with curtailment of public expenditure and/or increased financing for it. In these circumstances the question of financing the fiscal deficit and foreign debt determines the central definition of how the costs of the present crisis must be distributed.

It then has to be made clear which social sectors are to pay the external debt and finance the fiscal deficit. The latitude to put off identifying the social agents involved in the problem of distribution of the costs of the adjustment has contracted, for the fiscal deficit cannot continue to be financed with more external and/or internal debt and the creation of higher Ill-fare States in terms of unemployment-underemployment-falling real wages and contracting social expenditures appears to be reaching critical thresholds.

As we observe income distribution in Latin America and the evolution of returns to capital and labor (Table 4), there can be no doubt that the higher cost of the needed fiscal adjustments must be borne by the sectors with the highest incomes and wealth, for those adjustments must be proportional to the respective responsibilities of the different social groups for the external debt. Because of the high level of tax evasion and the dearth of information in the tax systems, it has been argued that this proposal is impractical. But then, just as it is advocated that the systems of statistical information on poverty and the poor be improved, it also appears necessary to develop better information on wealth and its reproduction to make it possible to identify those who should finance the fiscal deficit.

Moreover, any proposal for growth—with and without equity—needs to identify the social agents that can finance it. Proposals for the transformation of production with equity and the adjustment modalities implemented all assume that the business sector will be the dynamic focal point which will make the investments needed to propel growth. What is more, it is assumed that the entrepreneurial mentality can be easily spread around to the medium and small-scale firms serving the domestic market, and that management techniques will improve the productivity of microenterprises in the informal sector.

But let us see what role is demanded of Latin American entrepreneurs and whether they, with their present practices, are prepared to play it. In the approaches mentioned, the entrepreneur would essentially have to provide the capital needed for self-sustaining economic growth. In addition, he would have to put off his luxury consumption and provide wider margins of investment needed to place the countries on the international market for manufactures; bring in more technology to raise productivity and enhance competitiveness; modernize business management techniques, and stop realizing financial surpluses (especially those deposited abroad) and put them instead into high-risk investments in production with long recovery periods.

The facts appear to show that, in a context of decades of inflation and captive markets directly or indirectly guaranteed by the public sector, the businessman—especially if he is operating in sectors of tradable goods—is far from the desired paradigm. Indeed, he is a social agent who is out for high profits in the short run, rapid recovery of capital, monopolistic and oligopolistic control of the markets in which he operates (whether at home or abroad), response to demand with price incentives, production of goods whose competitiveness is defined by their variable costs (mainly wages), the exchange rate, and labor productivity (obtained by lowering the demand for labor).[9]

The sought-for hero, steeped in civic values, with a medium-term vision that prevails over quick realization of returns, dynamic and efficient, is not what obtains in real life in our countries. The point is that entrepreneurs are indispensable in capitalism, too, which means that the logic of profits is a necessary condition for maintaining the state and, in the end, the survival of democracy. For—and it is worth making this clear—with or without democracy, capitalism there will be.

We are touching here on complex problems bearing on the relationships between civil society and government, which are also beyond the scope of this paper. Beyond that, however, it can be posited that under capitalism the state is structurally dependent on capital and prone to advance its interests. Without denying this principle of structural dependence, however, one may conceive a relatively or operationally autonomous state in a stable democracy in which the different social sectors, and workers in particular, accept private property and the control of investment by businessmen, and who in turn accept democracy and therewith public policies favorable to the social sectors least favored by the state.

Thus, the concept of the relative autonomy of the state creates the possibility of proposing a mixed welfare economy. No economist could propose a development alternative based on the altruism of business or think of the state as independent of those interests. That is not to imply that those interests cannot be given direction through regulations which supersede the bureaucratic regulation of the state and regulation by the market. For a mixed welfare economy the point is that, starting from those selfish interests operating in the market, it is possible to develop public institutions relatively autonomous of sectoral interests and complex enough not to become their one-to-one counterparts. The essential principle of a mixed welfare economy is based on the following: the highest form of interest consists in not placing one's own interests foremost. There would then be restraint and responsibility that would not be dictated by the principles of the economic rationality of private enterprise or an exclusively corporate logic.[11]

The "mixed" character postulated is associated less with ownership of the means of production and more with the configuration of an institutional space in which to define the profile of the sectors that would generate a new economic dynamism of high productivity and synergism. So propounded, the idea is that the flows of finance attracted by the public sector through external and/or chiefly internal savings are linked with private foreign and/or domestic savings in restarting capital formation on a stable and sustainable basis. This all implies a legal and political framework that clearly specifies the role of the public and private sectors, labor unions, and different social groups and, above all, an explicit agreement on welfare, that is, how the fruits of economic growth and technical progress are to be distributed.

Let us return to our two basic themes, the fiscal deficit and recovery of investment. In a mixed welfare economy, it appears prudent to think that the foreign debt and the budget deficit—assuming a lack of relaxation of foreign restrictions—should be financed as proportionally as possible with regard to revenue distribution. In the same way, investment in a mixed welfare economy will be able to be restored at strategic points of articulation where the scant public savings available can be linked to private savings.

It would be naive to posit a moral reform and assume that financial assets deposited abroad will return home if there is no institutionally formalized guarantee of profits. In both cases, therefore, the fiscal deficit and the recovery of investment realistically presuppose a public sector that will have its own direction that will be unable to ignore the specific social agents that finance it. Even so, the creation of a mixed welfare economy—in a context such as Latin America's of rising poverty and social inequalities—is grounded on the possibility of imparting a social direction to appropriation of the surplus by the private sector.

The surmounting of hypertrophied state regulation is not a return to the status quo ante of a market economy,[6] nor is it a reduction in the size of the Welfare State conducive to a reduction of social inequalities.[7] Under present conditions, investment will not be recovered if the state takes marginal action and does not actively involve capital in a positive development process. The basic hypothesis is that it would be possible to define a political space through the articulation of suprasectorial enclaves that have risen above the factional corporate logic and so make a mixed welfare economy feasible. These "universality spaces" may be partly identified in sectors of the government's bureaucracy, in technicians, intellectuals, and the academic community, in certain groups of businessmen and labor unions, in parts of political parties, and in the wide gamut of nongovernmental organizations. Hence, a mixed welfare economy will require political engineering capable of identifying those interests and "weaving" them into a state-private business structure which will generate investment and the recovery of economic dynamism with social integration. A mixed welfare economy would thus imply a new form of collective regulation which is partly privatized and decentralized but not without universal and public direction. Obviously, this point requires elaboration beyond the scope of this paper.

In conclusion, the decline and fall of the Welfare State through creation of the Ill-fare State is neither economically nor politically sustainable. The forces motivating the market together with government action can combine to generate investment in human, physical, and technological capital—and their synergism among themselves—to generate development with increasing social integration. A mixed welfare economy conceived as a macroregulation space in which articulations between government, business, and other social sectors are organized under a post-profit logic appears to be a socially feasible alternative for the recovery of investment and growth in Latin America.

References

1. Albánez, T., et al. Economic decline and child survival: the plight of Latin America in the Eighties. Florence, Italy, Spedale degli Innocenti, Innocenti Occasional Papers No. 1 (1989).

2. Altimir, O. Desarrollo, crisis y equidad en América Latina. *In:* Gurrieri, A., and E. Torres-Rivas, *Los años noventa: ¿Desarrollo con equidad?* San José, Costa Rica, Latin American School of Social Sciences (FLACSO) and U.N. Economic Commission for Latin America and the Caribbean (ECLAC), 1990.

3. Barbeito, A. C. Crisis, distribución de ingresos y estado de bienestar. Buenos Aires, Centro Interdisciplinario para el Estudio de Políticas Públicas (CIEPP) mimeo, 1990.

4. Bustelo, E. S. *Política social en un contexto de crisis: ¿Será que se puede?* Buenos Aires, United Nations Children's Fund (UNICEF), 1988.

5. Bustelo, E. S., and E. A. Isuani. *El ajuste en su laberinto: Fondos sociales y política social en América Latina.* Buenos Aires, United Nations Children's Fund (UNICEF), 1990.

6. Friedman, R. R., et al. *The modern welfare state: A comparative view, trends and prospects.* New York, New York University Press, 1987.

7. Krugman, P. *The age of diminished expectations: U.S. economic policy in the 1990s.* Cambridge, Massachussetts, MIT Press, 1990.

8. Londoño, J. L. Distribución nacional del ingreso en 1988: Una mirada en perspectiva. Bogotá, Colombia, Fedesarrollo, Coyuntura Social No. 1, 1988.

9. Lo Vuolo, R. M. Economía política del estado de bienestar: Mitología neoliberal y Keynesianismo populista. Buenos Aires, CIEPP mimeo, 1990.

10. Nelson, J. *Fragile coalitions: The politics of economic adjustment*. Washington, D.C., Overseas Development Council, 1989.

11. Offe, C. *Partidos políticos y nuevos movimientos sociales*. Madrid, Editorial Sistema, 1988.

12. Regional Program on Employment for Latin America and the Caribbean (PREALC) (International Labor Organization). *Empleo y equidad: Desafío de los '90*. Document 354. Santiago, Chile, PREALC, 1990.

13. United Nations Children's Fund (UNICEF). *Efectos de la recesión mundial sobre la infancia*. Madrid, Siglo XXI, 1984.

14. United Nations Children's Fund (UNICEF). *Ajuste con rostro humano*. Madrid, Siglo XXI, 1987.

15. United Nations Development Program (UNDP). *Human development report, 1990*. New York, Oxford University Press, 1990.

16. United Nations Development Program (UNDP). *Desarrollo sin pobreza*. Document presented at the I Regional Conference on Poverty in Latin America and the Caribbean, Quito, Ecuador, November 20-23, 1990.

17. United Nations Economic Commission for Latin America and the Caribbean (ECLAC). *Endeudamiento externo y crecimiento económico en América Latina y el Caribe: Consecuencias económicas de la propuesta de reducción de la carga de la deuda formulada por la secretaría permanente del SELA comparadas con las de escenarios alternativos*. Document LC/R 841. Santiago, Chile, ECLAC, 1989.

18. United Nations Economic Commission for Latin America and the Caribbean (ECLAC). *Anuario estadístico de América Latina y el Caribe, 1989*. Santiago, Chile, ECLAC, 1989.

19. United Nations Economic Commission for Latin America and the Caribbean (ECLAC). *Balance preliminar de la economía de América Latina y el Caribe, 1990*. Document LC/G 1646. Santiago, Chile, ECLAC, 1990.

20. United Nations Economic Commission for Latin America and the Caribbean (ECLAC). *Transformación productiva con equidad: La tarea prioritaria en América Latina y el Caribe en los años noventa*. Document LC/G 1601-P. Santiago, Chile, ECLAC, March 1990. United Nations Publication S.90II.G.6.

21. United Nations Economic Commission for Latin America and the Caribbean (ECLAC)-United Nations Development Program (UNDP). América Latina: La

política fiscal en los '80. Proyecto regional de política fiscal CEPAL-PNUD. Serie Política Fiscal 2. Santiago, Chile, ECLAC-UNDP, 1989.

22. United Nations Economic Commission for Latin America and the Caribbean (ECLAC)-United Nations Development Program (UNDP). Magnitud de la pobreza en América Latina en los años '80. Document LC/L 533. Santiago, Chile, ECLAC, 1990.

Economic Policies and Social Policies

Frédéric Lesemann

I ought to make three observations by way of introduction to this presentation.

First, I should make it clear that I have assumed that the organizers of this seminar wanted this presentation to be an attempt at a comparison between what is going on in the northern and southern hemispheres in terms of economic and social policies and, more specifically, as regards developments and trends in government intervention in the social/health sector. One might suppose that there is a certain North-South convergence regarding concerns and analysis in the management of social and health programs, approaches to organizing these programs and services, financial and budgetary constraints that are limiting the scope of public interventions, the "health culture," and models for training personnel in the health and social services. To what degree is this convergence occurring and why, and what are some of its implications? But also, to what extent are there profound differences of outlook, and what are the social and political consequences of this? The analysis that I will offer should throw some light on these questions.

Secondly, I had the opportunity, for which I thank the organizers of this seminar, to read Mr. Bustelo's address while I was preparing my own text. This was fortunate, because otherwise I would basically have repeated what he has just told us. I agree with the essential thrust of his analysis, as an economic analysis. Since this economic frame of reference has now been established for our discussions, I can concentrate directly on an analysis of political sociology rather than political economy, an approach both different from and complementary to that developed by Mr. Bustelo.

Thirdly, in my analysis I will draw heavily on the work by the French sociologist Alain Touraine, *La parole et le sang, politique et société en Amérique latine* (Paris, Odile Jacob, 1988). Touraine knows Latin America very well and is one of the best French-speaking specialists in that area. I did my own doctoral studies under Touraine in the 1970s, at the time when he published his work on Chile under the Popular Unity Government and when he was analyzing dependent societies. This was a period when we were studying the particular situation of Quebec's society in the context of North America as a whole, using dependent societies as an analytical framework. Touraine was moving backwards and forwards between Quebec and Latin America, and many intellectuals from that province established very close links with a number of Latin American countries. There was at that time a real circuit, a "connection," and this was no accident. Perhaps we will have the chance to discuss it together.

In preparing this presentation, I had occasion to read *La parole et le sang*, with which I was not familiar, and once again I discovered how magnificent and reinvigorating Touraine's analysis is, at a time when we have been rendered powerless by economic analysis, which makes us forget that, beyond the terrible constraints of the debt, structural adjustment programs, and the ascendancy of the neoliberal laisser-faire ideology, there are societies that are living and suffering, but which, as Touraine says, "define themselves" through their very conflicts. This is a much more active than passive view of these societies, whose existence goes far beyond the *diktats* of the International Monetary Fund or the World Bank. It is a perspective that raises profound questions regarding the conceptual frameworks that we intellectuals and planners who are fascinated, positively or negatively, by the logic of world economic relations, use to structure and organize our perceptions.

In very summary fashion, I will suggest, following Touraine, that, in order to arrive at worthwhile reflections on our societies, we must assume the existence of at least three "actors," in the collective sense of the term: capital, the state, and communities. These three actors can, in Latin America, be symbolized by three current events: first, the debt, of course, and what it indicates concerning the economic relations between the center of the financial empire and its peripheral regions; second, the transition from dictatorships to more democratic regimes; and third, the persistence of community resistance that is linked to the non-integration of large, marginalized social groups. What is important is that we focus our attention on all three of these "actors," not just one of them, and take account of their interrelationships. Although this schematic framework is in theory valid for all contemporary societies, it is apparent that in Latin America these three actors each play an important specific role, while in North America, on the other hand, economic considerations directly determine both the nature of the state and social relationships, which are strongly dependent on the logic of the market.

Let us describe each of these actors a little further.

First of all, there is capital, the "market is everything," or unbridled consumption. It is Wall Street, with its pressure from the banks on countries to repay their debts and promote a kind of development that is exogenous to the national economies. Capital is an actor which attempts to extend its logic to all aspects of human behavior and imposes itself on any approach to the development of services and any evaluation of their relevance and effectiveness. It is the Western model of modernization, and its triumph is the extension of market relationships.

As for the state, its original role in Latin America was that of agent of revolutionary change and modernization. But this modernization has often been associated with an authoritarian and repressive bureaucracy which suffocates civil society, crushes attempts at participation, and eliminates institutions that channel social demands, such as labor unions or political parties. This is an authoritarian approach to modernization.

The third actor is the one which defends the community identity against the destructive universality of the market or the equally destructive authority of the state. It does so by attempting to establish a nationalist or religious order and by appealing to that sense of identity that wants to resist the domination, both external and internal, associated with modernization. This can give rise to the spectacular development of forms of religious expression, sects, charismatic phenomena, and identity-creating myths, as well as to mutual assistance and self-defense in the shanty towns.

The identification of these actors and the recognition of their coexistence in Latin American societies has, it seems to me, the virtue of adding a proper complexity to our understanding of the political, economic, and social phenomena at work, and therefore of broadening the scope for analysis of strategies for change. It rules out any excessively simple and pessimistic analysis of Latin American societies as being principally determined by the external economic constraint. It brings back to the center of the analysis the change agents, namely financial, industrial, and commercial elites; the technocratic elites in the public sector, middle-class service providers, professional groups, labor unions, parties; community movements, protest movements of those who are excluded and marginalized. In this sense it invigorates our perceptions and expands them. For, although what the IMF or World Bank decide in Washington may be decisive for the future of these societies, it is also very evident that their basic dynamics are not controlled or governed by Washington or its local ambassadors. We may be fascinated by this idea, but we should be clear-sighted enough to recognize that this is the direct result of our great cultural proximity to these elites.

This analytical approach also enables us to achieve a more complex understanding of the crisis of modernization in Latin American societies and of our perceptions of development. There is indeed much discussion and disagreement regarding the objectives of access to modernization and about the notion of well-being. This is true not only of the modes of access, i.e. via the market or through more or less authoritarian planning, but of the consequences of this access, in terms of the very selective and unequal extension of the logic of the marketplace to goods and services which are supposed to lead to "well-being" and "freedom." This logic in fact entails the destruction of community identity and the exclusion of entire social groups. In this sense, "development" destroys. This being so, the social movements that take root in the threatened communities are not anachronistic expressions of underdevelopment, but rather a living contestation of the very purposes of development and the elites promoting it.

Finally, this analysis, based on the multiplicity and diversity of social actors, namely, economic elites, the state, and social movements, also allows us to stress the basic differences that exist between the societies of North America and those of Latin America. North America, almost by definition, is essentially characterized nowadays by the dominance of the laws of the market over almost all aspects of life, and by the penetration of the logic of the marketplace to almost all forms of behavior, both private and public. In North America there are no government party and no revolutionary movements. Charismatic and sectarian phenomena are very limited and marginal; the state is highly integrated into the market. This is what is known as liberal democracy, which our powerful neighbors to the south do not hesitate to promote as a universal model and an ideal to which all nations should aspire. I feel that it is hardly necessary to belabor the fact that the spread of liberal democracy is by definition inseparable from the expansion of markets. If a few decades or centuries ago it was the missionaries who paved the way for the colonial conquerors, it is now the standard-bearers of liberal democracy who are opening the way to intracontinental free trade.

Another consequence of this conjunction of the market and liberal democracy that is typical of the North American and Western model of development is the formidable expansion of the middle classes, which is an expression of the huge capacity for integrating marginal elements in these kinds of societies. These middle classes are properly defined both in terms of their broad access to markets (their power of consumption), their considerable influence over the political system and their cultural participation. The expansion of the welfare state in the education, health, and social service sectors is the direct result of this influence and, in my view, the guarantee of its permanence.

By comparison, Latin American societies are characterized to a much greater extent by their polarized, not to say explosive, nature. The middle classes are far smaller and their participation is essentially political and cultural, much more so than economic. Above all, having developed through their access to education systems, and frequently as a result of the expansion of the public sector and of social security systems, the middle classes have over the last two decades become increasingly polarized. In a number of countries, the interventionist state and its national/populist goals are in crisis. While that part of the middle class linked to large corporations and international trade is prospering, the part associated with the civil service, salaried professionals, and also small traders is declining sharply and in some cases has sunk back into the informal sector of the economy. The very existence of this sector and its expansion are a direct result of the increase in social inequality, and constitute a living proof of the non-integrated nature of Latin American societies. The marginalization of a growing proportion of the population, in terms of employment, housing, political influence, education, culture, and—most definitely—health, reflects the radical differences between the societies in the center and the south of the continent and those in the north.

In light of this analytical approach, we can now comment briefly on some features of recent changes in public health programs in both the north and the south. If we were to analyze these strictly from an economic standpoint, it would be impossible not to be struck by the considerable element of convergence in the changes going on in both regions; the differences noted would essentially be restricted to questions of intensity and impact. However, having inserted the political and social components into the analysis, I think that we must talk explicitly about differences of kind.

Thus, while certainly the debt is a basic determinant of changes in public investment programs, we know that the U.S. or Canadian debt is considerably larger than that of the Latin American countries, in both absolute and relative terms. So how is it that the impact of these debts on American or Canadian public programs is infinitely smaller than in the case of the southern hemisphere countries? Clearly, it is not the debt in itself, in other words as an economic and financial fact, that is the problem; rather, it is the power relationship between the countries at the center and those on the periphery that determines the relative significance of the debt. In other words, the debt is not primarily an economic phenomenon, but a political or even a geopolitical one. If the debt must first be grasped in terms of international political relationships, it also has to be understood in terms of its internal political dynamic.

Concretely, Canada is from an economic point of view as much on the periphery of the United states as any Latin American country; its dependence is extreme. However, over the course of its history, which is intimately linked to the development of society in the United States,

Canada has developed large, powerful middle classes; by developing its social programs, it has worked actively to promote the economic and social integration of its marginalized groups. Consequently, no political party today can seriously consider the electoral risks of a drastic reduction in social programs. Canada's economic structure is not necessarily sounder or more successful than that of a number of Latin American countries, in fact quite the contrary; yet, despite an enormous public federal debt ($400 billion, to which must be added the debts of the provincial and municipal governments), an astounding level of private personal debt ($30,000 per head), and a growing trade deficit, the major public programs (education, health, and social programs) are continuing to expand, although moderately, it is true. There have even been some reductions in the area of programs to combat poverty, but on a limited scale.

In very summary terms, the same can be said of the United states. Notwithstanding the ideological fanaticism of the Reagan administration, the major social programs suffered only a few cuts, except in the area of housing and certain anti-poverty programs. It is true that American society has become somewhat more inegalitarian as a result of fiscal changes and the growing tendency for services to be privatized. Nonetheless, when certain changes became too unfavorable to the poor and risked damaging the electoral interests of the Republican party, they were corrected.[1] In other words, the very high degree of social and political integration of the classes in North American societies prevents any sudden and radical change in the status quo. Political regimes and consumption structures basically need the middle classes, and the social programs that cater to them, in order to sustain and reproduce themselves.

In the context of strategies to control the costs of public services—I deliberately said control, and not reduce—there will of course be attempts in the area of health to promote preventive programs and encourage recourse to primary health care, rather than maintain direct access to specialized forms of care (I am referring here to programs providing free, universal access, as in Canada); in other words, to promote a more rational use of resources. Efforts will be made to control the expansion of medical manpower and to promote a better spatial distribution of that manpower. The duration of hospital stays will be reduced, and the merits of household care, the role of families, and voluntary assistance will be reasserted. Likewise, resources will be decentralized and certain service sectors will be privatized to some extent. Overall, however, these modifications will be introduced from the standpoint of preserving guaranteed universal access to services and to the benefits of the programs in question, enhancing the effectiveness of the resources applied, and thus keeping firm control of the growth of costs. This is what is happening in Quebec and, with a few slight differences, in the rest of Canada as well. The situation in the United states is different in the sense that there is no aim to offer universal services, but nonetheless, some kind of basic protection is guaranteed to the entire population in principle.

Clearly, the issues of reducing expenditure, decentralization, privatization, and recourse to the family have absolutely nothing in common with what is going on in the Latin American countries, as already indicated by Mr. Bustelo in his description of the "Ill-Fare state". The risk of radical splits does not exist in North American society, at least in the practical sense that the notion is acquiring in the southern part of the continent. There is practically no informal sector in the economy; everybody participates in the formal production and consumption circuits. Indeed, it might be maintained that a substantial part of the poverty that exists in North America is linked to the absence of an informal sector. In general terms, there are no sections of the population (except perhaps among the clandestine Latin American immigrants) who do not benefit even in some small way from governmental protection programs.

The northern part of the continent remains socially integrated. For this reason, many public health, employment, and social service programs make effective use of more or less extended forms of participation by individuals or groups. This participation in no way implies any disengagement by the public sector, but rather a recognition of the right and ability of individuals and groups to define what is most relevant for them. It involves a collaboration, a recognition of the limits of the competence of experts and professionals, and a sharing of responsibilities, since the state is constantly providing financial support and expertise. There could be no more eloquent demonstration of a high level of political and social integration.

Before I conclude, let me make one further reference to the significance of the ascendancy of the economic viewpoint in our societies and its consequences in the area of public health. In North America, as I have stressed and illustrated, the market is king. It colors all our analyses and judgments. It has penetrated our entire culture and all our values, including our professional behavior. What is valued is what is economically effective. This influence of the market economy in the countries of North America is made possible (which does not mean that it is necessarily accepted) because it represents a practical reality: social groups have very wide access to private and public consumption of goods and services. It is indeed this very access that constitutes them.

It is not, therefore, surprising that a practical area like public health, being conceptualized and developed in the north, should also be shaped by economic considerations, specifically evaluation criteria and objectives that are strictly defined in terms of economic costs and benefits. What happens when this northern paradigm, developed in the context of a socially and politically integrated society, is uncritically exported and incorporated into Latin American societies marked by their polarization and low level of economic, political, and social integration? There is a danger that this model will only be able to function in relation to that very limited range of social services to which a small middle class, isolated from the rest of the society, has access. There is a risk that program managers may become blind and deaf, in other words incapable of understanding and recognizing the social demand for participation from sectors that are not integrated into the society, and therefore incapable of adequately responding to it, for example by turning for support to popular health practices, or recognizing specific needs and unsuspected resources that do not match the norms and criteria developed in the northern countries. Paralysis may afflict managers who, having learned and absorbed northern attitudes according to which nothing can be done without significant amounts of funds, are thrown into disarray by the budget cuts imposed on them.

In conclusion, I would like to suggest some areas for action in relation to each of the three actors I have identified.

In the economic sphere, where the interdependence between the north and the south finds its most direct expression, it should be clear that the debt question can only be settled politically, since, as I have indicated, it is a profoundly political issue. The debt burden is unbearable and its consequences for the domestic economies of the southern countries, for their internal social relationships, and for the polarization if not the disintegration of their societies, are intolerable. The implications of this situation for both the south and the north—we have only to think of the migratory flows from the south to the north—are incalculable. There has to be strong pressure on the banks in the north that have already made enormous profits out of the Latin American debt, and also on the IMF and World Bank, to move away from a strictly financial approach to a political approach to solving the debt problem. Given the impact of the debt on public health programs and the actual health of these countries' populations, international health organizations cannot regard the debt as outside their sphere of competence and responsibility.

As regards states, political relationships, and the conditions for the blossoming of democracy, it would seem that the state's capacity for action is becoming more important than ever. Action must be taken to protect the economies of the southern countries against the distortions created by the debt and to defend their national integrity; but action is also required to combat the unequal distribution of national income, the growing polarization of these societies, and the uncontrolled expansion of the informal sector. To achieve this, the state must work to reintroduce informal sector wage earners into the productive sectors, support the development of these sectors, and train and protect the labor force. In total contrast to an economic philosophy of laisser-faire, which can only be catastrophic for the future of these societies, these states must be provided with the management capacity and resources required to construct true economic and social participation.

From this standpoint, structural adjustment policies must be negotiated so that they guarantee:

- support for levels of production, investment, and satisfaction of basic human needs throughout the entire adjustment period;
- the introduction of sectorial policies designed to restructure the productive sector so as to increase employment and raise the productivity of low-income activities (small-scale agriculture, informal sector in industry, and services);
- the introduction of policies designed to make the health and social sector more efficient, by emphasizing basic services;
- the protection of basic social and health services, by creating compensatory services designed to protect the health and nutrition of vulnerable groups, particularly by subsidizing certain products for specific groups, with children of course as a top priority;
- the establishment of a very sensitive system of indicators of the nutritional and health status of the population, which is as important for guiding decisions as the rates of inflation or growth of GNP.[2]

Finally, as regards communities, their very recognition raises the question, familiar to all those involved in international development, of the role of the populations concerned in determining needs and program orientations, establishing priorities, recognizing traditional practices in the area of health, food, and housing—in other words, cultural habits—and their articulation with external health assistance. This recognition of the primacy of the role of communities and the development of modernizing actions that respect traditional practices are the basis for any effort to improve health and living conditions. These technically simple and inexpensive initiatives, which communities easily sustain on their own, are extremely effective. But they are not free. The public sector must have the financial resources to support them and in this sense must give community care very clear priority over any other form of care. The recognition of these communities cannot be allowed to legitimize further disengagement by the state from these necessarily priority sectors.

If the economic, political, and social components are inseparable from an analytical point of view, they are equally so in relation to strategies for solutions.

References

1. See F. Lesemann. *La politique sociale américaine.* Paris, Syros, and Montreal, St. Martin, 1988.

2. These suggestions summarize some of those put forward by R. Jolly and D. Caillaux in *Le Monde diplomatique*, January 1987, p. 15.

The Environment and its Effects on Health

Alfredo Gastal

Investments in health in Latin America and the Caribbean declined by close to 61% between 1979 and 1984. Nevertheless, the "lost decade"—as it is called by the United Nations Economic Commission for Latin America and the Caribbean (ECLAC) in its document *Productive Transformation with Equity*[1]—is not yet over. During the Eighties, characterized by the burden of the foreign debt and the reduction of fiscal revenues, unprecedented inflationary processes took place in the region and led to the application of often draconian policies. These processes also affected the health and nutrition sectors to an extent never seen before. We are thus beginning a new decade, the last of the century, with an economic and social deficit of such proportions that it is difficult to predict what its consequences will be in fields as diverse as health, politics, education, and the environment.

A 1988 epidemiological study[2] which looked at the effects of air pollution in Santiago, Chile, pointed out that in comparison with the neighboring city of Los Andes, there was a greater relative risk of irritative and obstructive respiratory disease and pneumonia in Santiago. It was also noted that "There was a general increase in the relative risk (RR) (the relationship between incidence rates of a given disease: rate in Santiago/rate in Los Andes) of irritative illnesses, whose incidence rose during the months of high pollution." The population groups most affected were students (with an RR of 1.87, which means that a child in Santiago is almost twice as likely to contract a disease of this type as a child in Los Andes) and the elderly (RR 4.39). Bronchial obstructions registered an annual RR of 1.76, and this increased to 2.41 in winter, mainly affecting milk-drinking minors (RR 2.5) and the elderly (RR 8.95). Neuropathies, with a general RR of 3.72, were also shown to be affected by air pollution levels. The groups most affected were milk-drinking adults (RR 5.54) and preschool children (RR 4.56). It was also noted that in Santiago a large number of deaths attributable to respiratory diseases are also associated with high air pollution levels.

Elsewhere, in Mexico, according to information contained in the National Program for Protection of the Environment 1990-1994, 36% of biochemical oxygen demand is of municipal origin, while 64% comes from industry. It is estimated that by the year 2000, the volume of waste waters will reach 207 cubic meters per second, while the present treatment capacity of municipal discharges is only 15.7% and of industry,

15.5% of that. In 1989, there were 8 million motor vehicles in the country which consume 57.5 million liters of gasoline a day.

The air in the Mexico City metropolitan region daily receives 5 millions tons of pollutants: 4 tons from motor vehicles, 570,000 tons from industry, and the rest from "natural" phenomena (dust storms, particles coming from garbage dumps, excrement exposed to the open air, etc.). As a result, the average air quality has been unsatisfactory for almost 45% of the time that the Air Quality Monitoring Network[3] has made observations. In 1989, 20% of the industrial establishments, 40% of total industrial investment, and 42% of the economically active population were concentrated in Mexico City. Also, the city consumes more than 30% of the federal investments to subsidize food, water supply (60% of the meters do not work), and public transportation. Almost 11 million inhabitants of Mexico City do not have access to a drinking water supply system, and only slightly more than 35% of the population has sewage services. Faced with this situation, it is not surprising that diarrhea and respiratory ailments are the main cause of death in Mexico City.

The list of this kind of examples in the region is long, but the two cases presented are enough to establish that there is a close relationship between environmental problems and health. This, in turn, is a reflection of the development models adopted and the state of the economy. Likewise, it becomes clear that traditional ways of dealing with environmental and sanitary problems by sector have had a negative effect by isolating those sectors from the national development process. This, in general, is assessed only on the basis of economic progress indicators which in turn are frequently considered to be outside the context of the social and political realities of each country.

The relationship between environment, health, and the economy is often shown by the economic cost to society of the inadequate treatment of the first two of these sectors, and by the vicious circle created in this way, determined by environmental decay, an increase in illnesses secondary to environmental problems, and growing economic restrictions on both sectors.

In the region, urban concentration is a phenomenon which has occurred with a speed and intensity that has no comparison in the develop world. At present, the degree of urbanization in a number of countries is over 60%, to the extent that 30% of the regional urban population is concentrated in 12 metropolitan areas, each with a population over 2.7 million (Table 1).

In spite of this accelerated urbanization process—due at times to low investment capacity or even to deliberate actions—the necessary public policies have not been developed to provide the infrastructure and basic services needed or to regulate where investments and people should be located (territorial organization). These environmental and sanitary problems have risen with the inappropriate occupation—whether industrial or residential—of hills, valleys, and river bank areas. This results in water pollution, floods, and soil erosion. In addition, there is

Table 1
**Population of the main urban concentrations
of Latin America**
(millions of inhabitants)

		Population		
Rank	Urban area	1950	1985	2000
1	Mexico City	3.0	17.3	25.8
2	São Paulo	2.7	15.8	23.9
3	Buenos Aires	5.2	10.8	13.2
4	Rio de Janeiro	3.5	10.4	13.2
5	Lima/Callao	1.0	5.7	9.1
6	Bogota	0.7	4.5	6.5
7	Santiago	1.4	4.2	5.3
8	Caracas	0.7	3.7	5.0
9	Bello Horizonte	0.5	3.2	5.1
10	Guadalajara	0.4	2.8	4.1
11	Porto Alegre	0.7	2.7	4.0
12	Recife	0.8	2.7	3.6

Source: United Nations. *The Prospects of World Urbanization.* Revised as of 1984-85. Population Studies Series No. 101 (ST/ESA/SER.A/101). New York, United Nations, 1987. United Nations Publication Sale No. E.87.XIII.3.

the problem of household refuse which, in low-income areas like *favelas*, *barriadas*, and *poblaciones*, becomes a breeding ground for infectious diseases. As well, such mounds of refuse usually cause tragic disasters when they slide down hillsides, killing tens and even hundreds of victims as has often happened in the *favelas* of Rio de Janeiro.

This vicious circle is created because human life and its development are not normally considered indispensable development capital in our societies. If human capital is not valued, why then value the natural capital made up of the environment and natural resources? Or why place value on the discreet and silent work of preventive public health if it does not raise per capita income in the short term?

Since national accounts systems were adopted in the western world over half a century ago, per capita income has been the most best known indicator of economic progress. Although at first this indicator could to a certain extent measure the growth of social well-being in the countries of the North where political institutions developed with economic progress, the appearance of other economic and social phenomena detracted from it, making it less and less satisfactory for assessing real progress, especially in developing countries. For example, it does not allow for measurement of environmental decay, the distribution of wealth, the health levels of the population, or its degree of literacy or social organization. In the specific case of the Latin American and Caribbean region where the predominant style of development has favored the emergence of enclaves of modernity which stand in radical contrast to the vast area of poverty around them, to speak only of per capita income borders on the ironic.[4]

Because of its interdisciplinary nature, this meeting on international health is without any doubt a unique opportunity to point out, even though only in principle, the need to establish a more direct and harmonious relationship between the health and environment sectors in a development context. Progress in both fields depends a great deal on scientific and technological advances, on the availability of adequate human resources for systematic investments, and finally, on the participation of broad strata of the population in promoting and working on it. This can only happen to the extent that democratic states are consolidated in the region.

Besides the considerations mentioned above, a fact that should be acknowledged is that many environmental problems do not have frontiers; they go beyond political boundaries and their consequences join together to cause transborder effects of a regional and even global nature. Thus, the importance of the processes of consolidating inter-regional cooperation in both the economic and the environmental and health spheres should be considered. Also, taking into account some of the global aspects of environmental problems—such as the destruction of the ozone layer and the greenhouse effect, just to mention two—makes it necessary to begin to propose new parameters for international cooperation and to be innovative with development conceptions. The debate about both topics should place a priority on the environmental sustainability of the planet and, as a result, seek ways in which to restrict the overconsumption and waste which frequently characterize the development models in place in the developed countries, and which have been copied by many countries in Latin America and the Caribbean.

Perhaps in order to understand the dilemma of the ambiguity of development in the region, it should first be accepted that it is rooted in some of the very features of our cultures. Since independence, long periods of strongly centralized government and many years of dictatorship have resulted in the theme of development often being manipulated by an elite whose paradigm for progress is represented by the consumer societies of the developed West.

Likewise, lack of knowledge about the cultural diversity in each country has led to an erroneous interpretation of national realities. This has favored the emergence of development models conceived of from the top down. Now, with the implementation of these development models—often imported uncritically from the industrialized countries—the capacity for resistance by the cultures of the great national majorities has been ignored. Since time immemorial, they have lived by their own means, marginalized from the enclaves of modernity created by cultural, political, and economic elites in line with their paradigm for progress.

This situation is occurring in practically every activity: health, housing, industrialization, exploitation of natural resources, etc. In the health field, for example, there is a notable disproportion between investments in preventive and curative medicine. Meanwhile, the number of neighborhood and rural health posts is dropping or remaining stable in spite of population growth. Given the lack of preventive measures, epidemics which had been controlled or eradicated in the past are recurring, while public resources are spent on very sophisticated areas such as organ transplants, depite the fact that their care capacity is very limited due to lack of technical and human resources. In this way, we have created societies which, though they are able to incorporate the most complicated scientific and technological advances of the century's end, still contain social structures which can only be compared with those of the European Middle Ages.

The basic goal of our region's industrialization has been to enter the external market, and very little has been done to develop domestic markets. The costs of maintaining this model, especially since the crisis cut the flow of investment towards the region and it became a net exporter of capital, have been paid by reducing budgets for the social sector, mainly health, education, housing, infrastructure, and urban services.

In order to maintain this model, albeit precariously, and service the debt, the public sector has often resorted to the overexploitation of the country's natural resources, without much consideration of the environmental effects of such methods of exploitation. Parallel to this, foreign industrial groups, pressured by the increasing limitations imposed on them by environmental legislation in the developed countries, are trying to get into countries in the region where rules are more flexible, not just because of technical inability but also because the demand for foreign exchange and creating jobs makes this an apparently advantageous trade-off.

An overview of the region does not just reveal these situations, which though real are not very promising and do damage the economic, social, and political future. For example, it is notable that the restoration of democratic processes has demanded an effort of social organization from the national populations that has no precedent in the history of the region. The proliferation of nongovernmental organizations has allowed the creation of new social organizations which are more aware of their rights as citizens and are more active politically. In addition, because of the political and social events they have lived through, the elite now has a more objective knowledge of national realities, and the governments which have emerged from this process have found themselves compelled to find new ways of practicing politics and of planning the development of their societies. It should also be recognized that much of this evolution has had the decided support of the international community, whether officially at the government level or through nongovernmental organizations.

One of the most important recent changes has been the recognition that defense of the environment and the welfare of the population are not just moral or ethical problems. Both environmental sustainability and social development are deeply rooted in the economic development process and are therefore closely interdependent. According to the document presented by ECLAC to the Regional Preparatory Meeting for the United Nations Conference on the Environment and Development held in Mexico, "Achieving sustainable development leads towards a dynamic equilibrium between all forms of capital taking part in the development process. That is, human, natural, physical, and finance capital, as well as the institutional capital and cultural patrimony."[5]

At that meeting, the Latin American and Caribbean countries belonging to ECLAC approved, through their ministers, the Tlatelolco Platform on Environment and Development. It is once again pointed out in this document that there are links between the fields of international health and the environment, and it stresses some basic prerequisites for both processes: development of regional scientific and technological capacity and international conditions which would allow the region to access advanced technologies, obtain additional resources to ensure sustainable development, and intensive training of human resources.

To end this brief presentation, it is necessary to reiterate the importance of using a multisectorial approach to solutions proposed for both environmental and health problems in the region. On this point, it is worth suggesting that more emphasis be given in international health education programs to the study of and research into environmental problems and their interrelationship with the health situation of the population, linking both topics with the cultural and economic aspects of development. Both can contribute in a positive or negative way. In other words, it is necessary to make clear that the public health problem, more than an ethical or moral one, is an economic problem which affects one of the main capitals for development: human capital. People are both the primordial subject and object of development and of any work in this field.

References

1. U.N. Economic Commission for Latin America and the Caribbean (ECLAC). *Transformación productiva con equidad: La tarea prioritaria de América Latina y el Caribe en los años noventa* [Productive Transformation with Equity. The priority task for Latin America and the Caribbean in the nineties]. Document LC/G.1601 P. Santiago, Chile, ECLAC, March 1990. United Nations Publication Sales No. S.90.II.G.6.

2. This study, made for the Metropolitan Regional Intendancy, was carried out by a consortium composed up of the companies ARA, SEEBLA, and CONSECEL, Santiago, Chile, and distributed as a mimeograph in December 1989. Cited in the document "La contaminación del aire y sus efectos sobre la salud" [Air pollution and its effects on health], Document LC/R.1025 (Sem.61/24), written by the consultant Hernan Sandoval for the Joint United Nations Economic Commission for Latin America and the Caribbean (ECLAC)/United Nations Environmental Program Unit for Development and Environment, Environment and Human Settlements Division, ECLAC, Santiago, Chile, July 1991.

3. Pan American Health Organization, *Las condiciones de salud en las Américas* [Health Conditions in the Americas]. Washington, D.C., PAHO, 1991. Scientific Publication 524.

4. According to Lester R. Brown, there are two recent interesting efforts in this field. They are the *Human Development Index*, suggested by the United Nations, and the *Index of Sustainable Economic Welfare* developed by Herman Dayly and John Coob, and noted in: Worldwatch Institute, *State of the World*, New York, W. W. Norton, 1991.

5. U.N. Economic Commission for Latin America and the Caribbean (ECLAC). *El desarrollo sostenible: Transformación productiva, equidad y medio ambiente* [Sustainable development: productive transformation, equity, and environment]. Document LC/G.1648 P. Santiago, Chile, ECLAC, February 1991. United Nations Publication Sales No. S.91.II.G.5.

Problems of Insurance Coverage and Health Care Costs in the United States

E. Richard Brown

Despite the apparent attraction many nations find in proposals to privatize their largely public systems for financing health care, the United States is moving in the opposite direction. In almost all OECD countries, public expenditures account for more than three-quarters of health spending, compared to only about 40% in the United States.[1] There is now nearly universal consensus in the United States that the present, largely private health care financing system is a failure. This view is shared by nine out of ten Americans, including the same proportions of the general public and the chief executive officers of the nation's largest corporations.[2]

In many countries, debate centers on whether to privatize some or all public health services insurance or national health service programs. In the United States, there is wide consensus that government must provide social insurance for health services to a far greater share of the population than ever before. The political debate focuses on whether this public insurance program should supplement an expanded private insurance system or replace private insurance. The public policy debate is between establishing a government-mandated system of employment-based health insurance, with the expanded public program covering those left out of private insurance coverage, or instead creating a universal national health insurance program, thus expanding government involvement to cover the entire population.

During the 1980s, the United States and most of its individual states were battered by two fundamental problems related to the financing of health services. One is the soaring cost for health care and health insurance, a problem which it shares to some extent with most industrialized nations. A second problem is the growing number of people who are uninsured for health care expenses, a problem that, among the industrialized countries, is virtually unique to the United States and the way it finances health services. The combined pressure of these two forces has generated growing political support for broad reforms to solve these problems and is bringing the country to a critical choice point.

Health insurance coverage

Most people in the United States have some type of health insurance coverage. Nearly the entire elderly population, 65 years of age or older, is covered by Medicare, a federal social insurance program which covers about half the health care costs of the elderly. To pay for some of the expenses that Medicare does not cover, most elderly persons also have private insurance or rely on Medicaid, a welfare-based program which covers about half of the poorest population (mainly those who are eligible for federal public assistance).

The uninsured population is large and growing. Among the nonelderly population, however, coverage is much more variable, and many people have no protection at all against medical expenses. In 1989, 74% of the nonelderly population had private insurance coverage, including 64% who obtained their own employment-based health benefits or were covered through employment of a family member and another 10% who had privately purchased insurance coverage. Still another 10% of the nonelderly population were covered by Medicaid, a federal-state welfare-related program that covers about half of the poor, or another public program (Figure 1).[3]

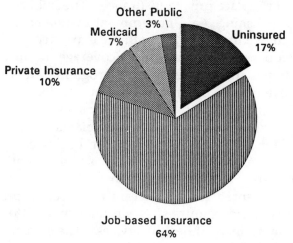

Fig. 1. Distribution of Nonelderly Persons by Insurance Coverage and Source of Coverage, U.S., 1989

Other Public
3%

Medicaid
7%

Uninsured
17%

Private Insurance
10%

Job-based Insurance
64%

But 17% of the nonelderly population—more than 35 million Americans—have no coverage of any kind: not private insurance, not Medicare, not Medicaid, not any other. These people thus have no protection against the costs of medical care for themselves or their families.

The problem in some regions and states, especially the southern and southwestern states, is even more severe than in the country as a whole. In California, for example, 22.5% of the population under 65 years of age—5.9 million persons—are uninsured, and in Los Angeles County, one in every three nonelderly persons is without any coverage.

The uninsured are disproportionately young, low-income, and ethnic minorities. One-third of all the uninsured are children under the age of 18, almost another third are between 18 and 29 years of age, and the rest are between 30 and 64 years of age (Figure 2). Young adults are most at risk for being uninsured; one in four persons 18-29 years of age is without any protection (in California, one in every three young adults is uninsured). (Figure 3)

Fig. 2. Distribution of Uninsured Nonelderly Persons by Age, U.S., 1989

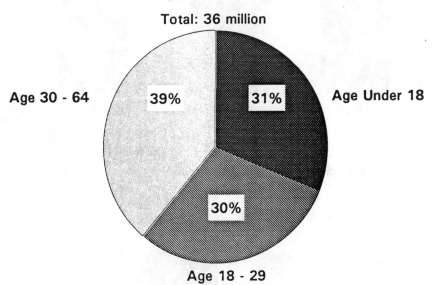

Total: 36 million

Age 30 - 64   39%   31%   Age Under 18

30%

Age 18 - 29

Nearly half (47%) of all the uninsured in the United States are poor or near-poor children and adults (in 1989, an annual income of about $19,000 or less for a family of four). The relative poverty of the uninsured is important to the public policy debate because it is unlikely that most of the uninsured can afford to pay much, if anything, for their coverage. Nevertheless, a large proportion of the uninsured are not poor at all: 22% of the uninsured have family incomes at least three times the poverty level (about $38,000 or more for a family of four).

Low-income persons are much more likely to be uninsured than the more affluent population. In 1989, 35% of those with family incomes below the poverty line ($12,675 for a family of four) and 36% of those just above the poverty line had no coverage, compared to 19% of those with family incomes between 150% and 299% above the poverty line and just 7% of the more affluent population.

Fig. 3. Uninsured Nonelderly Persons by Age, U.S., 1989

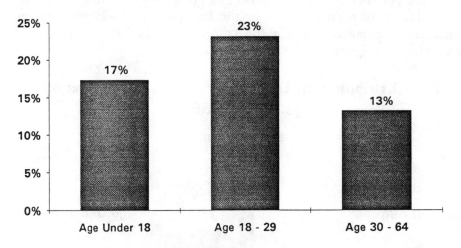

Fig. 4. Distribution of Uninsured Nonelderly Persons by Work Status of Adults in Household, U.S., 1989

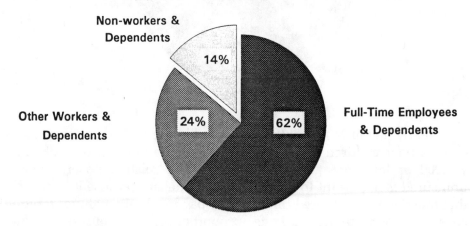

Thirty-eight percent of all nonelderly Latinos were uninsured in 1989, the highest rate among all ethnic groups (three times as high as the rate for non-Latino whites). Although lower than the rate for Latinos, the proportions of uninsured blacks, Asians, and other ethnic minority groups are two-thirds higher than the rate for non-Latino whites.

Nearly nine out of ten of the uninsured are workers or in families headed by a worker. The uninsured are overwhelmingly workers and their families. Nearly 9 out of every 10 uninsured people—86% of the uninsured—are workers or in a family headed by at least one worker. Sixty-two percent of the uninsured are full-time employees and their dependent spouses and children. Another 24% are other workers— part-time employees and the self-employed—and their dependents (Figure 4).

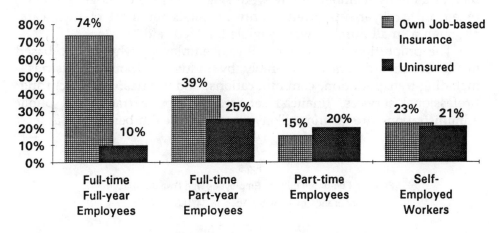

Fig. 5. Percent Full-time Full-year Employees with Own Job-based Insurance and Uninsured, Ages 18-64, U.S., 1989

Although most Americans gain access to health insurance as a fringe benefit of employment, the very large proportion of the uninsured who are working people and their families is clear evidence that employment-based private, voluntary health insurance inadequately covers even the working population.

Employees who work full time for the full year (at least 35 hours per week and at least 50 weeks a year) are more likely than other employees or self-employed workers to get health benefits through their own jobs. It is therefore not surprising that 74% of full-time full-year employees were covered by their employer's health plan in 1989. Another 16% received coverage through the insurance of another family member or some other source, but that left 10% who were completely uninsured. Full-time part-year employees and self-employed workers are two and one-half times as likely to be uninsured (Figure 5).

Low-income employees are far less likely to have health benefits through their employment and are far more likely to remain completely uninsured. Even among full-time full-year employees, the more people earn, up to about $35,000 a year, the more likely they will be covered by their own or a family member's health benefits and the less likely they will be uninsured. More full-time full-year employees with personal incomes below $10,000 are uninsured than are covered by employment-based health insurance.

A 1988 survey of homecare workers in Los Angeles, for example, found that 65% of these low-income service workers were uninsured. These workers, who earned $3.72 per hour performing personal care services for elderly and disabled persons, received no health insurance through their jobs. Those who were not covered by the group health plan of a family member (many were single persons or single mothers) relied on taxpayer-supported county hospitals for most of their care, although a small number were eligible for Medicaid.[4]

The proportion of full-time full-year employees who get job-based health benefits differs considerably by industry. Some industries— including transportation, communications, and utilities; manufacturing; professional services; financial services; wholesale trade, and public administration—are far more likely to provide health benefits to at least

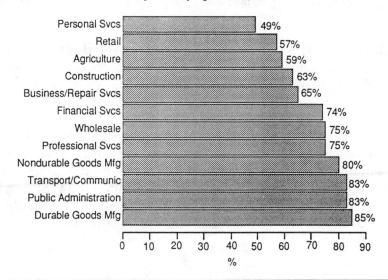

Fig.6
Percent Full-time Full-year Employees with Own Job-based
Insurance by Industry Ages 18-64, U.S., 1989

Personal Svcs — 49%
Retail — 57%
Agriculture — 59%
Construction — 63%
Business/Repair Svcs — 65%
Financial Svcs — 74%
Wholesale — 75%
Professional Svcs — 75%
Nondurable Goods Mfg — 80%
Transport/Communic — 83%
Public Administration — 83%
Durable Goods Mfg — 85%

%

their full-time full-year employees than are other industries, especially agriculture, forestry, fishing, and mining; construction; personal services; business and repair services, and retail trade (Figure 6). Those who work for private employers are much less likely to get health benefits as part of their jobs and far more likely to be uninsured than are public-sector employees.

Unionized workers are much more likely than nonunionized workers to get job-based health insurance. Among unionized workers, 82% get their own health benefits, compared to 56% of those who are not covered by a union. Historically, employment-based coverage, especially of blue-collar workers, was due to collective bargaining by unions on behalf of their members, accounting in part for the higher insurance coverage in the more unionized industries. But with only 19% of American workers in unions or covered by a union contract, this factor has lost some of its influence for the working population as a whole.

Employees who work in small firms are much less likely to get employer-sponsored health benefits. Although 8 out of 10 full-time full-year employees in firms of 100 or more workers get their own benefits, fewer than 7 in 10 in firms of 25 to 99 workers get these benefits, and less than half in firms with fewer than 25 employees receive them (Figure 7). Small firms are one of the central contributing factors to the problem of lack of insurance coverage. Although 22% of all employees in the United States work in firms with fewer than 25 workers, 42% of all uninsured employees work in firms of this size.

The decrease in employment-based insurance coverage among workers and their families is due in large part to a decline in jobs in

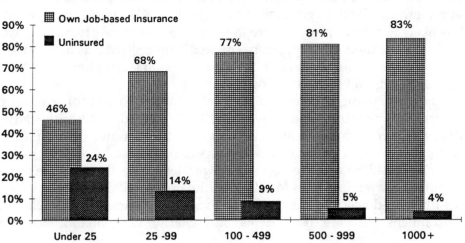

Fig. 7. Percent Full-time Full-year Employees with Own Job-based Insurance and Uninsured by Firm Size, Ages 18-64, U.S., 1989

manufacturing and other unionized, higher-wage sectors of the economy and an increase in employment in the retail and service sectors.[5] The shrinking of employment in industries that have traditionally provided health benefits, and the rapid growth of jobs in small retail and service firms, where low wages and seasonal employment are prevalent, has made increasing numbers of people question the continued reliance on private employment-based health insurance in the United States.

In addition to the population that is completely uninsured at any given time, a substantial portion of the population is inadequately covered by health insurance, leaving them exposed to major financial losses or debts due to expensive medical care. The most definitive analysis of this problem estimated that, including the inadequately insured and the completely uninsured, between 24% and 37% of the nonelderly population is underinsured against the predictable risks of large medical expenses. In 1977 these included about 9% of the population who were uninsured throughout the year, more than another 9% who were uninsured part of the year, and at least another 5% to 18% with private insurance coverage that left them vulnerable to significant risks of spending at least 10% of their family income on medical expenses.[6] It is likely that the underinsured now represent considerably more than the one-quarter to one-third of the population they were a decade and a half ago.

Why is the growing lack of health insurance a problem? Several factors make the lack of health insurance a serious problem for the uninsured themselves and for health care providers, local governments, and employers who do provide health benefits. First, compared to people with health insurance coverage, the uninsured have much less access to necessary medical care. They are less likely to see a physician in a year, less likely to get their young children adequately immunized, less likely to receive prenatal care in the first trimester of pregnancy, less likely to have their blood pressure checked, and only half as likely to see a physician within 30 days if they have serious symptoms, such as persistent high fever, nausea, or bleeding.[7]

Second, reduced access to medical care due to lack of insurance coverage may contribute to a severe decline in individuals' health status. Research studies have found that pregnant women and their children and persons with chronic illness are especially at risk.[8]

Finally, although the uninsured get less care than the insured population, everyone pays for care that the uninsured do receive. When the uninsured need urgent care, they usually go to hospitals and clinics. Uncompensated care (bad debts and charity care, mainly for the uninsured) cost hospitals in California, for example, $975 million in fiscal year 1985-86—84% more than in 1981-82, 49% more after adjusting for inflation.[9] Charity care cost U.S. hospitals more than $8 billion in 1988. Individual and business taxpayers shoulder the financial burden of uncompensated care provided by public hospitals, but these public facilities remain depressingly underfunded, understaffed, and ill-equipped to meet this population's needs in medical care.[10]

Employers and employees pay for much of the uncompensated care provided by private hospitals—that is, the costs of this care that are not paid out-of-pocket by the patient are shifted to the bills of insured patients, mainly employees of firms that do not provide health benefits. But as such "cost-shifting" has become more difficult over the last few years because employers are demanding discount rates from hospitals, more and more private hospitals have found ways to keep out uninsured patients. Hospitals in many cities throughout the country have sporadically closed their emergency rooms, others have downgraded them permanently, shutting their emergency room doors to "911" rescue ambulances, and many have closed their trauma centers. These actions affect the entire community—people with insurance as well as the uninsured.

Rising health care costs

The other major health care financing problem that plagues the United States is the rapid increase in expenditures for medical care. Health care in the United States has been consuming an ever greater share of our economic resources, from 6% of our gross national product in 1965 to more than 12% today.[11] Part of the increase in total expenditures is due to the rapid increase in the costs and prices of medical care, which have been growing at a faster rate than inflation in the rest of the economy. Much of this increase is due to an increasing "intensity" of services provided to each patient, many of which are neither necessary nor effective.

The United States spends more than any other country in the world on health care (Figure 8)—40% more per capita than Canada, the second most expensive health system, which covers its entire population through a universal government-run, tax-funded health insurance program in each province.[12]

Does the United States get adequate value for its higher spending? Despite greater per capita health care spending, health indicators in the United States demonstrate that it should be getting more for its money.

Many less developed countries have lower infant mortality and as good or better life expectancy than the United States. Nineteen other industrialized countries, for example, had lower infant mortality rates in 1987 than the United States. Although medical care contributes less to determining whether people are healthy or sick than do the social and physical environment—such as financial resources, living and working conditions, and culture—as well as personal lifestyle, many types of preventive and curative care have been shown to make a significant and important difference in determining who lives and who dies.

Fig. 8
Per Capita Health Spending,
Selected OECD Countries, 1989

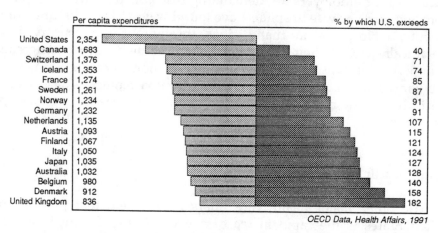

	Per capita expenditures	% by which U.S. exceeds
United States	2,354	
Canada	1,683	40
Switzerland	1,376	71
Iceland	1,353	74
France	1,274	85
Sweden	1,261	87
Norway	1,234	91
Germany	1,232	91
Netherlands	1,135	107
Austria	1,093	115
Finland	1,067	121
Italy	1,050	124
Japan	1,035	127
Australia	1,032	128
Belgium	980	140
Denmark	912	158
United Kingdom	836	182

OECD Data, Health Affairs, 1991

One reason the United States gets less value than it should for the amount it spends on medical care is that more of its health dollars are spent on administration than in other countries. In the United States, 1,500 separate private health plans and an estimated 175,000 self-insured employer plans[13] compete with one another for enrollees, each bearing substantial marketing costs, analyzing the financial risks of applicants, negotiating fees with individual doctors and hospitals, scrutinizing clinical decisions of physicians, and processing individual bills and claims from health care providers and enrollees. During the 1970s and 1980s, administrative costs took a rapidly increasing share of total health care spending.[14] The costs of administering health insurance are about 1% of total program expenditures in the public Canadian insurance system, about 3% of total costs in the United States public Medicare program, and about 11% to 12% for private insurance plans in the United States.[15] These insurance overhead costs do not include the much higher administrative costs of U.S. doctors and hospitals for billing and collecting from a fragmented insurance and payment system.[16] Higher administrative costs seem to be a corollary of a privatized health care financing system.

The fragmentation of "third-party" payers has prevented payers from negotiating collectively and effectively with hospitals and the medical profession. Only the federal Medicare program has a sufficient share of the market to give it substantial clout in reimbursement policy, enabling it to innovate payment reforms for hospitals and doctors that have had an impact on all payers, public and private alike. Until very recently even the Medicare program reimbursed hospitals their costs for all services performed and paid doctors their "usual and customary" fees for all covered services. Medicare's change in hospital reimbursement to a prospective pricing policy per admission, with the payment based on classification of the patient into one of several hundred diagnosis-related groups (DRGs), has influenced hospital care and expenditures under all third-party payers.[17] Payment for physician services is now also being reformed by Medicare, to a fixed-fee schedule designed with financial incentives to encourage more primary care at the expense of procedure-oriented specialists.[18]

Although Medicare reimbursement reforms have influenced other payers, competing private health insurance plans have themselves relied on competition among hospitals and doctors to negotiate prices individually. This strategy of a private competitive solution to the cost problem has left health services payers divided and medical care costs virtually uncontrolled.

Health insurance has become unaffordable for many. Higher medical care costs mean higher premiums. As costs of care escalated, health benefit costs rose accordingly. Between 1977 and 1987, average premium contributions for employment-based health benefits per person covered increased 49% in inflation-adjusted dollars, from $1,111 to $1,656 (both figures are in 1987 dollars).[19] Every year, employers get hit with substantial double-digit percentage increases in the costs of health benefits.[20]

Small firms have been hit very hard by rising health care costs and insurance premiums. Certainly one factor that contributes to the high cost of insurance for individual firms and employer trusts is experience rating,[21] which has isolated smaller risk groups and exposed them to ever escalating rates.

Rising costs have made it difficult for small businesses to purchase insurance. The health insurance market for small groups is drying up throughout the country: since 1988, at least 34 insurers have stopped selling group policies to small businesses in California.[22] Finding health insurance for small groups in which one or more members have a preexisting medical condition is difficult for even the most dedicated insurance broker. Moreover, as more insurers move from community to experience rating, employers have seen their health insurance premiums skyrocket.

Employers who do provide insurance have responded to rising health benefits costs by encouraging or forcing their employees to join managed-care plans. Employers also have shifted more of the costs of coverage to employees by increasing required cost sharing for premiums and for medical care.[23] Employers' increasingly desperate attempts to control their costs by altering formerly generous health benefits are a major source of conflict in labor-management relations, and have become a main factor in nearly 80% of all strikes.[24] Despite these efforts to control their own costs, many employers are at their wits' end. As the president of the California Council of Employer Health Care Coalitions has said, "We have tried a lot of things—utilization review, case management, cost sharing with employees, health maintenance organizations, preferred provider organizations, hospices—and costs are still going up 20 to 30 to 40%."[25]

These cost increases have extracted a greater share of workers' earnings and of corporate profits. Between 1965 and 1989, the cost of health benefits has grown from 2% of wages and salaries to 8% (Figure 9). And it has jumped from 8% of pre-tax corporate profits to 56% (Figure 10).[26] The financial losses inflicted on business and labor, together with increasing labor-management conflicts and strikes over health benefits, have pushed political pressure for health care reform to an all-time high.

Solving the problems: public policy options

These two health care financing problems are inextricably linked. A large and growing uninsured population has little access to necessary medical care. When they do get care, the uninsured add to the hospital bills, insurance premiums, and taxes of others. Universal coverage of the population would provide more equitable access to health care and end uncompensated care cost shifting to employers, employees, and government.

Rising health care costs, the second major health care financing problem, are straining the economic resources of employers, workers and their families, as well as all levels of government. The high costs of health care and health insurance make it increasingly difficult for small employers and low-income people to pay for health benefits. This problem, like the problem of insurance coverage, can be solved most effectively by major reforms in the health care financing system.

Fig. 9. Business Health Benefits Spending as Percent of Wages and Salaries, U.S., 1965-1989

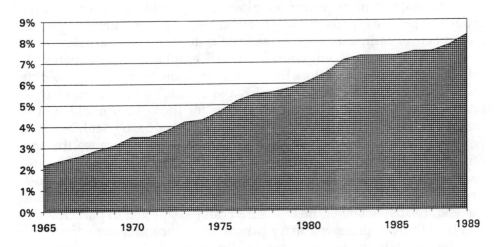

Fig. 10. Business Health Benefits Spending as Percent of Corporate Profits, U.S., 1965-1989

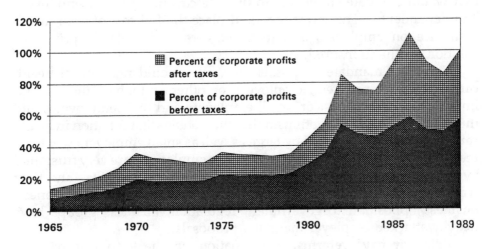

59

The approaches to the problem now being considered range from incremental, targeted strategies—proposals that would provide coverage for some groups of the uninsured—to strategies that would completely reform the financing of health care. These restructuring proposals would provide insurance to the entire population by completely reforming the health insurance market or by establishing a universal health services financing program.

Encouraging or requiring employers to provide coverage. Some states and private groups, hoping to avoid enacting mandatory programs, have been experimenting with tax credits to encourage employers to cover their uninsured employees. Small employers' participation is influenced by the very factors that now discourage them from providing this fringe benefit—low profit margins and the high cost of insurance[27]— adding up to a competitive disadvantage for those who might add to their products or services the increased labor costs due to health benefits. Few small employers are buying into such programs because the cost remains high, for both employer and employee, and because participation remains voluntary. Most of the tax credits for such programs go to employers who are already providing health benefits. In the end, relatively few of the uninsured can be expected to participate in and benefit from these voluntary private insurance programs.[28]

The most dramatic incremental policy option being considered is to require employers to provide health benefits to their workers. The high cost of government-subsidized health coverage programs has encouraged legislators in many states and members of the Congress to propose laws that would mandate employers to provide coverage to their employees and dependents. This strategy would place the full cost of such health insurance on employers and their workers, a completely privatized solution for the uninsured.

Employer mandate proposals, however, would not control health care costs for employers, employees or others. Rather, they would impose a significant cost on small employers and their employees, and they offer no reason for optimism that the double-digit inflation in health care premiums experienced by large as well as small employers would be restrained. Employers, together with their employees, are very frustrated by their inability to control the costs of their health benefits—and they want some relief. Because of its impact on small businesses and general business opposition to government regulation, business groups have heavily attacked employer mandate proposals.

"Play or pay" reforms. A variation on the employer-mandate approach is the play-or-pay strategy.[29] Designed to ameliorate the impact of the requirement on small firms with low profit margins, play-

or-pay would require all employers either to provide health benefits or to pay a special health care payroll tax, in most proposals set lower than the cost of purchasing health insurance. With the revenues from this and other taxes, the government would provide coverage in a "pay" program or purchase it for otherwise uninsured people from contract health plans. Although only Massachusetts and Oregon have enacted play-or-pay programs, but not yet implemented them, many states are considering such legislation.[30] Several proposals have been introduced in the Congress, including one by the Senate Democratic leadership.[31]

However, the play-or-pay strategy would require heavy government subsidizes to make it affordable to low-income workers and low-profit employers. If employers with higher risk workers dump their bad risks into the "pay" program, the need for subsidies would rise dramatically. This tendency toward increasing public-sector costs due to the dumping of bad risks is a threat to any mixed public-private financing system.

Play-or-pay proposals almost all include efforts to prevent some of the insurance industry's most egregious marketing and underwriting practices, particularly those inflicted on small firms. By requiring guaranteed renewal of policies, limiting or prohibiting exclusions of coverage for medical conditions, and limiting the range of premiums that an insurer may charge, these reforms are likely to bring small employer insurance costs closer to those of larger employers.

But play-or-pay proposals' other methods to control the costs of medical care are weak and very regressive. They almost always rely on market competition between health plans and hospitals and doctors to bring costs under control. Market competition, however, favors large groups with substantial shares of the market. And the competition among health care providers for this business encourages constant overinvestment in buildings and equipment, resulting in costly unused capacity, duplication of services, and bankruptcies among many hospitals. Moreover, administrative costs in a competitive, fragmented financing system are very high. These market-oriented proposals also impose heavy cost sharing on enrollees to encourage "cost-conscious" consumer behavior, a tendency that would make health care financing even more regressive.[32]

Finally, play-or-pay strategies would put the poor and mainly lower-income workers in a separate public health care program. Despite the improvements this would represent for those now covered by the underfunded Medicaid program, this limited public program would be politically isolated and would remain vulnerable to the budgetary axe.[33] Who would join the poor in the public program would depend upon whether only small, usually low-wage employers would be allowed to buy in, the rate at which the payroll tax is set, and how generous the benefits are. Past experience with Medicaid and other programs restricted to lower-income populations suggests that a new "pay" program would suffer a similar fate of political vulnerability.

The play-or-pay approach would be a halfway reform, ameliorating access and cost conditions caused by the present chaotic collection of very regressively financed private health plans and limited public programs. But it would perpetuate many of the current system's problems. Nevertheless, many analysts and political leaders believe that this approach, compared to more sweeping reforms, is more likely to be enacted, largely because it requires less dramatic changes for insurers, the medical profession and hospitals, and other powerful elements in the present financing system. Despite this optimistic political assessment, business groups have not liked play-or-pay requirements much better than straight employer mandates, and they have fought these proposals in state legislatures and the Congress with the same intensity.

Universal coverage through national health insurance. A more comprehensive reform strategy would establish a universal national health insurance program, an approach that long has had a substantial core of political support in the United States but that has been defeated when periodically proposed.[34] National health insurance (NHI) proposals typically would replace the payment of premiums by employers and individuals to myriad private insurance plans with a government-run health care financing program supported by tax revenues.[35]

These NHI proposals would provide a comprehensive package of benefits covering essentially the entire population in one financing program which would pay for care obtained from independent practitioners and facilities or organized health plans. For example, Rep. "Pete" Stark's (D-Calif.) "Mediplan" proposal, H.R. 650, would extend Medicare-type coverage to all U.S. residents, and Rep. Marty Russo's (D-Ill.) "Universal Health Care Plan," H.R. 1300, would adapt the Canadian national health insurance program to the United States.[36] Sen. Bob Kerrey's (D-Neb.) "Health USA" proposal, S. 1446, would establish a federal-state NHI program, enabling every resident to enroll in any approved private or state prepaid health plan, with the state health insurance program paying a capitation fee to the enrollee's plan and the plan paying for doctor and hospital services and other covered benefits.

The complete NHI approach has several advantages (see chart below). First, health insurance coverage would no longer depend on or be tied to employment. People would be covered because they are residents of the country, and their coverage would not terminate or change due to changes in their employment status or marital status. A universal financing system that separates coverage from employment, covering the entire population in one program, would provide protection for the poor and other politically less powerful groups, avoiding the inequities of separate, politically vulnerable programs. Even two of the most widely cited authors of the play-or-pay approach acknowledge that an employment-based financing program is not the ideal way to cover a population.[37]

Second, a public NHI program would permit effective control of health care costs and spending. It would channel most health care dollars through a government financing program with negotiated fee schedules and expenditure targets for doctors and some form of budgeted payment of hospitals. These reimbursement methods have been used effectively by Canada and Germany to control their health care expenditures.[38] Such methods also are administratively much simpler and more economical than complex efforts to control utilization by reviewing physicians' clinical decisions.

Third, tax financing would shift the burden of paying for health care from a very regressive system of premiums, which are essentially a flat amount irrespective of income or earnings, to a system that is more progressive, related to ability to pay. Fourth, employers' and employees' liabilities for health care expenditures would be limited and their total health benefits costs greatly reduced to a specified tax. Employers' administrative costs related to their present role of health insurance brokers would be completely eliminated. Fifth, cost shifting between payers would end because providers would receive equal payments for all persons they serve, regardless of the person's source of coverage.

Finally, a tax-funded government financing program would be more accountable than the present financing system which relies on many privately run insurers. Employer mandates and insurance market reforms leave people vulnerable to the "accountability" of the marketplace, a particularly weak position given the regressiveness of the financing system and the limited choice of plans made available to most employees by their employers. A public financing program could actually expand market accountability by providing a virtually unlimited choice of providers, like the Canadian system, or by giving each person a very wide choice of health plans, as in Senator Kerrey's proposal.

Of course, any large organization or program, whether a government agency or a private corporation, has a tendency toward bureaucratization and unresponsiveness. But government financing and operating control are subject to the accountability of the democratic political process, while oligopolistic insurance companies are not. A public financing program with expanded market choice and political accountability is thus more likely than the private marketplace to serve society's needs, as well as the interests of private providers and health plans.

Many state legislatures have been considering variations of these basic national NHI and market-reform approaches. The pressure for state action has grown in the absence of leadership from the White House and the Congress. Most advocates see state-level reforms simply as a necessity to come to grips with the growing crises facing almost every state. Many, however, see state health insurance as a way to begin to solve national problems of access and cost containment in those few states that have the economic base and political will to act—much as Saskatchewan's leadership in health insurance reform was followed by other Canadian provinces, ultimately leading to a national health program. Although the Bush Administration seems to share its predecessor's reluctance to deal with the growing health care crisis, there is new political momentum behind health care reform in the Congress, reflected in the spate of broad play-or-pay and national health insurance bills. It is difficult to say whether the states or the Congress will enact significant reform first.

Public support for major health insurance reform is growing. More Americans are very dissatisfied with their health care system, and more likely to support dramatic restructuring, than people in most other industrialized countries. Of 10 industrialized democracies surveyed in a recent study, fewer Americans were satisfied with their system than were the citizens of any other country, despite the fact that the U.S. spends more money per capita on health care (Figure 11). In the United States, 89% of respondents believed that fundamental change or complete rebuilding of the nation's health care system is needed (compared, for example, to 69% of Britons and 43% of Canadians).[39] This view is shared by 91% of the chief executive officers of the nation's largest corporations; 73% of them say the problems cannot be solved by companies working on their own, that government must take a bigger role in this sector.[40] The leaders of four major national business organizations recently made a joint appeal to the Congress to "do something" about health care costs.[41]

Although there is clear and consistent evidence of strong dissatisfaction with the present system, there is less consistent public support for any particular solution.[42] A majority of the public supports a government national health insurance program, while a majority also supports a play-or-pay approach or some other employer mandate, including about a third who support both.[43] The public opinion polls demonstrate that—driven by fears of potentially ruinous financial losses, inability to obtain care, and weariness with the confusion and fragmentation of the present system—people want the problems resolved, but they are poorly educated about the substance and consequences of alternative solutions.

COMPARISON OF REFORM STRATEGIES

Advantages and Disadvantages

	Employer mandate	"Play or Pay"	NHI
Employment-based?	Yes	Yes	No
Population coverage	Some left out	All have access to insurance	All are covered
Coverage of low-income population	Separate programs/plans	Separate programs/plans	One universal program for all
Revenue sources	Highly regressive	May be more progressive	Much more progressive
Cost containment	None or very little	Moderate, but complex	Effective and less complex
Allocation of resources	Market only	Market only	Planning and market
Accountability	Market control	Market plus some added regulation	Direct political control plus market

Political pressure is growing rapidly to control health care costs and extend coverage to the uninsured. At the same time, elected officials fear that new coverage would increase fiscal demands on already strained government tax revenues, and business leaders worry that new programs would add to employers' labor costs and fuel inflation in health care prices and total expenditures. This apparent political dilemma can be solved by legislation that addresses both problems together in a

comprehensive way. There is growing consensus, at least among health
policy analysts and many

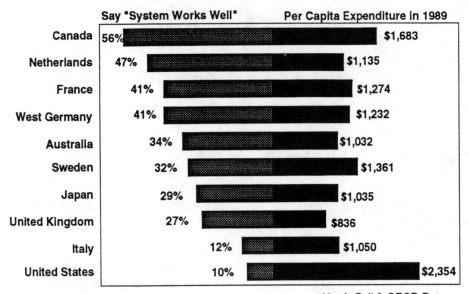

**Fig. 11. Public Views & Health Spending
In Ten Countries**

Say "System Works Well"   Per Capita Expenditure in 1989

Country	Say "System Works Well"	Per Capita Expenditure in 1989
Canada	56%	$1,683
Netherlands	47%	$1,135
France	41%	$1,274
West Germany	41%	$1,232
Australia	34%	$1,032
Sweden	32%	$1,361
Japan	29%	$1,035
United Kingdom	27%	$836
Italy	12%	$1,050
United States	10%	$2,354

Harris Poll & OECD Data
Health Affairs, 1990 & 1991

political leaders, that legislation must be enacted simultaneously to
provide coverage for the uninsured and underinsured and to control
health care spending. But medical industry interest groups have thrown
their substantial political weight against reforms that would limit their
earnings and profits, as almost any effective cost controls must.

Despite the present impasse, more and more Americans are looking
to government either to severely regulate the private insurance industry
and operate a very large public health insurance program or to create a
universal national health insurance program that would completely
replace the present mainly private financing system. It is ironic that,
while other countries with predominantly public financing of health
services are considering privatizing their health care financing systems,
political support for public sector financing and control is rapidly building
in a nation with one of the most privatized systems.

References

1. Schieber, G. J., and J. P. Poullier. Overview of international comparisons of health care expenditures. *Health Care Financing Rev* 10:Annual Supplement (1989). Pp. 1-7.

2. Blendon, R. J., et al. Satisfaction with health systems in ten nations. *Health Affairs* 9:185-192 (Summer 1990).

3. Brown, E. R., R. B. Valdez, H. Morgenstern, W. Cumberland, C. Wang, and J. Mann. Health insurance coverage of Californians in 1989. Berkeley, California Policy Seminar, University of California, 1991. Unless otherwise noted, all data on health insurance coverage are taken from this report and additional analyses by the author.

4. Service Employees International Union. *The hidden story of taxpayer subsidies for low-wage employers*. Washington, D.C., Service Employees International Union, 1988.

5. Congressional Research Service, Library of Congress. Health insurance and the uninsured: Background data and analysis. Washington, D.C., Government Printing Office, May 1988.

6. Farley, P. J. Who are the underinsured? *Milbank Memorial Fund Q* 63(3):476-503 (1985).

7. Davis, K., and D. Rowland. Uninsured and underserved: inequities in health care in the United States. *Milbank Memorial Fund Q* 61:149-176 (1983); H. E. Freeman, *Americans report on their access to health care: The 1986 Wood Johnson Foundation survey* (Los Angeles, Institute for Social Science Research, University of California, Los Angeles, May 1987); and H. E. Freeman, et al., Americans report on their access to health care, *Health Affairs* 6:6-18 (1987).

8. Lurie, N., N. B. Ward, M. F. Ward, M. F. Shapiro, and R. H. Brook. Termination from Medi-Cal: Does it affect health? *N Engl J Med* 311:480-484 (1984); N. Lurie, N. B. Ward, M. F. Shapiro, C. Gallego, R. Vaghaiwalla, and R. H. Brook, Termination of Medi-Cal benefits: A follow-up study one year later, *N Engl J Med* 314:1266-1268 (1986); and P. Braveman, et al., Adverse outcomes and lack of health insurance among newborns in an eight-county area of California, 1982 to 1986, *N Engl J Med* 321:508-513 (1989).

9. Sofaer, S., T. G. Rundall, W. L. Zellers. Restrictive reimbursement policies and uncompensated care in California hospitals, 1981-1986. *Hosp and Health Services Admin* 35:189-206 (1990).

10. Brown, E. R., and G. Dallek. State approaches to financing health care for the poor. *Annu Rev Public Health* 11:377-400 (1990); D. W. Baker, C. D. Stevens, and R. H. Brook, Patients who leave a public hospital without being seen by a physician: causes and consequences, JAMA 266(8):1085-1090 (1991); A. B. Bindman, K. Grumbach, et al., Consequences of queuing for care at a public hospital emergency department, JAMA 266(8):10-1096 (1991).

11. Levit, K. R., H. C. Lazenby, S. W. Letsch, C. A. Cowan. National health care spending, 1989. *Health Affairs* 10(1):117-130 (1991); U.S. Department of Commerce, International Trade Administration, *1991 U.S. Industrial Outlook,* Washington, D.C., Government Printing Office, January 1991, pp. 44-1 to 44-6.

12. Schieber, G. J., and J. P. Poullier. International health spending: Issues and trends. *Health Affairs* 10(1):106-116 (1991).

13. McDonnell, P., A. Guttenberg, L. Greenber, and R. H. Arnett. Self-insured health plans. *Health Care Financing Rev* 8(Winter):1-16 (1986).

14. Levit, K. R., et al. *Op. cit.*

15. U.S. General Accounting Office. Canadian health insurance: lessons for the United States. Document GAO/HRD-91-90. Washington, D.C., GAO, June 1991.

16. Woolhandler, S., and D. U. Himmelstein. The deteriorating administrative efficiency of the U.S. health care system. *N Engl J Med* 324:1234-1258 (1991).

17. Lave, J. R. The effect of the medicare prospective payment system. *Annu Rev Public Health* 10:141-161 (1989).

18. Iglehart, J. K. The new law on Medicare's payments to physicians. *N Engl J Med* 322:1247-1252 (1990); P. B. Ginsburg, L. B. LeRoy, and G. T. Hammons, Medicare physician payment reform, *Health Affairs* 9(1):178-188 (1990).

19. DiCarlo, S., and J. Gabel. Conventional health insurance: a decade later. *Health Care Financing Rev* 10(3):77-89 (1989).

20. Gabel, J., S. DiCarlo, S. Fink, and G. de Lissovoy. Employer-sponsored health insurance in america: preliminary results from the 1988 survey. Washington, D.C., Health Insurance Association of America, January 1989; and Health Care Benefits Survey, 1988, *Medical Benefits,* February 28, 1989, pp. 1-2.

21. Under "experience rating", the insurer bases the premium in part on the costs of health benefits used by that covered group. This is distinguished from "community rating," in which the insurer averages the costs of all covered persons as one "risk group," rather than considering the experience of particular subgroups.

22. Reich, K. Allstate's dropping of small group health coverage stings many. *Los Angeles Times*, July 15, 1989, part II, pp. 1, 4; and G. White, The uninsured: health gamble affects 1 in 5, *Los Angeles Times*, January 29, 1990, pp. A1, A16.

23. Short, P.F. Trends in employee health insurance benefits. *Health Aff* 7:186-96 (1988); and G. A. Jensen, M. A. Morrisey, and J. W. Marcus, Cost sharing and the changing pattern of employer-sponsored health benefits, *Milbank Q* 65:521-550 (1987).

24. Service Employees International Union. *Labor and management on a collision course over health care.* Washington, D.C., Service Employees International Union, February 1990.

25. Holzman, D. Rising cost of insuring workers. *Insight* 5(3):54-55 (January 16, 1989).

26. Author's analysis of unpublished data from the Health Care Financing Administration.

27. U.S. Small Business Administration. *The state of small business.* P. 152.

28. Brown, E. R., and G. Dallek. *Op. cit.*

29. U.S. Bipartisan Commission on Comprehensive Health Care. *A Call for Action, Final Report.* Washington, D.C., Government Printing Office, September 1990; A. Enthoven and R. Kronick, A consumer-choice health plan for the 1990's, *N Engl J Med* 320:29-37 and 94-101 (1989); A. Enthoven and R. Kronick, Universal health insurance through insurance reform, JAMA 265(19):2532-2536 (1991).

30. Brown and Dallek, "State approaches to financing health care for the poor."

31. U.S. Senate. S.1227. 102s Congress, 1st Session. "Health America: Affordable Health Care for All Americans."

32. J. C. Cantor, "Expanding Health Insurance Coverage: Who Will Pay?" *J Health Polit Policy Law* 15(4):755-78 (1990).

33. E. R. Brown, "Medicare and Medicaid: The Process, Value and Limits of Health Care Reforms, *J Pub Health Policy* 4(3):335-66 (1983).

34. R. Fein, *Medical Care, Medical Costs: The Search for a Health Insurance Policy* (Cambridge, Massachusetts, Harvard University Press, 1986), pp. 33-51; and P. Starr, *The Social Transformation of American Medicine* (New York, Basic Books), pp. 235-89.

35. See Fein, *Medical Care, Medical Costs*; and E. R. Brown, "Principles for a National Health Program: A Framework for Analysis and Development," *Milbank Q* 66(4):573-617 (1988).

36. For another adaptation of the Canadian NHI to the United States, see D. U. Himmelstein and S. Woolhandler, "A National Health Program for the United States: A Physicians' Proposal," *N Engl J Med* 320:102-108 (1989).

37. Enthoven and Kronick, "A Consumer-Choice Health Plan for the 1990s," pp. 94-101.

38. R. G. Evans, J. Lomas, M. L. Barer, et al., "Controlling Health Expenditures—The Canadian Reality," *N Engl J Med* 320:571-77 (1989); V. R. Fuchs and J. S. Hahn, "How Does Canada Do It? A Comparison of Expenditures for Physicians' Services in the United States and Canada," *N Engl J Med* 323:884-90 (1990); B. L. Kirkman-Liff, "Physician Payment and Cost-containment Strategies in West Germany: Suggestions for Medicare Reform," *J Health Polit Policy Law* 15:69-99 (1990); J. K. Iglehart, "Germany's Health Care System," *N Engl J Med* 324:503-508 and 1750-56 (1991).

39. Blendon, et al., "Satisfaction with Health Systems in Ten Nations."

40. J. C. Cantor, N. L. Barrand, R. A. Desonia, et al., "Business Leaders' Views on American Health Care," *Health Aff* 10(1):98-105 (1991).

41. R. A. Rosenblatt, "Business Groups Plead for Health-Care Support," *Los Angeles Times*, November 16, 1989, A20.

42. C. Jajich-Toth and B. W. Roper, "Americans' Views on Health Care: A Study in Contradictions," *Health Aff* 9(4):149-57 (1990).

43. E. Echholm, "Health Benefits Found to Deter Job Switching," *New York Times*, September 26, 1991, A1, A12; G. Pokorny, "Report Card on Health Care," *Health Management Q* 10:3-7 (1988). See also R. J. Blendon and H. Taylor, "Views on Health Care: Public Opinion in Three Nations," *Health Aff* 8:149-57 (Spring 1989).

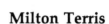

The Health Situation in the Americas

Milton Terris

The present health situation in the Americas must be described in terms of a spectrum rather than a fixed point because of the great variation between countries. The position which any country occupies in the health situation spectrum is based on the interaction of a number of determinants, each of which also exists on a spectrum or continuum.

These determinants include the specific hazards to health: infectious and noninfectious diseases, injuries, occupational and environmental hazards and addictions; the determinants of these specific hazards in the physical and social environments, and genetic factors.

The health situation determinants also include the health services which have been organized to deal with the specific hazards: prevention, medical care, and rehabilitation.

Furthermore, there are general determinants which influence both the hazards and the services; the economic development of both industry and agriculture: the living standards of the population, and the political-ideological commitment of the country to improved living standards, preventive services, medical care, and rehabilitation.

Table 1 defines the determinants of the health situation in more detail. Two hypothetical countries (A and B) are described. For each determinant, the range is from 5, the most favorable, to 1, the least favorable for the country's heath situation.

Country A is an industrial country, while country B is a so-called developing country. You will note that, both for health services and general determinants country a has a more favorable situation than country B. You will also note that the degree of disparity between A and B is quite variable for the specific determinants listed. You will note further that the picture for health hazards is quite different, with country B having a more favorable situation for major hazards such as noninfectious diseases, injuries, occupational and environmental hazards, and addictions.

These are hypothetical countries. But for every country one can attempt to estimate the situation with regard to the specific hazards, the specific services, and the general determinants of the specific hazards and services. This is difficult to accomplish, but the approach is essential, for it is based on the complex "web of causation" which determines the health situation in each country.

Table 1. Health Situation Determinants

Health hazards

Specific hazards to health
    Infectious diseases
    Noninfectious diseases
    Injuries
    Occupational and
        environmental hazards

Determinants of specific hazards
    Physical environment
    Social environment
    Genetic factors

Health services

Prevention
    Infectious diseases
    Noninfectious diseases
    Injuries
    Occupational and
        environmental hazards
    Addictions

Medical care
    Personnel
    Facilities
    Quality
    Accessibility

Rehabilitation
    Medical
    Vocational
    Social

General determinants of hazards and services

Economic development
    Industry
    Agriculture

Living standards
    Education
    Nutrition
    Housing
    Employment

Income
Rest and recreation
Transportation
Communication
Participation

Political-ideological commitment
To living standards
To prevention
To medical care
To rehabilitation

The result of all the forces involved in the "web of causation" is expressed in a measure of health status which is available for all countries, i.e. mortality as expressed in expectation of life. Although incomplete, since morbidity is excluded because of lack of adequate information, and since mortality data are inaccurate for some countries, this measure is nevertheless the best we have. For the countries of the Americas, the data are given in Table 2.[1]

Table 2 underscores the importance of Table 1. How, without a painstaking review and analysis of all the factors listed in Table 1, can one explain the fact that two poor countries, Cuba and Costa Rica, with a real GDP per capita of $2,500. and $3,760 respectively[2] have essentially the same expectation of life as the United States, one of the richest countries in the world, with a real GDP per capita of $17,615.? Or that Brazil, with a real GDP per capita of $4,307 has an expectation of life which is 10 years shorter than that of Cuba and Costa Rica? It appears to me that such thorough study and analysis are a necessary prerequisite for effective professional practice in international health.

The changing pattern of disease in the Americas

In the United States and other industrial countries, it became increasingly apparent in the second quarter of this century that, with the conquest of many of the major infectious diseases, the leading causes of death and disability were noncommunicable diseases. Table 3 demonstrates that this process has now taken place throughout the Americas, where the leading causes of death in 1980-1984 were heart disease, cancer, stroke, accidents, and perinatal conditions.[3] Intestinal infections, still the leading case of death in the world today, was the first cause of death only in Ecuador and Guatemala, the second cause in

Honduras and the third cause in Mexico, the fourth cause in Paraguay and the fifth cause in El Salvador and Suriname.[3]

The mortality structure by broad group of causes in selected countries around 1985 is given in Table 4.[4] Of the countries listed, only in Guatemala, Mexico, and Chile were communicable diseases responsible for more than 10% of deaths from defined causes.

Mortality from noncommunicable chronic diseases continues to rise as a percentage of mortality in the Americas, as indicated in Table 5,[5] which excludes injuries, a major contributor to mortality. The greatest increases in the percentage of mortality due to noncommunicable chronic diseases are occurring in those countries with the lowest initial percentages. Noncommunicable diseases are rapidly becoming the dominant causes of death throughout the Americas.

The data presented in the tables above reflect a profound shift in the character of the environmental hazards to health. In the past, there were in large part naturally existing, animate agents—both micro and macro-organisms—the effects of which were potentiated by changes in human society such as migration, trade, urbanization, industrialization, and war. In the current period, many of the important hazards are produced by humankind itself; there are inanimate agents, physicochemical in nature, such as nuclear energy; radiation; numerous toxic chemicals, not the least of which are tobacco, alcohol, and saturated fats; and vehicles, other machinery, etc.

Furthermore, though they are not communicable in the same sense as diseases caused by microorganisms, these agents can be spread very rapidly. The Chernobyl disaster did not respect national boundaries, nor, as Canadians have learned to their sorrow, does air pollution from the northern United States. We now know that chemical weapons like Agent Orange in Vietnam, nerve gas, bacteriological weapons, and both conventional and nuclear bombs can be carried swiftly by airplanes to destroy entire cities, entire countries, and entire regions of the world. That people will also be destroyed is now being accepted as "collateral damage." These monstrous international hazards need to be given major attention in the study and practice of international health.

Epidemiologically oriented health planning

The changing character of health hazards and changing patterns of disease make it essential that we change our approach to health planning. If we do so, our efforts will be crowned with extraordinary success in preventing disease, disability, and death. We are no longer

Table 2. Life Expectancy in
Countries of the Americas, 1985-90

Subregions, groups and countries	Life expectancy at birth, 1985-90
Latin America	66.6
1. Bolivia	53.1
Haiti	54.7
2. Peru	61.4
Guatemala	62.0
El Salvador	62.2
Nicaragua	63.3
Honduras	64.0
3. Brazil	64.9
Ecuador	65.4
Dominican Republic	65.9
Paraguay	66.9
Colombia	68.2
Mexico	68.9
Venezuela	69.7
4. Argentina	70.6
Chile	71.5
Uruguay	72.0
Panama	72.1
5. Costa Rica	74.7
Cuba	75.2
Non-Latin Caribbean	72.4
1. Suriname	69.5
Guyana	69.7
Trinidad and Tobago	70.2
2. Guadeloupe	73.3
Barbados	73.9
Jamaica	74.0
Martinique	74.2
North America	76.1
United States	75.4
Canada	76.7

Table 3

Rank Order of Frequency of the Five Leading Causes of Death in 33 Countries in the Americas, 1980-1984

Rank	Score*	No. of Countries					
		1	2	3	4	5	Other
1. Diseases of the heart	146	23	5	3	1	-	1
2. Malignant neoplasms	98	3	13	7	3	4	3
3. Cerebrovascular disease	84	-	8	13	4	1	7
4. Accidents	73	4	4	6	6	7	6
5. Perinatal conditions	28	-	1	2	6	6	18
6. Influenza and pneumonia	26	1	1	-	4	9	18
7. Intestinal infections	25	2	2	1	1	2	25
8. Homicide, legal int. & war	20	-	1	2	1	1	29
9. Diabetes mellitus	10	-	-	-	3	4	26
10. Chronic liver dis. & cirrhosis	8	-	-	-	1	-	32
11. Benign neoplasms, ca. in situ	8	-	-	-	1	-	32
12. Mental disorders	8	-	-	-	1	-	32

*Score = 5 x no. of 1s + 4 x no. of 2s + 3 x no. of 3s + 2 x no. of 4s + 1 x no. of 5s.

Source: Pan American Health Organization. *Health Conditions in the Americas, 1981-1984.* Washington, D.C., PAHO, 1986. Volume 1.

powerless, for in the past four decades epidemiologists have forged powerful weapons to combat most of the major causes of death.

Heart disease, the first cause of death in the Americas, results from high serum cholesterol caused by a diet rich in saturated fat and cholesterol; high blood pressure; cigarette smoking, and lack of physical exercise. All of these are amenable to public health action programs.

Cancer is the second major cause of death in the Americas. Etiologic agents have been discovered for some of the most important cancer sites; they include radiation, tobacco, and many other chemical carcinogens. All of these are amenable to public health action programs based on the epidemiologic triad, that is, preventing the agent from reaching the host through the establishment of environmental barriers.

**Table 4. Mortality Structure by Broad Groups of Causes
in Selected Countries, around 1985**

	Gua	Mex	Arg	Chi	Uru	Cos	Cub	Can
Defined causes, total	100%	100%	100%	100%	100%	100%	100%	100%
Communicable diseases	46.5	19.6	6.2	12.1	5.4	7.5	8.4	4.0
Circulatory system	6.6	18.7	47.8	30.0	43.9	28.7	43.7	44.3
Neoplasms	3.6	9.1	18.0	19.9	24.4	21.6	19.2	26.3
Perinatal conditions	12.1	5.4	3.7	2.7	2.5	5.9	1.7	0.7
Existing causes:								
injury and poisoning	13.8	15.9	6.5	13.2	5.9	11.3	11.6	7.7
All other diseases	17.4	31.2	17.8	22.1	17.8	25.1	15.4	17.0

**Table 5. Percent of Total Mortality in the Americas
Due to Noncommunicable Chronic Diseases,
1970 and 1980**

		% increase	
Subregion	1970	1980	1970-80
North America			
(USA & Canada)	74.7	75.0	0.4
Temperate South America			
(Southern Cone countries)	54.0	60.0	11.1
Caribbean area	47.0	57.0	21.3
Tropical South America	22.0	45.0	104.5
Middle America			
(Central America, Mexico,			
and Panama)	18.0	28.0	55.6

Cerebrovascular disease, the third major cause of death in the Americas, can be effectively prevented by treating the risk factor, high blood pressure.

Accidents are the fourth major cause of death in the Americas, but rank first in terms of potentially productive years of life lost. Furthermore, they are not accidental; each type of so-called accident is the result of specific agent, host, and environmental factors. Many of these can be eliminated through appropriate public health programs.

Chronic obstructive pulmonary disease, the sixth cause of death in the United States (data are not available for the Americas), results almost entirely from cigarette smoking, and is therefore preventable.

Chronic liver disease and cirrhosis, the tenth cause of death in the Americas, is caused almost entirely by alcohol, and is therefore also preventable.

In most countries of the Americas, and of the world, health planning is still oriented toward medical care. The concern is with input, i.e., resources—the number of hospital beds, the number of physicians, etc. Recently concern has focused on expenditures: cost containment has become the main goal of the planning and policy effort, and privatization has become the slogan behind which the budget cutters carry on their destructive activities. The Reagan-Thatcher ideology now current in the industrial nations is being exported to the developing countries by the World Bank and the International Monetary Fund.

The need to shift to epidemiologically oriented health planning, to planning for outcomes—that is, to results in terms of illness, disability, and mortality in the population—was first formulated by the Canadian Government in the Lalonde Report in 1974. That report pointed out that "vast sums are being spent treating disease that could have been prevented in the first place." It proposed a goal-setting strategy which included: "The development of specific reductions in the incidence of major mortality and morbidity" and "The establishment of specific dates by which reduction in mortality and morbidity are to be achieved."

This goal-setting strategy was formally adopted by the U.S. Public Health Service in 1979,[6,7] but it had already begun its campaigns to prevent noninfectious diseases in the 1960s. From 1965 to 1987, the pre-adjusted prevalence of cigarette-smoking declined from 52% to 31% for men, and from 34% to 27% for women.[8] Table 6 shows that from 1970 to 1987 the age-adjusted death rate from heart disease declined by 33%, from cerebrovascular disease by 55%, from accidents by 35%, and from liver diseases and cirrhosis by 40%. As a result, the overall death rate fell by 25%.[9]

These remarkable, unprecedented successes reflect a great deal of experience which needs to be studied and analyzed by scholars and practitioners of international health throughout the Americas. Our failures need also to be studied, particularly our limited impact on the less highly educated sections of the population.[10]

Epidemiologically oriented, specific health objectives have been established by Australia, India, and probably by other countries as well. They are conspicuously absent in almost all countries in the Americas.

Table 6. Age-adjusted Death Rates in the United States, 1970-1987

	Deaths per 100,000 resident population		
	1970	1987	% change
Heart disease	254	170	-33%
Cerebrovascular disease	66	30	-55%
Accidents	54	35	-35%
Chronic liver disease and cirrhosis	15	9	-40%
All causes	714	536	-25%

The reason for this absence was made clear to me when I had the privilege of attending five congresses of epidemiology during the past two years in Venezuela, the Dominican Republic, Brazil, Cuba, and Guatemala. At all the congresses I attended, and at the congresses in Chile and Argentina which I did not attend, there were surprisingly large numbers of participants.

I am convinced that a great renaissance of epidemiology is now occurring in the Americas. The meetings I attended were of high quality: the epidemiologic studies presented were well designed from a scientific point of view, and the conclusions drawn were very thoughtful. Of the greatest importance was the fact that most of the people who came to the congresses were not epidemiologists in the narrow sense, but public health workers who came to learn how epidemiology could help them in their work. Indeed, in every instance the Ministry of Health helped in the financing and sponsorship of the congress.

However, in not all of the congresses was there sufficient emphasis on the implications of the epidemiologic findings for public health administration, for public health programs, for public health policy. The divorce between theory and practice, the separation of the academic milieu from the field of action, continued to be evident. There was very little discussion of applied epidemiology: the use of epidemiology in determining priorities, in designing action programs, in evaluating the programs and services. This must be changed!

Health promotion

A major development in recent years is the recognition that health promotion—the achievement of healthful living conditions—is essential for all four of the basic tasks of public health: enhancing well-being and functional capacity, preventing disease and injury, treating illness, and rehabilitating the disabled. That is why the Ottawa Charter for Health Promotion, adopted at the first International Conference on Health Promotion in November 1986, stated that "The fundamental conditions and resources for health are peace, shelter, education, food, income, a stable eco-system, sustainable resources, social justice and equity. Improvement in health requires a secure foundation in these basic prerequisites."[11]

Living standards have a profound effect on positive health, which is not only a subjective state of well-being—including such elements as vitality, freedom from excess fatigue, and freedom from environmental discomforts such as excessive heat, cold, smog, and noise—but also has a functional component, namely, the ability of the individual to participate effectively in society at work, at home, and in the community.

The standard of living also plays a major role in the prevention of disease and injury. Infant diarrhea, for example, the single most important cause of death in the world today, is caused only secondarily by salmonellae, shigellae and other microorganisms; it is caused primarily by underdevelopment, poverty, lack of basic sanitation facilities, undernutrition, illiteracy, and ignorance of personal hygiene.

The state of nutrition is a major factor affecting the resistance to many diseases. Inadequate education, resulting in both formal and functional illiteracy, is a serious obstacle to learning the use of preventive measures such as personal hygiene, immunization and lifestyle changes. Poor working conditions and hazardous environments are the cause of much preventable disease and injury. Dead-end jobs, inadequate incomes, poor housing, discrimination and segregation, and lack of educational, cultural, and recreational opportunities combine to produce low self-esteem, mental dysfunction, alcoholism, drug addiction, suicide, homicide, wife and child abuse, and other violence directed against self, family, and community.

Access to medical care is markedly affected by factors other than financial barriers. Educational levels, transportation problems, and overcrowded, inadequate clinical facilities are particularly important in preventing optimal utilization of available resources.

Rehabilitation cannot stop with physical measures; it must include social and vocational rehabilitation as well. Societal facilities—buildings, sidewalks, buses, cars, parking lots, etc.—must incorporate provisions to meet the needs of handicapped persons. Jobs must be available to them, a difficult task to accomplish when a significant portion of the able-bodied workforce is unemployed.

Studies of multisectorial programs to improve living conditions in different countries—their successes and their failures—need to be pursued vigorously by scholars and practitioners of international health.

Medical care

Similar studies need to be carried out in the field of medical care, not only of financing and cost containment, but in the key areas of organization of services, quality of care, and democratization of control. For example, two very important innovations have taken place in the Americas which deserve intensive study by all scholars and practitioners of international health: the development of the network of CLSCs (Centres Locaux de Services Communautaires) in Quebec, which provide both health and social services in a single community[14] and (2) the new family physician and nurse teams housed in individual neighborhood health centers, each serving 600 to 800 people, which will be extended throughout Cuba in the next few years.[15]

Questions of priority

Finally, scholars and practitioners of international health must help us learn from world experience to determine priorities for public health action. In all countries of the Americas, as indeed in the rest of the world, treatment services are given priority, preventive services receive only a pittance, and the importance of health promotion through the improvement of living conditions may be honored in theory but is neglected in practice. This results from the domination of public health policy by the medical profession, which is treatment-oriented. Unfortunately, also, governments identify medical care as the most important aspect of health policy because it is politically the most popular; they pander to the opinion of the public which, in its ignorance, follows the medical profession in focusing attention and concern on treatment service.

Equity in medical care has clearly failed to assure equity in health, however. In England and Wales, the inequality in mortality of social classes has actually widened since the establishment of the National

Health Service. The two highest social classes (I, professional, and II, managerial) comprised 18% of the adult male population in 1951, 19% in 1961, and 23% in 1971; their standardized mortality ratio (SMR) was 91 in 1951, 80 in 1961 and 80 in 1971. The two lowest social classes (IV, semiskilled, and V, unskilled workers) comprised 29% of the adult male population in 1951, 29% in 1961, and 26% in 1971; their SMR was 110 in 1951, 115 in 1961, and 121 in 1971. The difference in SMRs more than doubled from 19 in 1951 to 41 in 1971.[12]

Nor has the universal Canadian medical care system achieved equality in health. Russell Wilkins and Owen Adams have calculated disability-free life expectancy for Canada in the late 1970s by income level. Disability-free life expectancy is the difference between life expectancy of all states of health and the sum of expected years of institutionalization plus expected years of disability not involving institutionalization. Their results are given in Table 7.[13]

In the late 1970s in Canada, the difference in life expectancy between people in the lowest and highest income levels was 4.5 years; for disability-free life expectancy, the difference was 11 years. Poor people in Canada have, on the average, only 5 years of healthy life, that is, life free of disability, as compared with 66 years of healthy life for rich Canadians.

**Table 7. Life Expectancy and Disability-Free
Life Expectancy, Canada, late 1970s**

Income level (fifths)	Life expectancy (years)	Disability-free life expectancy (yrs)
Lowest	71.9	54.9
Second	73.6	59.9
Third	74.7	62.7
Fourth	75.5	63.1
Highest	76.4	65.9
Total	74.6	61.0

These data underline the fact that medical care is the least significant of the basic triad of public health. The most important determinants of health status are health promotion through higher living standards, and the prevention of disease and injury.

Unfortunately, there is much confusion about the terms "health promotion" and "prevention." To add to the confusion, the terms are used interchangeably. In the United States, health promotion is officially defined as changing lifestyles for disease prevention. In Canada and Europe, it is, according to the Ottawa Charter for Health Promotion, focused on the improvement of living standards, i.e., "peace, shelter, education, food, income, a stable eco-system, sustainable resources, social justice and equity."

In the United States, disease prevention is pursued, but living standards are hardly considered. In Canada and Europe, living standards are emphasized, and epidemiologically based disease prevention has tended to receive less attention. Indeed, there are voices in Europe calling for a "new public health" which mistakenly characterize epidemiology and disease prevention as "the medical model" to be avoided at all costs.

In Latin America, too, there are voices raised against epidemiologically based prevention programs on the ground that no significant changes in health status can occur in the absence of profound political and social changes. Like their counterparts in Canada and Europe, they denigrate the value of preventive programs without understanding their scientific basis in epidemiologic research.

Which is more important, disease prevention or living standards? The answer is: Both. In the short run, prevention is more important because we can achieve major declines in illness, disability, and death in a relatively short time at minimal cost. Living standards are probably more important in the long run, but we should not delude ourselves into thinking that we will achieve higher standards quickly. It will take decades for us to realize—in the industrial countries as well as the developing nations—the goals envisaged in the Ottawa Charter for Health Promotion for "peace, shelter, education, food, income, a stable ecosystem, sustainable resources, social justice and equity."

It is essential to work for both disease prevention and health promotion, putting major emphasis at this point on utilizing the powerful tools forged by our epidemiologists to prevent the major killers: infectious diseases; heart disease, cancer, stroke, injuries, chronic obstructive lung disease, and cirrhosis of the liver; and occupational and environmental diseases. We must at the same time adopt a multisectorial approach by joining forces with other elements of society that are concerned with the improvement of living standards, so that we may indeed achieve healthy communities, healthy cities, and healthy nations in the Americas.

In this great effort, the scholars and practitioners of international health have a major responsibility: to study and analyze experience on a world scale in order to help their own and other countries achieve health for all. In this era of rampant, destructive nationalism, we must go against the tide, we must serve the people—not only of our own countries or the Americas, but of the whole world. We must become, indeed, citizens of planet Earth.

References

1. Pan American Health Organization. *Health Conditions in the Americas, 1990 Edition.* Washington, D.C., Pan American Health Organization, 1990. Vol. 1, p. 26.

2. United Nations Development Program (UNDP). *Human Development Report 1990.* New York and Oxford, Oxford University Press, 1990. P. 129.

3. Terris, M. Epidemiology and leadership in public health in the Americas. *J Pub Health Policy* 9:250-60 (1988).

4. *Pan American Health Organization. Op. cit.* P. 39.

5. *Pan American Health Organization. Op. cit.* P. 95.

6. *Healthy People: The Surgeon's General Report on Health Promotion and Disease Prevention, 1979.* U.S. Department of Health, Education and Welfare, Public Health Service, 1979.

7. *Promoting Health/Preventing Disease: Objectives for the Nation.* U.S. Department of Health and Human Services, Public Health Service, 1980.

8. *Health United States 1989.* U.S. Department of Health and Human Services, Public Health Service, 1990. P. 165.

9. Ibid., p. 121.

10. Ibid., p. 166.

11. *Ottawa Charter for Health Promotion.* Ottawa, Canadian Public Health Association, 1986.

12. Wilkinson, R. G., ed. *Class and Health: Research and Longitudinal Data.* London, Tavistock Publications, 1986. P. 14.

13. Wilkins, R., and O. B. Adams. Health expectancy in Canada, late 1970s: Demographic, regional and social dimensions. *Am J Pub Health* 73:1073-80 (1983).

14. Bozzini, L. Local Community Services Centers (CLSCs) in Quebec: Description, evaluation, perspectives. *J Pub Health Policy* 9:346-75 (1988).

15. Gilpin, M. Update - Cuba: On the road to a family medicine nation. *J Pub Health Policy* 12(1):83 (1991)

Cost and Equity of Health Systems

A. P. Contandriopoulos

Introduction

The concepts of equity and cost are at the heart of the field of study represented by international health. Of these two concepts, the one most often studied and most directly accessible is cost. Comparative analyses of health service costs have proliferated,[1,2,4,6,7,11,22] yet the results of these works are often disappointing, for three main reasons:

1. The concept of cost varies from country to country.[8,27] The disaggregation of costs by major categories is not always consistent. For example, what one country calls medical services may include services provided by doctors in hospitals, while these are excluded from that category in another country, etc.

2. The indicators used to compare countries are often difficult to interpret. The most traditional indicator is the ratio of total health expenditure to gross national product or gross domestic product (GDP). Changes in this indicator depend, of course, not only on the numerator—health expenditure—but also on the denominator—the collective wealth. It can be misleading to use this ratio to compare changes in the volume of health services to which different populations have access, since even if it is the same in two countries, the quantity of health services available to the population of a country in which economic development is occurring rapidly is larger than that for a population in a country with low economic growth.

This kind of difficulty is clearly illustrated by a comparison of Figures 1 and 2. Changes in health expenditure as a proportion of the GDP of a number of developed countries, from 1960 to the end of the 1980s, are shown in Figure 1. It is apparent, for example, that Japan's health expenditure tended not to rise much during the 1980s, the same being true for Germany from the mid-1970s onwards. This apparent control of health expenditure disappears, however, when one examines Figure 2, which shows health expenditure per capita deflated by price changes and adjusted to take account of differences in the growth of the GDP in the countries concerned. Figure 2 indicates that the volume of health services enjoyed by the Japanese and Germans during the 1980s increased significantly, while that available to Canadians tended to stabilize or even to decline. Nevertheless, the two figures show very clearly that health

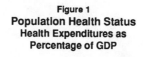

Figure 1
Population Health Status
Health Expenditures as
Percentage of GDP

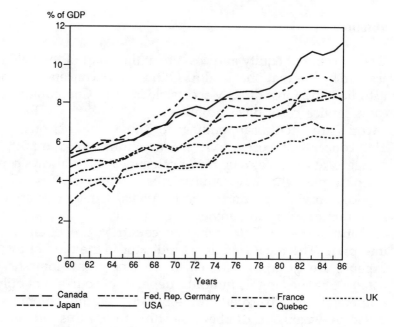

Sources: S. Sandier, *Eco-santé*, Paris, Medsi/McGraw-Hill, 1989, and and G.
J. Schieber and J. P. Pouiller, International health spending and
utilization trends, *Health Affairs* 7(3):105-112 (Fall 1988).

expenditure is growing more rapidly in the United states than in
other countries and that per capita expenditure is highest there.
Furthermore, it is difficult to attach much significance to the cost
differences revealed; it is not clear whether a higher per capita cost
reflects a greater quantity of health services per capita or higher-
priced services, in other words a higher level of remuneration for
health service professionals. [11,29]

3. Costs are merely a reflection of the efforts made to obtain a
    particular good. They have no meaning unless they are related to
    a result. From an international health standpoint, what results
    should therefore be considered in order to understand the
    significance of the cost differences that exist among different
    countries, and what indicator should be used to arrive at judgments
    regarding the relative performance of different health systems?

In what follows, we will suggest that this indicator should be the notion of equity in relation to health. I shall therefore begin by specifying what I understand by this concept. I will then put

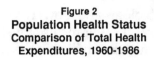

Figure 2
Population Health Status
Comparison of Total Health
Expenditures, 1960-1986

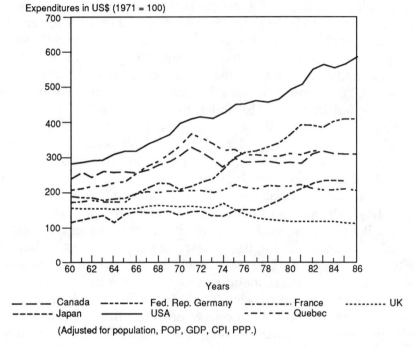

Expenditures in US$ (1971 = 100)

(Adjusted for population, POP, GDP, CPI, PPP.)

Sources: S. Sandier, *Eco-santé*, Paris, Medsi/McGraw-Hill, 1989, and and G. J. Schieber and J. P. Pouiller, International health spending and utilization trends, *Health Affairs* 7(3):105-112 (Fall 1988).

forward an analytical framework to facilitate an understanding of thesources of inequality in relation to health. Next I will return to costs in order to discuss the question of the financing of health services; I will try to identify which mechanisms are most consistent with improving the equity of the health system. Finally, I will touch briefly on the question of the role of the state in the general organization of health systems by asking whether the centralization and standardization that characterize most national health insurance programs do not in fact, paradoxically, generate new forms of inequity.

Why equity?

In a small work on biology and power, which partly takes up the analyses of Michel Foucault,[14] François Ewald says: "One of the characteristic features of modern civilization is the great attention given to the problems of the living, to the biological expression of men and their environment. The authorities are not asked to fight for or against values, because these divide the population. It is sufficient if they ensure the proper conservation of human beings, who have become citizens, and if they enable them to fulfill their potential as human beings."[13] This is also what is proposed in the "Ottawa Charter for the promotion of health" adopted in 1986. The states that subscribe to this charter are committed among other things to "reducing the current disparities in health status and providing all individuals with the same resources and opportunities to realize their health potential in full," in other words to promoting equity where health is concerned.

This statement formalizes what is in fact the raison d'être of the welfare state. The state must "manage the life of the population in order to protect it as well as possible against itself, and enable it to realize its potential."[13] Among the rights of man, the right to life and health are essential. A modern state sees itself as the doctor of society; its responsibility is to correct malfunctions in the natural relations among men in societies: "It is the society's task to establish itself as the remedy for the evils that in the natural course of things threaten life."[13] In the twentieth century "it is life that is emphasized and made an objective, life being understood as basic needs, the essence of humanity, the fulfillment of its qualities and potential. It is life, much more than the law, that has become the focus of political struggles."[14]

It is the combination of this ideology and the expansion of knowledge which during the first half of the twentieth century justified the introduction of large-scale health insurance and social security programs. The aim of these programs was to offer everybody (universality) a full range of services (completeness), without ability to pay, place of residence, social class, ethnic origin, etc., resulting in anybody's exclusion (accessibility). These large-scale programs are officially designed to improve the health of each individual, to put all citizens on an equal footing in their striving for health, in a word, to promote equity in relation to health.

During this first period, up to the mid-1970s, the emphasis was on the quantity of services; states invested massively in building hospitals, training doctors and installing a comprehensive health infrastructure in all countries.[12]

During the 1970s there was a significant change in approach. The rise in health costs became an ever-increasing source of concern to public authorities, all the more so as economic growth lost momentum and criticisms of the medical system became more and more virulent.[19] Instead of trying to correct health problems, it was now seen as desirable to prevent them.[20] It was no longer a matter of developing the health system, but of regulating it so as to find the best possible equilibrium among quantity, quality, and cost containment. At the same time, the notion of equity, which when large-scale health insurance programs were introduced consisted, in operational terms, of making accessible to everybody all the services that the medical profession regarded as appropriate, became more precise. Nowadays, a health system is regarded as equitable if it gives everybody access to those health services which make the most efficient contribution, in time and space, to improving the health of the population and putting all the individuals in a society on more equal terms as regards health.

This definition meshes with an egalitarian approach to utility.[24] It entails, first, that there are opportunity costs attached to health services and that it is important to assess the effectiveness of a good or service in improving health before making it universally available.[12] Second, it implies that the temporal and spatial dimensions of health must be considered, and third, that the state has an essential role to play in promoting equity in health.

It is therefore natural that different health systems should be evaluated in terms of their contribution to achieving equity. To do this we must analyze the principal causes of inequality in health, and ask what role the health system can play in reducing these inequalities.

Sources of inequality in relation to health

Individuals and organizations working in the area of international health are constantly confronted by two problems. The first is that there are considerable disparities in health status not only between the populations of different countries but between groups within a given country. The second concerns the resistance of these disparities to efforts made to reduce them. A lack of information is at the root of these problems; we know too little, among other things, about the role of the health care system in reducing inequalities.

This section begins by giving some examples of inequalities in health and then proposes a conceptual framework for a systematic analysis of inequalities in health and their determining factors.

Inequalities in health are numerous and varied. Figure 3 shows how life expectancy has changed between 1960 and 1986 in a number of developed countries. In interpreting this figure it is interesting to compare it with the changes in costs illustrated in Figures 1 and 2. It is particularly striking that there is no relation between the level of health expenditure and life expectancy, and that life expectancy in Japan is growing more rapidly than in any other of these countries.

House[18] shows that the social environment in which a population lives has a significant influence on its health. He analyses the results of a number of longitudinal studies comparing social support and mortality, and notes that the relative risk of dying is from two to four times greater among those with a low level of social integration than it is among those who are highly integrated.

Hertzman and Ward[17] analyzed the relationship between marital status and mortality. They note that death rates among persons who have never been married or are divorced or are widows are clearly and systematically higher than for those who are married.

Aïach et al. show that socioeconomic status and health, measured by the rates of perinatal, neonatal, and post-neonatal mortality, are not unrelated.[3] The higher the social class, the lower the mortality rate, and inversely.[21]

Wilkinson suggests that mortality is linked not merely to the level of income but also to its structure.[32] There is a significant correlation between the degree of disparity in income and life expectancy in the developed countries. The countries in which income differences are low have a higher life expectancy than those in which these disparities are large.

There is a broad consensus on the fact that very numerous differences exist between the health status of different populations, both among countries and within a given country. The question then arises as to how to organize the available information so as not only to compare equity in health among different countries but to determine the best strategies that should be introduced to reduce these inequalities.[5]

An analytical model of health disparities. To go beyond a description of inequalities to an analysis of their causes and to approaches to correcting

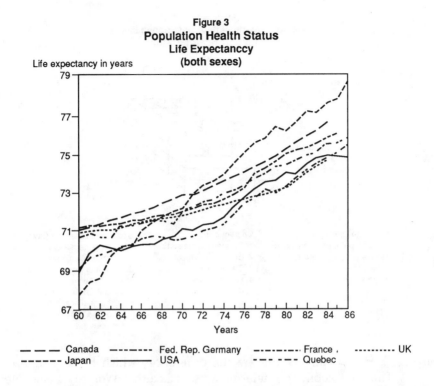

Figure 3
Population Health Status
Life Expectanccy
(both sexes)

Life expectancy in years

Years

— — — Canada   ------- Fed. Rep. Germany   --------· France ,   --------- UK
------- Japan   ———— USA   --- --- Quebec

Sources: S. Sandier, *Eco-santé*, Paris, Medsi/McGraw-Hill, 1989, and and G. J.
 Schieber and J. P. Pouiller, International health spending and
 utilization trends, *Health Affairs* 7(3):105-112 (Fall 1988).

them, we need a systematic investigation model. I am adopting that
developed by Clyde Hertzman[16] to analyze heterogeneities in the health
status of populations (Figure 4). He suggests analyzing heterogeneities
using three dimensions.

The first dimension involves the *life cycle of individuals*. Hertzman
suggests dividing the life cycle into four periods within which health
problems are relatively homogeneous: (1) from conception to one year,
i.e., a period during which health problems are linked to conception,
pregnancy, birth, and the first year of life; (2) from age one to 44, i.e., a
period during which individuals should only temporarily be affected by
illness; (3) from age 45 to 74, a period marked by the appearance of
chronic diseases; (4) from 75 years onwards, a period dominated by the
complex diseases of old age.

Figure 4
Model for Investigation of Heterogeneities in
Population Health Status

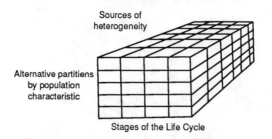

Stages of the Life Cycle	Characteristics	Sources of Heterogeneity
1. Perinatal: pre-term to one year	1. Socioeconomic status	1. Reverse causality
2. Misadventure 1-44 years	2. Ethnicity/migration	2. Differential suceptibility
3: Chronic disease 45-74	3. Geographic	3. Individual lifestyle
4. Senescence: 75 + years	4. Male/Female	4. Physical environment
	5. Special Populations	5. Social Environment
		6. Differential access to response to health care services

Source: C. Hertzman. Where are the differences which make a difference? Thinking about the determinants of health. Working Paper No. 8. Toronto, Canadian Institute for Advanced Research, 1990.

The second dimension used to analyze heterogeneities in health status involves *the different characteristics of the population*. Health status may vary according to the country or region of residence, sex, socioeconomic status, ethnic group, or culture.

These first two dimensions enable us to classify a population to some extent as a function of its age and certain of its characteristics and to note, within each of the resulting cells, the importance of heterogeneities in relation to health status.

The third dimension is designed to provide *major explanatory factors* for the differences in health status. These factors are lifestyles, the physical environment, the social environment, access to health services, human biology as reflected in greater or lesser individual susceptibility to the environment and ability to resist diseases more or less effectively, and, finally, a category which he calls reverse causality. This allows us to ask whether differences in health are determined by the fact that an individual belongs to certain population categories, or whether instead a difference in health status is responsible for membership in a particular category. For example, does being unmarried lead poorer health, or does the fact that an individual enjoys poorer health explain why he or she is not married?

This framework for analyzing heterogeneities in health status is particularly useful, first because it permits systematic comparison of the results of a vast number of works dealing with health inequalities of all kinds, but above all because it illustrates the fact that differences in health are an astonishingly complex matter. They should therefore be studied using approaches that allow their complexity to be grasped, as opposed to the tendency, too prevalent in the case of epidemiology, to explain a health difference in terms of a single cause while assuming everything else is constant. There has to be a way of determining the influence of various configurations of causes on groups of health differences. This kind of analysis may make it possible to devise realistic health policies that take account of the complexity and diversity of local situations.

While recognizing that current knowledge and research methods do not yet permit this goal to be reached, and that the studies and training now under way must be continued, we should nevertheless consider which directions the health care systems of different countries should take in order to contribute as effectively as possible to reducing health inequalities.

Costs, financing, and equity of health care systems

The work done on the costs and methods of financing the various health care systems in different countries has made it possible to reach certain conclusions regarding their ability to reduce health inequalities or not.[4,8,15]

1. In very general terms, it is impossible to establish a connection between the level of total expenditure on health, or the percentage of the collective wealth allocated to health, and equity as regards health. This is an unexceptional conclusion insofar as, first, equity is essentially a concept linked to the distribution and allocation of resources rather than their absolute level, and, second, very little is known about the influence of health services on reducing inequalities.

2. Financing methods may or may not help to promote equity in access to health services. It can be said that financing health services from public funds is a necessary condition for an equitable system, although it is in no way a sufficient condition. The greater the redistributive effect of the system of financing among social classes, the

more likely it is that the system will be equitable: the richer groups are to some extent financing the health services of the poorer groups, which on average are in poorer health. Conversely, recourse to private financing necessarily excludes certain segments of the population, which runs counter to the objective of equity.

3.   The ways in which system resources are paid out also affect the level of equity.[9,26] In proportion as a health system is financed by budgetary allocations determined a priori as a function of the populations to be served, it will tend to be more equitable. Conversely, to the extent that resources are paid out after the fact on the basis of the services provided, as in the case of fees for services and the financing of hospitals by diagnosis-related group (DRG), the system is potentially more inequitable. In such circumstances, it is in particular very difficult to allocate resources equitably across the country. Furthermore, it is hard to control the costs of health systems in which resources are paid after the fact and in part directly by those who are sick. This entails increasingly large transfers of resources to the health system, often to the detriment of other areas such as education, employment, and economic development which could help reduce health inequalities.[5,29]

4.   It is more likely that a health care system will be equitable if it incorporates mechanisms facilitating the relatively systematic collection, analysis, and diffusion of information on the health results it achieves and on the effectiveness of goods and services it provides.[28]

Conclusion

We have attempted to show that, from the standpoint of international health, equity in relation to health should be the principal criterion for evaluating the relative performance of health systems in different countries, and that equity between countries should be the goal of international health activities. We have based this argument on an analysis of the welfare state, whose purpose is to promote and protect the life of its citizens. Following the same logic, insofar as the health of a population is affected by phenomena that cross national boundaries (e.g., pollution, epidemics, external debt, migratory flows, tourism, wars), we are faced with the question of the need for an international organization which can legitimately intervene to promote greater equity among countries. But this development, which strengthens the responsibility of national states and the need for an international order paradoxically also risks giving rise to new differences. Let me explain.

Firstly, we must realize that at the end of the twentieth century the welfare state is doing better than ever. It is notable that, in very many countries, the share of government expenditure in total wealth continues to rise, despite all the talk of privatization.[10] The increasingly large role played by the state often takes the form of universal, centralized programs that theoretically aim to offer the same kinds of services to all citizens. The natural consequence of this development is an increasing standardization of society: "A standardizing society is the historic effect of a technology of power centered on life."[14] This standardization is apparent within every country and, to an increasing extent, throughout the world, where the practice in the developed countries is becoming the rule, often as a result of international assistance, in the southern countries. Paradoxically, however, this standardization is creating new forms of inequity.

In the area of health, for example, the introduction of comprehensive insurance programs has established the monopoly of the medical profession at the expense of the role of other health professionals who, before these programs were introduced, could exercise their skills independently. The consecration of an official, recognized, legitimate health system banishes those who are not part of it into a marginal and sometimes even illegal situation.

In the developed countries, the trend towards standardization raises serious questions, not to mention the extreme situations recently observed in the eastern countries (inefficiency, waste, deplorable health results). The justification for the power and/or autonomy enjoyed by the medical profession lies in the fact that medicine remains an art, despite considerable advances in its knowledge. Diagnosis is not the result of the application of a single algorithm, but rather the result of the conjunction of confidence, skill, and conscience at a given moment in a given context. The progress of a disease, in the shape of the effects of treatment of a patient's health problem at a given moment, is not a priori entirely predictable. Medicine is not a technique, and the doctor is not an engineer. In light of all this, society, in order to ensure that the decisions taken about the health of its citizens are the best possible, has delegated to the medical profession the responsibility of making sure that the skills of each of its members are adequate and that they are all bound by a strict professional ethic.

However, the efforts currently being made to rationalize medical activity, using scientific methods derived from basic research and epidemiology to evaluate the effectiveness of medical services, are in basic contradiction with the raison d'être of professionalism. Of course, the desire to find a scientific criterion which can be applied in order to reduce the uncertainty inherent in medical activity is attractive to doctors. But this norm, intended as a guide for each doctor to interpret and adapt in light of the situation of each patient, will quickly be regarded by the state, through its financing organizations and regulatory structure, as the only way of dealing with a given health problem. Any deviation from this norm will be regarded with suspicion; a doctor who departs from it may well be required to justify his action, and it may become tempting for patients to require that the standard treatment be applied to the letter, even if this is not appropriate in a particular case. The type of treatment suggested by the norm becomes the rule, thereby depriving the doctor of that margin of autonomy which is precisely what justifies his professional status. The state no longer needs to delegate self-regulation to the medical profession, since it is now sufficient, through administrative arrangements, to ensure that standard treatments are applied. The objective to be achieved is no longer health but observance of the norm; anything outside the norm is excluded. In this situation, it may be more sensible to do nothing than to offer services that do not conform to the norm, even if care is denied as a result to individuals who need it. These dangers of standardization are all the greater insofar as the society in question is highly developed and the state has significant powers.

Hence the challenge facing societies on the threshold of the twenty-first century is to rethink their health systems in order to find new ways of doing things that improve equity. We must devise health systems in which an adequate level of decentralization will find a place for innovation and allow the initiative of different communities to express itself. One can imagine systems in which common objectives would be accepted but in which a significant level of decentralization would allow much to be left to the independent decisions of professionals as regards how things should be done, with the corollary that the regional authorities could ask for an account of the results achieved. From this standpoint, the ongoing reforms in Quebec and the concept of local health systems seem very promising.[23,25]

References

1. Abel-Smith, Brian. Maîtrise des coûts dans 12 pays européens. *World Health Stat Q* 37:351-468 (1984).

2. Abel-Smith, Brian. Who is the odd man out?: The experience of Western Europe in containing the costs of health care. *Milbank Memorial Fund Q* 63(1):1-17 (1985).

3. Aïach, P., R. Carr-Hill, S. Curtis, and R. Illsley. *Les inégalités sociales de santé en France et en Grande-Bretagne.* Paris, Documentation Française, 1987.

4. Berthod-Wurmser, M. (ed.). *Systèmes de santé. Pouvoirs publics et financeurs: qui contrôle quoi?* Commissariat Général du Plan, Paris, Documentation Française, 1987.

5. Canadian Institute for Advanced Research. *The health of populations and the program in population health.* Population Health Publication No. 1. Toronto, Canadian Institute for Advanced Research, 1989

6. Commission d'enquête sur les services de santé et les services sociaux. *Rapport de la Commission d'enquête sur les services de santé et les services sociaux.* Quebec, Publications du Québec, 1988.

7. Contandriopoulos, A. P. Cost containment through payment mechanisms: The Quebec experience. *J Pub Health Policy* 7(2):224-238 (1986).

8. Contandriopoulos, A. P., A. Lemay, and G. Tessier. *Les coûts et le financement du système socio-sanitaire.* Dossier thématique. Quebec, Commission d'enquete sur les services de santé et les services sociaux, 1987.

9. Contandriopoulos, A. P., F. Champagne, and I. Baris. Physician compensation and health care system objectives: An appraisal of international experiences. Montreal, GRIS Cahier no. 90-14 (1990).

10. *The Economist*, March 2, 1991, p. 71.

11. Evans, R. G. *Strained mercy: The economics of Canadian health care.* Toronto, Butterworth, 1984.

12. Evans, R. G., and G. Stoddart. *Producing health, consuming health-care.* Toronto, Canadian Institute for Advanced Research, 1990.

13. Ewald, F. Le bio-pouvoir. *Magasine littéraire* 218:42-43 (1985).

14. Foucault, M. *Histoire de la sexualité, la volonté de savoir.* Paris, Gallimard, 1976.

15. Glaser, W. *Health insurance in practice.* San Francisco, Jossey-Bass, 1991.

16. Hertzman, C. Where are the differences which make a difference? Thinking about the determinants of health. Working Paper No. 8. Toronto, Canadian Institute for Advanced Research, 1990.

17. Hertzman, C., and H. Ward. Selected tables of mortality in Canada, programme in population health. Document 4A. Toronto, Canadian Institute for Advanced Research, 1989.

18. House, J. S., K. R. Landis, and D. Umbreson. Social relationship and health. *Science* 241:540-546 (July 29, 1988).

19. Illich, I. *Némésis medical: l'expropriation de la santé.* Paris, Seuil, 1975.

20. Lalonde, M. *Nouvelles perspectives de la santé des canadiens.* Ottawa, Santé et Bien Etre Social Canada, 1974.

21. Marmot, M. G. Social inequalities in mortality: the social environment. *In:* R. G. Wilkinson (ed.), *Class and Health*, London, Tavistock, 1986.

22. Marquez, P. Containing health costs in the Americas. *Health Policy and Planning* 5(4):299-315 (1990).

23. Ministère de la Santé et des Services Sociaux du Québec. *Une réforme axée sur le citoyen.* Québec, Gouvernement du Québec, 1990.

24. Mooney, G. Qu'est-ce que l'équité en matière de santé? *World Health Stat Q* 40:296-303 (1987).

25. Pan American Health Organization. *Development and strengthening of local health systems in the transformation of national health systems.* CE101/25. Washington, D.C., Pan American Health Organization, 1990.

26. Pouvourville, G. de. Gérer l'hôpital: outils et modes d'emploi. *Sciences Sociales et Santé* 8(2):33-65 (1990).

27. Pouvourville, G. de. L'approche comparative des systèmes de santé: réglementation ou régulation. Colloque sur les comparaisons internationales des politiques et des systèmes de sécurité sociale, Paris, MIRE et AISS, June 13-15, 1990.

28. Rachlis, M., and C. Kushner. *Second opinion.* Toronto, Collins, 1989.

29. Reinhardt, U. E. Resource allocation in health care: The allocation of lifestyle to providers. *Milbank Memorial Fund Q* 65(2):153-177 (1987).

30. Sandier, S. *Eco-santé.* Paris, Medsi/McGraw-Hill, 1989.

31. Schieber, G. J., and J. P. Pouiller. International health spending and utilization trends. *Health Affairs* 7(3):105-112 (Fall 1988).

32. Wilkinson, R. G. (ed.). *Class and health.* London, Tavistock, 1986.

33. World Health Organization. Ottawa Charter for health promotion. An international conference on health promotion sponsored by the World Health Organization, Health and Welfare Canada, and the Canadian Public Health Association at Ottawa from November 17-21, 1986. *Bull Pan Am Health Organ* 21(2):200-203 (1987).

PART TWO

THE CONCEPT AND PRACTICE OF INTERNATIONAL HEALTH WITH SPECIAL REFERENCE TO TRAINING EXPERIENCES

A Survey of International Health

Lise Gravel
Paul-A. Lamarche

The sociosanitary sector has not escaped the worldwide trend toward interdependence and the globalization of markets. Indeed, economic development and health are becoming more inextricably intertwined, thus compelling many governments to review the role of the state as a provider of services. As a result, an international awareness has developed of the need to enhance the state of health and the well-being of peoples, perceived as a prerequisite for peace and greater solidarity among nations. Moreover, the burgeoning of new means of communication is facilitating the dissemination of knowledge and the sharing of experience, and obliges us to review the scope of our methods of thinking and training programs aimed at health workers.

The past few decades have witnessed significant changes in mortality and morbidity, accompanied by a marked increase in life expectancy. New problems have arisen in the industrialized and developing nations, however. The wide array of problems are not perceived in the same manner, although there is a common concern to enhance the health and well-being of everyone.

Under the circumstances, international health is unquestionably a field of study and of professional practice. Three factors confirm this observation:

1. We are all subject to the effects of interdependence and globalization, population shifts, geopolitical changes, proliferating trade, and methods of communication.
2. We are all facing the same challenge, i.e., to satisfy unlimited health needs with the knowledge that the necessary resources are very limited.
3. We recognize that knowledge is changing rapidly, thus encouraging the sharing of experience and the development of vast information and exchange networks.

While a question does arise as to the true meaning of "international health," in our opinion it is possible to reflect at length on three issues: enhancing the state of health of a population, pinpointing the specific means of achieving this end, and respecting the ability to pay of various communities and their cultural traits. The foregoing question clearly imposes limitations on our knowledge but does enable us to channel experience gained in numerous sectors.

Bearing in mind these factors, let us examine "international health" in light of six themes that reflect many of the concerns of researchers, decision-makers, clinicians, or teachers.

First theme: The search for new indicators related to current sociosanitary conditions

We all know and use numerous traditional indicators of mortality and morbidity to compare the state of health of populations. Moreover, we acknowledge that health and well-being are determined by biology, the health care system, the physical, economic, and social environment, and lifestyles. Many health problems are attributable to social factors.

It would be useful to elaborate new indicators to better delimit new problems. Take, for example, mental health, violence, and the problems related to adaptation and rehabilitation affecting growing numbers of disabled people.

In the same vein, a team of researchers representing various countries and international organizations is seeking to harmonize the use of a new indictor, life expectancy in good health. In our view, these new indicators are essential to monitor the state of health of various populations.

Second theme: The reformulation of the objectives of various sociosanitary systems with a view to overcoming problems

We believe it is hard to manage a health and welfare system efficiently without first defining, in conjunction with a health and welfare policy, objectives pertaining to the reduction of health problems.

Such objectives must precisely, realistically establish the results expected in terms of reducing mortality due to the main health problems pinpointed. In addition to these objectives, a health policy must stipulate strategies and the means of carrying them out.

The elaboration of a health and welfare policy makes it possible to approach health problems in a different manner. We say "different" because, until now, the notion of services has been at the forefront of our concerns to such an extent that it has become an objective in itself, thus overshadowing the true purpose of such services, i.e., to solve sociosanitary problems. Moreover, the elaboration of objectives provides a rational, solid foundation on which to arbitrate various demands for the development of services at a time when resources are scarce.

We have used the term "different" because thinking in terms of the results to be achieved rather than services to be offered enables us to demonstrate that the health care system is not the only factor that contributes to solving sociosanitary problems.

By setting objectives centered on results, it is possible to more extensively involve individuals, families, and communities in solving health problems.

A trend has been noted in a number of countries toward the elaboration of health and welfare policies and could serve as a basis for exchanges and the sharing of experience.

Third theme: Interrelationships between economic development and health

Growing numbers of studies are revealing the impact of economic crises on health. The past decade saw a broad movement aimed at harmonizing the economies of the industrialized nations and adjusting the economies of the developing nations under the guidance of major financial institutions. All of these countries have experienced, in varying degrees, the consequences of economic change, repercussions which have led among other things to a reduction in government intervention and public spending in the fields of health and education.

Under the circumstances, a discussion of health cannot be confined solely to the organization of services. We must also take into account factors that, sooner or later, alter health and well-being and relate to an increase in or the appearance of new problems, e.g., malnutrition, violence, drug abuse, pollution, homelessness, unemployment, and so on. Sociosanitary services alone cannot solve these problems, which call for the establishment of new alliances between professionals in order to bolster cooperation and defend each group's rights. In this way, we are compelled to develop new means of intervention and initiate alliances with various groups and communities.

Fourth theme: The role of the state, methods of financing, and procedures aimed at decentralizing health care systems

Each country has its own perception of how to organize sociosanitary services. Some countries opt for a universal system, while others maintain several systems.

We have clearly chosen a universal health care system, which assumes a network of interconnected establishments offering an array of general, specialized, and ultraspecialized services, based on a clear notion of the links between different levels of responsibility, and financing derived by and large from public funds and covering a broad range of services. As a result, the state must clearly commit itself to playing a leading role in ensuring public health.

However, we do acknowledge that it is a complex task to establish such a system, enable it to attain its objectives, and at the same time tailor services to the changing needs of users. The challenges to be met are daunting. To meet these challenges means not only that we must take into account various facets of the system and those who operate it, but that we must deal with our own political and economic environment. The latter factor is of crucial importance to the government and obliges us regularly to review operations, resource allocation, and the role of intervening parties.

A number of research teams are analyzing health care systems, and we feel that such interest should grow in the Americas.

Decentralization is a concern in a number of countries and is carried out according to each country's political and administrative attributes. The trend nonetheless reflects a single concern, that of aligning decision-making power and intervention as closely as possible. In this vein, the greatest virtue of decentralization is that it achieves greater flexibility when the means of satisfying widely divergent needs are selected. By decentralizing, we acknowledge diversity and make possible the adoption of different strategies demanded by different situations. Furthermore, decentralization makes it possible to heighten the complementarity and availability of services.

Fifth theme: The involvement of individuals in organizing health services and improving their health

We noted earlier that knowledge is evolving rapidly. It should also be noted that knowledge is not the prerogative of specialists. More and more people are becoming concerned about the development of certain health problems, are seeking to participate in community groups, and are questioning the management of the health care system.

We must find ways to further involve individuals in the decision-making process as it pertains to their health. While the means adopted will vary from one country to another, we are convinced that broad participation can only be achieved through decentralization in which decision making and intervention are as closely aligned as possible, and the democratization of knowledge. We must bear in mind that the individual will always be the focal point of our initiatives, and that individuals give legitimacy to our initiatives and knowledge.

We could envision the participation of individuals as a theme of discussion by defining it in relation to our respective societies, the importance we attach to it, the sharing of knowledge, and the place reserved for nonprofessionals, community groups, traditional medicine, and new therapies.

In this way, we will have to accept the attendant changes in our professional practices.

Sixth theme: Technological research and development and pressure on the allocation of financial resources

Whether it is basic, clinical, epidemiological, evaluative, or organizational, research underpins the planning, management, and evaluation of sociosanitary programs and services and provides essential support will regard to professional practice. It also ensures that the public has access to better adapted, more efficient services. Moreover, we fell it is essential that the results of research be widely disseminated.

Still, research often suffers from underfinancing; governments alone cannot provide the necessary funds. Furthermore, technological development and the ever-growing use of technology oblige us to reach difficult decisions and establish processes for selecting and applying such technologies. How can we reconcile human considerations and notions of cost and efficiency? What information do we need to reach enlightened decisions and explain them to managers, health care workers, and the public at large? How can we predict the cost of quickly introducing increasingly sophisticated technologies? These questions should encourage us to combine our efforts and find ways of furthering collaboration between research teams in the Americas.

One valuable way is to foster technical cooperation which, when it respects cultural affinities, makes it possible to heighten solidarity among peoples, share experience and review development models centered for too long on the notion of assistance. We believe that technical cooperation projects aimed at organizing sociosanitary programs and services should be effected using a multisectorial approach which, without being exhaustive, seeks to reflect the needs and capacities of the communities where the projects are being carried out.

Based on several themes related to "international health: a field of study and of professional practice," we outlined a framework for discussion applicable not only to public services, but to the training of health care workers and the dissemination of information to the public. While the ultimate meaning of the concept warrants further reflection, we do believe that the discussion cannot be avoided. Current conditions compel us to examine the matter.

To discuss international health means to acknowledge that health extends largely beyond the organization of sociosanitary services. It implies questioning the efficacy of medical services and, as a result, rethinking the very foundations of medicine. It also means reviewing the meaning and utility of our initiatives, from the national to the local level. It entails realizing the importance of multidisciplinary studies that focus by and large on concepts of work that are often different from our own. Finally, it involves recognizing the important role played by women in improving family health and in providing health care.

To discuss international health also means comparing our policies, programs, and infrastructures and agreeing to call them into question to take into account the complexity of our societies and take advantage of the numerous contributions the social sciences can make. It implies strengthening a community-oriented bias in our initiatives, fostering universal access to knowledge, ensuring that those we train receive sound basic knowledge, and reviewing methods of learning and disseminating knowledge. It also entails recognizing that knowledge is democratizing itself and that not only are our decisions being called into question but the way in which we share knowledge as well. Individuals are demanding more and more to participate in decision making with respect to the choice of treatment, the management of establishments, and so on.

To discuss international health also means learning, as Jacques Attali would have it, to manage the globalization of problems, which demands a new culture, a new political perception and, indeed, new institutions. It involves seeking solutions to crucial problems such as inadequate distribution networks, social inequality, the management of external debt, environmental protection, the fight against epidemics and so on. It entails influencing power: this influence can be channeled by focusing fully on different levels of social and political life within various groups and our countries, expressing our opinions, and disseminating and popularizing knowledge.

Finally, to discuss international health is a matter of accepting our differences and limitations; of understanding the dead end into which current development models have led us, in which little concern has been shown for the impact of development on human beings; of questioning our initiatives and acquiring the ability to think, see, and act in a medium- and long-range perspective, and of adapting our practices to the introduction of innovative devices which will foster the greater autonomy of individuals and the accentuation of their differences.

Just as computers have made educational, health promotion, and development programs accessible, these innovative devices, distribution of which will be tied to socioeconomic conditions, will broaden the notion of self-diagnosis. Breathalyser and pregnancy tests are now widespread. Other tests will be introduced, for example, to quickly measure a parameter. Once miniaturized, these innovative devices will be readily available to consumers.

Thus, individuals will be less and less frequently excluded from the act of caring and teaching. Moreover, they will be increasingly subject to behavioral standards such as "being fit" and "being informed." They will carry with them their complete identity. A smart card will enable consumers to store a wide array of confidential information, which, in addition to being more readily accessible, will democratize knowledge and legitimize individual autonomy. The role of health professionals will be significantly altered; they will have to listen more extensively than at present.

This electronic revolution is already widespread and is permeating all spheres of endeavor. It has made it necessary to organize the development of the use of human faculties. This is the challenge facing us: to capture, process, and disseminate information requires numerous well-trained men and women, thus creating the need for new exchanges, communication, and knowledge. It compels us to place human beings at the forefront of our concerns.

The revolution also obliges us to review the role and responsibilities of the state, the private sector, NGOs, and each and every one of us to encourage complementarity, find new forms of development, and bolster exchanges of information and human resources.

The foregoing reflections coalesce around the theme "international health: a field of study and of professional practice."

We cannot overemphasize the importance of fostering exchanges among professionals, institutions, and governments and of encouraging discussion which will clarify the concept of international health.

International Health and Schools of Public Health in the United States

Charles Godue

It is in the United States of America that the idea of international health has prospered the most. The term "international health" first appeared and gradually gained ground following the establishment in 1913 of the International Health Commission in the then only just established Rockefeller Foundation. The Commission also supplanted the Rockefeller Health Commission, itself established in 1909 for the eradication of ankylostomiasis; its initial purpose was to spread to other countries and peoples the experience acquired by the Health Commission in the southern states of the United States.[1]

To better support its massive public health operations abroad, the Commission played a leading part in the opening in 1917 of the first school of public health in the United States at Johns Hopkins University. The School was immediately given an international mission with the training of the technical staffs of the Commission and its own research work. Nevertheless, no specific subject matter was assigned to international health; indeed, it was not until 1960 that an international health division was established in the School.[2]

International health operations have multiplied considerably since then, and have involved an ever growing number of actors and organizations which, moreover, have been widely diverse in kind and interests. For the last three decades, however, international health has been a field of study and training in its own right. The trajectories of many American teaching institutions have been fairly identical in this regard: the former school of tropical diseases or its equivalent has become a school or department of public health, which since the Sixties has become interested in international health and the teaching thereof.

This development is the source of the residual pathologies hypothesis, according to which the recent establishment of international divisions or units in schools of public health stems from the need to group together within an institution the experts in the so-called tropical diseases, which were endemic in the United States at the turn of the century but have become progressively dated as the national epidemiological situation has evolved. The international aspect refers not just to the fact that the work is done outside the country, as it did for the Rockefeller Foundation, but also designates pathologies of a type that are likely to die out under the combined weight of industrialization and development or, in a word, modernization. A review of the history of these units quickly demonstrates the inadequacy of this explanation.

In any case, some professionals are asking questions and taking a second look at international health as a field of training and research because of confusion over the object of study, the lack of distinct limits to the field, and its want of theoretical substance. These assertions are borne out indirectly by the scarcity in the literature of health and medicine of discussions of the nature of international health, its defining features, supporting disciplines, central themes, and explanatory power. There is, to our knowledge, but one book specifically on the subject.[3] International health is for many an assemblage of health initiatives and practices which bring together health workers of different nationalities but is otherwise an empty shell, devoid of any method or body of knowledge specific to itself.

Before inquiring how schools of public health in the United States approach and conceive international health, it is useful to isolate the principal meanings of the term in the literature. This exercise will provide a background against which we can best grasp where the schools of public health stand.

International health: Principal meanings of the term

> International society has existed for only three centuries.
> All that time it has been in the throes of its own birth,
> and only it the last few years has it become truly universal.
> We are today only at the dawn of the universal and
> multidimensional international society.[4]

To speak of international health is to speak of international society. The meaning given to the term "international health" varies with the writer and his or her place in a national or international institutions, but it is implicitly inspired by the leading paradigms of the nature of international society and the relationships that nations establish among themselves.

The predominant notion of international health refers to the interactions in the health field that occur on the global scale, on the scale of humanity as a whole. The proposition is predicated on the interdependence of the states of health of individuals and populations owing to the mobility of health hazards and people.[5] This interaction of states of health justifies an analysis of the factors that can affect the health of peoples, including protective measures.[6] For some, international health refers primarily to the most frequent world health problems: overpopulation, malnutrition, and infectious diseases.[7] More generally, however, the study of international health bears on such elements as the states of health of populations and their determinants, the internationalization of pathologies and their causes and of the phenomena of epidemiological transition, comparative analysis of health policies and systems, and the importance of cultural elements in living habits and the use of services.

The comprehensive and sweeping scope of this proposition makes it somewhat less interesting. International health becomes more distinct, more practical, when placed in geographic context; it is then seen as consisting in the health activities carried on between two or more countries.[8] The notion of the country is here broader than that of a government or even of a nation-state. The dividing line follows the borders between states, but the political actors who establish and defend their borders are secondary. Much more important are the health workers and health organizations. Thus, the notions of international health and international collaboration are frequently merged, for the latter assembles around a single project health workers from two or more countries.[9]

The most frequent division is not geographical, however, but socioeconomic and is based on the fact of underdevelopment. International health is then associated with the health problems of the developing countries.[10] This proposition is rooted in humanitarian values which affirm the universal right to health, which are at the source of the widespread solidarity expressed in practices of international cooperation aiming at improving the health status of the deprived populations in poor countries.[11] In this context international health sometimes takes on an aura of a spiritual or moral crusade.[12] The social sciences—anthropology in particular—will have an important impact on the nature of and forms taken by international health assistance.[13] They will contribute to an improved understanding of the dynamics of local communities and of the political, economic, and ideological factors that can make a project succeed or fail.[14] This is the sociocultural model of cooperation, which emphasizes the importance of adapting health technologies to local situations and cultures.[15]

This predominant concept of international health, with its numerous variants, is based on the paradigm of international society as a global society. The primary subjects of this society are men and women; the states play their parts and carry on their activities, but on the same footing as individuals, groups, and organizations because human beings antedate states and retain basic rights and prerogatives. International society is actually transnational; borders attenuate and the rights of man are asserted.[16]

The idea contains an important contradiction, however. Whereas the opening proposition places the accent on the interactivity and interdependence of states of health and their determinants worldwide, the more restricted interpretation associating international health with the health problems of the developing countries largely confines this interaction to aid, and to the knowledge needed to provide it. International health, rather than favoring a global vision, separates the partners and processes into "modern" and "traditional" societies; for the latter, the idea loses all meaning. "International" equals that which is extranational or foreign in the one-way view of countries at the center looking at those on the periphery.

A second concept of international health—less frequently heard, to be sure—associates international health with health activities that result from agreements between two or more countries for their mutual benefit.[17] The idea of the state is used in its strict sense as the government apparatus. These states are entirely free to sign agreements and to become members of and participate in international and intergovernmental organizations. The study of international health is concerned with the process of framing these agreements, with their purpose and implementation: the International Sanitary Code, international health institutions and their different programs and activities; international health policies and strategies, particularly the goal of Health for All by the Year 2000 and the strategy of Primary Health Care; travelers' health, and other elements of multilateral relations. It also covers bilateral agreements such as health control measures at borders and health cooperation carried out or funded by government agencies.

This proposition can be reconciled with the view of international society as constituted by the coexistence of independent and sovereign states, which are the leading—though not the sole—actors. Primacy is accorded to defense of the national interest, which is expressed in strategies of cooperation, accommodation, or confrontation. One important characteristic of this theory is recognition of the specific nature of the international society relative to the domestic polity, the former based on the coexistence of independent entities and the latter integrated and hierarchically organized.

In the literature reviewed there appears to be little interest in the relationship between agreements entered into between two or more countries and the foreign policies of those countries. What is more, few authors wonder about the existence of connections between the two senses previously presented; put differently, those who see themselves as actors in international health in the sense of cooperation with developing countries act as if what they did was unrelated to national interest, or to their own government's foreign policy, or, in some cases, as if it counterbalanced that policy. When the possibility of a connection between foreign policy and international health is raised at all, it is to decry the lack of any and to promote one. International health is then claimed to be a legitimate instrument of foreign policy.[18]

A third sense of international health considers the development of a world system resulting from the spread of the capitalist mode of production as a central analytical element, the one best fitted to account for changes in the states of health of populations and in health systems. This world system structures relationships and arrays them in hierarchies not just among nations but also among the different social groups within each. This system brings about an international division of labor and a structuring of production between the countries of the center, the countries at the periphery, and those in between. Its dynamic is impelled by a quest for the increasing accumulation of capital and the formation of monopolies. The objects of study in regard to its impact on health are many: malnutrition of commercial origin, linked to the growth of reliance on single crops for export, or the substitution of milk powder for breast-feeding, the growth of drug companies, the transfer of hazardous substances and high-risk technologies, human production processes and life habits, and birth-control campaigns, to name but a few. To these direct effects on the health of populations must be added the effects on the configuration of care systems, in particular through exportation of the biomedical model by way of the medical-industrial complex.[19] The proposition asserts that health in a given society is determined first and foremost by how resources are distributed in it, which itself depends on profiles of accumulation worldwide.[20]

This approach to international health makes reference to a view of international society based on the development of a hierarchically organized national and world system. The capitalist rationale, which carries with it a need to reproduce itself more widely, cannot remain confined within the borders of one country: through international relations and multinational dynamics it has contributed to the creation of national domains integrated at the world level and to globalization of the world economy (and of the ideological, cultural, and institutional factors therein implied). Each economic activity, whatever the economic system that characterizes it and its level of involvement (local, regional, or national) in the reproduction of a social group, is increasingly influenced by capitalism, which is spreading around the globe. We are witnessing a disappearance of diversity all over the world.

Schools of Public Health in the United States

In recent years international health has grown more important in the United States, not just in terms of activities and exchanges but also as a field of study and research. Schools of public health are taking the lead in coordinating the international health projects of universities and in promoting international health as an area of training. These training programs are a relatively recent phenomenon, the first of them dating from the beginning of the Sixties, and differ from the more traditional training in tropical medicine. Besides, interest has rapidly spread to undergraduate medical education and to the specialty of family medicine.

The importance of the phenomenon is clear from the status of international health in the internal structure of the schools of public health. Of the 24 schools of public health accredited by the Council of Education for Public Health, international health is ranked as a major division in five of them, on a par with, for example, epidemiology, maternal and child health, and health administration.[21] It is interesting to note the frequent association in the name of the division between international health and population planning. Five more institutions have subdivisions of international health as a field of specialization in a larger division. International health is generally under a division of population and family health, or even of community health development, hence of units concerned with populations. Finally, there are three other institutions which have set up units (called "Programs" or "Offices") of international health which bring together the faculty members concerned and whose principal functions are to coordinate all activities and projects in this domain, ranging from teaching to cooperation abroad. Such units are generally responsible for raising extrabudgetary funds. The other universities have no formal structure for international health, but all the schools offer one or more courses regarded as relevant to international health. It is also interesting to note that one school is a collaborating center of the World Health Organization and that two others offer a joint program with the Peace Corps (Peace Corps M.P.H. Program). The sources consulted yield no information on the contribution of international health activities to the raising of extrabudgetary funds; in some cases it does seem as though such funds are of respectable size and are an important factor in the institution's development.[22]

The formal pronouncements of the schools of public health broadly concur in their conceptions of international health, which refer explicitly to health problems in developing countries and partake of the same stream of humanism, universalist in outlook and sometimes of religious inspiration. Underdevelopment implies a host of obstacles to the attainment of a satisfactory state of health and to the organization of effective health services. The poverty associated with underdevelopment gives rise to particular profiles of morbidity and mortality that are dominated by the infectious and deficiency diseases, which themselves are aggravated by unchecked population growth; the obstacles to health are sociocultural, environmental, and economic in nature and among other things are manifested in severe deficiencies of hygiene, public health, and schooling, and in the administrative complexities frequently associated with developing countries. The object of study of international health is illuminated by the use of contrasts and contraries that partake of the dichotomous: industrial vs. nonindustrial countries, urban vs. rural regions, rich populations vs. populations steeped in poverty, and chronic diseases vs. infectious and parasitic diseases. International health corresponds in a way to public health for the deprived and poor populations, to the adaptation of techniques, methods, and skills of public health for operation in adverse settings where resistances and difficulties are pronounced.

The motivations and values that underlie the development of international health stem largely from a sense of responsibility for reducing the socioeconomic disparities observed in the world of today in quest of equity and social justice. These disparities exist not just between nations but also within them. This fact of life explains why poor and poorly served communities in the United States are frequently included within the purview of international health, because they require the same theoretical knowledge for the solution of public health problems as third-world populations do.

There is thus yet another motivation for the development of international health: the professional trained in this field is particularly suited for work with national minorities. In the same sense and by extension, training in international health and the experience of work in the third world are regarded as relevant strategies for promoting primary health care at the national level, that is, within the United States, and for the development of community-oriented services with a view to participation and accessibility. Finally, the contribution of international health to the protection of household health is mentioned, of course, but as a secondary concern.

This conception of international health is closely linked to, and even identifiable with the idea of international aid, assistance, or cooperation in health, for which the terminology varies with the times. The body of knowledge and skills conferred by training in international health is to an extent limited by demands for the execution of projects and programs in underdeveloped settings. As an example, some institutions give more importance to transcultural communication and the adaptation of operational techniques to the local situation and its dynamics in order to enhance the chances of success.

Though a more searching examination of the courses and programs offered would certainly bring out a wider diversity of approaches and analyses, the fact remains that the convergence among statements by schools of public health is real, and this raises a fair number of questions.

International cooperation, international health, and global health

The first concept or meaning of international health presented briefly at the beginning of this paper, which refers, it may be recalled, to health as a transnational phenomenon, prevails in all the formal utterances of the schools of public health, but in its narrowest sense, that of the developing countries. No reference is made to international health as an aspect of relations between states or as a manifestation of a hierarchical world system, and no question is raised about the incompleteness or delimitation of the object of study. The latter is defined by a particular subdivision of the world population based on the levels of development or modernization attained and is equated with the notion of international cooperation.

International health is thus closely associated with aid and underdevelopment, with the opening of a sociocentric gulf between "us" (the developed) and "the others" (the underdeveloped). From the perspective of the latter, international health has nothing to concern itself with. This dissociation is reinforced by the inclusion in its purview of deprived groups at home. It has to be recognized that this inclusion has tactical value in making international health domestically relevant. One can also understand the use of international health as a strategy for reorganizing health services in the United States. Though admittedly of secondary importance, the inclusion muddles the concept without offering any assurance of effectiveness.

We are forced to recognize the operational character of this definition. The structures for training and work in international health have emerged in the schools of public health at the instigation of and with funding from the Agency for International Development (AID) in its search for operational authorities to implement health programs in developing countries. The object of study is thus defined operationally on the basis of geopolitical interests and strategies of the early Sixties. Foreign aid is an instrument of foreign policy; its rapid growth, it must be remembered, coincides with decolonization and independence processes, chiefly in Africa, and with the rise of revolutionary movements and wars of liberation in many third-world countries in a setting of intensifying cold war and rivalry between the superpowers.

Whereas the concept of international health was engendered, spread, and institutionalized at the turn of the century through a private foundation in response to economic imperatives associated with an expansion of world trade,[23] after 1960 the pace of this advance was determined more by the geopolitical interests promoted by AID, a public agency. In each case the motivation was supplied by a different paradigm: in the first by confidence in science and technology as an engine of modernization and development, and in the second by the attribution of greater importance to local characteristics and sociosanitary dynamics, since it is these factors that largely determine the modalities of transfer of new technologies and the likelihood of their success.

The interpretation that international health is the operational expression in the schools of public health of a segment of foreign policy, if proved correct, bodes ill for the further development of the concept and of operations under its banner in coming years as the premises of foreign policy are completely overhauled in the wake of the collapse of communism in Eastern Europe. The debates of yesteryear on the theory of dependence, concern over projects for national independence and development, and the struggle against communism have given way to discussion of interdependence, economic integration, globalization of markets, and liberalization of terms of trade. Among other ways, this thematic shift is expressed in a reduction of government aid and the channeling of sizable sums of money to the Eastern European countries to facilitate their integration into the market economy.

The debate on the object of study has already started: a shift from a dissociative, sociocentric approach to one that focuses on health at home. Supported by arguments of shared vulnerability and mutuality of interests, the proposition of interdependence centers the discussion on global problems in reflection of a rising tension over domestic repercussions of international issues.[24] Particularly disquieting are deterioration of the environment (planet warming, ozone depletion, etc.), the great pandemics, most of all the Acquired Immunodeficiency Syndrome (AIDS), and migrations. The term "global health" is being used to promote this new trend and signal a break with the earlier sense of the term.

Interestingly, this new thinking around the idea of interdependence seeks to develop in integration with the formulation of an appropriate post-cold war foreign policy. The national security policy of the United States in the Sixties, underpinned by geopolitical and military imperatives, was aimed primarily at eradicating communism; the events of the last few years appear to clear the way to a widening of the idea of security to take in, among others, considerations of public health.[25]

While some assert the legitimacy of using international health as an instrument of foreign policy, our thinking leads us to reason in the opposite direction: is there an elaboration of international health that is in some degree autonomous of foreign policy interests? A collaborative effort to produce a theory of international health with explanatory power valid in other national and international contexts seems urgently needed here. The foreign policy review now going forward in the United States presents an ideal opportunity for redefining the object and field of international health.

Universities, and most particularly schools of public health, have a primary responsibility in this redefinition. The relatively recent emergence of international relations as a field of study promises a richly instructive experience. To elicit a response, any further elaboration of international health may require a closer association with international relations. Without knowledge and analysis of the nature and history of international society, there is nothing that can be referred to specifically as international health.

References

1. On the origins of the International Health Commission, see John Ettling, *The germ of laziness: Rockefeller philanthropy and public health in the New South* (Cambridge, Massachusetts, Harvard University Press, 1981), in particular Chapter 8, "Henceforth Thy Field is the World." As for an expansion of the Foundation's work to the international sphere and its connection with the teaching of public health in the United States, see E. R. Brown, Public health in imperialism: Early Rockefeller programs at home and abroad, *Am J Pub Health* 66(9):897-903 (1976).

2. For a stimulating discussion of the establishment of the School of Hygiene and Public Health of Johns Hopkins University, see Elizabeth Fee, *Disease and discovery: A history of the Johns Hopkins School of Hygiene and Public Health, 1916-1939*, Baltimore, Johns Hopkins University Press, 1987.

3. P. Basch. *International health*. New York, Oxford University Press, 1978.

4. Huntzinger, J. *Introduction aux relations internationales*. Paris, Editions du Seuil, 1987. Pp. 73-74.

5.   John Last sums up the best of this thinking in writing that "International Health refers to the interlocking and interrelated health status of people throughout the world and to efforts to improve the health of all people of every country." *In:* J. M. Last (ed.), *Maxcy-Rosenau Textbook of Public health and preventive medicine*, 12th ed., New York, Appleton-Century-Crofts, 1986, p. 1793.

6.   This is the option of Basch's book: "The systematic comparison of the factors that affect the well-being of the peoples of the world, and of the steps that can be taken for its improvement." *Op. cit.*, p. v.

7.   Seah, S. K. K. Canada and international health. *Can Med Assoc J* 115:377-8 (1976).

8.   Last himself puts forward this definition the second time around: "Therefore, a general understanding of the term international health would include activities between two or more countries to detect or counteract disease problems and to enhance health." *Op. cit.*, p. 1794. See also T. Baker, C. Weisman, and E. Piwoz, United States health professionals in international health work, *Am J Pub Health* 74(5):438-41 (1984).

9.   One example of this is the issue of *JAMA* devoted to international health, and especially the editorial by Philip Schambra, entitled "Seeking New Dimensions in International Health Research." In it the author associates research in international health with international collaboration in research projects in different areas such as human genetics and hepatitis non-A non-B. See *JAMA* 263(24):3325-6 (1990). Another example is an issue of the *American Journal of Public Health* also devoted to international health. International health refers to the fact that the articles are signed by foreign authors whose research was done in their own countries. See *Am J Pub Health* 81(1) (1991).

10. This is Last's last proposition, which determines the content of his chapter: "A more limited definition of international health, as used in this chapter, refers specifically to the health problems of developing countries. In this chapter, we will define international health as the branch of public health that deals with current and projected health problems of developing countries, rather than with the general conditions existing throughout the world. As will become apparent, however, health problems of developing countries can affect us all wherever we live in the world." *Op. cit.* p. 1374. This is clearly the bias of the issue of *Infectious Diseases of North America* devoted to international health, with Dr. Anvar Velji as guest editor. See *Inf Dis Clin North Am* 5(2) (1991).

11. In their volume on international cooperation for health, Reich and Marui write: "The health gaps between rich and poor countries persist alongside the economic and political chasms that separate the so-called developed and developing worlds. The main objective of international cooperation for health is to close those gaps through efforts that go beyond national boundaries." See Michael R. Reich and Eiji Marui, Overview and Introduction, *in:* Michael R. Reich and Eiji Marui (eds.), *International Cooperation for Health: Problems, Prospects and Priorities*, Dover, Massachusetts, Auburn House, 1989, p. 1.

12. Perhaps the most eloquent spokesman of this view is Dr. Anvar Velji, from whom international health evokes bursts of compassion and generosity. In one article he characterizes international health in the following terms: "International Health can best be described as health care that is shared between nations (international) and encompasses multiple disciplines and sciences... Unlike the component disciplines, it has a moral and spiritual component." See A. M. Velji, International health (editorial), *West J Med* 155(3):308-9 (1991). Elsewhere he writes: "More and more it is defined as the study and application of what makes a human being the global being (regardless of his ethnic origin, background, or place of residence on this planet) enjoy his or her inalienable right in achieving health as a state of physical, social, mental and spiritual well-being and not merely the absence of disease or infirmity, as proclaimed in the World Health Organization chapter." A. M. Velji, International health, *Infect Dis Clin North Am* 5(2):xiii-xv (1991).

13. Foster, G. M., Applied anthropology and international health: Retrospect and prospect, *Human Organization* 41(3):189-97 (1982).

14. Giovannini, M. J., and A. T. Brownlee, The contribution of social science to international health training, *Soc Sci Med* 16:957-64 (1982).

15. Foster, G. M., Bureaucratic aspects of international health agencies, *Soc Sci Med* 25(9):1039-48 (1987).

16. Dr. Bernard Kouchner, the founder of Médecins du Monde, speaks of a duty to interfere. See his fascinating book containing the presentations made at an international conference held in Paris in 1987 under the aegis of Médecins du Monde and the Faculty of Law of Paris-South: M. Bettati and B. Kouchner, *Le devoir d'ingérence: Peut-on les laisser mourir?* Paris, Denoel, 1987.

17. Isaza, P., *Salud internacional*, manuscript, PAHO/WHO, Mexico, June 1988. The author writes: "International health designates the set of health activities that transcend the area under the responsibility of a country so that, through mutual agreements at the subregional, regional or world

level, these activities and their components are shared with one or more countries."

18. Pust, R. R., "U.S. abundance of physicians and international health," *JAMA*, 252(3):385-8 (1984). Pust writes: "Apart from its humanitarian value, international public health programs can be cost-effective as foreign policy. Among the 1,417 American physicians serving abroad in 1981, there were 659 clinicians, many of them volunteers; these bedside doctors also are impressive ambassadors of goodwill in the region they serve." P. 386.

19. The best defender of this proposition is Ray Elling. See R. H. Elling, The capitalist world system and international health, *Int J Health Serv* 11(1):21-51 (1981).

20. See J. W. Ratcliffe and J. C. Merrill, The impact of U.S. energy policy on international health: Alternate paths into the future, *Int Q Comm Health Educ* 3(1):27-43 (1982).

21. These schools have emerged in the following institutions: the Universities of Alabama at Birmingham, of California at Berkeley, of California at Los Angeles, Loma Linda, State at San Diego, Yale, South Florida, Hawaii at Manoa, Illinois at Chicago, Tulane Medical Center, Johns Hopkins, Boston, Harvard, Massachusetts at Amherst, Michigan, Minnesota, Columbia, North Carolina at Chapel Hill, Oklahoma, Pittsburg, Puerto Rico, South Carolina, Texas at Houston, and Washington State. The remarks that follow are based on the general syllabi of the different schools in 1988.

22. The Dean of the School of Public Health of North Carolina at Chapel Hill writes, for example, that "the benefits of such international research are many. Of course, our international efforts have brought millions of dollars in grant funds to UNC—dollars that support our faculty and facilities and allow us to continue vital research around the world." See M. A. Ibrahim, International health is everybody's business, *Pursuit*, School of Public Health, University of North Carolina at Chapel Hill, 1989, p. 3.

23. Fee, E. International health in historical perspective. *In: Proceedings of the World Federation of Public Health Associations*, Sixth International Congress, November 10-14, 1991, Atlanta, Georgia.

24. Gellert writes: "If the domestic public health of Western nations is to be maintained, a vision of global interdependence—economic, environmental and epidemiological—must become central to domestic policy." See G. A. Gellert, A. K. Neumann, and R. S. Gordon, The obsolescence of distinct domestic and international health sectors, *J Pub Health Pol* 10:421-4 (1989).

25. Gellert writes: "Interdependence argues for broadening the scope and definition of security, adding economic, environmental, demographic, and public health factors to the traditional military and geopolitical model." See G. A. Gellert, Global health interdependence and the international physicians' movement, *JAMA* 264:610-13 (1990).

The International Health Program of the Pan American Health Organization

María Isabel Rodríguez

In October 1985 the Pan American Health Organization (PAHO) launched a program of personnel development in the field of international health,[5] which in more than five years of operation has contributed not only to the enrichment and reorientation of groups of young public health workers in the region, but also to the generation of new knowledge in the field of international health and most particularly to more intensive study of one of its basic practices—technical cooperation in health.

This paper will provide information for an examination of the program, starting with its background and features and setting out why it emerged and developed in an intergovernmental agency such as PAHO.

Background

The development of a body of knowledge about the region's health problems and the work of technical groups in PAHO itself in continuous interaction with different groups of officials, educators, and researchers in the countries, in different areas of health work at PAHO's headquarters and in the countries and regional centers has created opportunities for personnel development. A sizable portion of those personnel have shown interest in learning more about the forms and options of the approach taken at the international level to the complex health problems of the countries in the region and to their determinants and limitations.

Recognition of that potential in the region has prompted the undertaking in PAHO over the last 20 years of a variety of experiments in personnel training and development through internships of varying duration in specific technical units. In this way PAHO has been building up experiences such as the Young Professional Internships Program at the Pan American Center for Sanitary Engineering (CEPIS) in Lima, teaching experiences at other Pan American centers such as the Center for Human Ecology and Health (ECO) at Toluca, Mexico, the Institute of Nutrition of Central America and Panama (INCAP) in Guatemala City, and a variety of internships in PAHO's technical units at its headquarters in Washington, D.C.

As stated in an internal document on "Health Manpower Development in the Context of International Technical Cooperation,"[6] the key feature of all these experiences is the active and involved participation of personnel who join in PAHO's work for varying periods of time. This involvement enables those people to learn more about the particular or the general problems, as the case may be, in the health situations in the countries: their trends, the ways in which problems are addressed, and the characteristics of the technical cooperation that PAHO provides at the national, subregional, or regional level.

Thus, the object of study and work is precisely this experience and the ways of addressing the health problems in the countries. This effort can hence in no wise be viewed as duplicating the training function of institutions in the countries, whether they are universities, centers, or institutes, which PAHO supports as part of its functions, thereby helping to strengthen the processes for the development of personnel in different fields of health.

Frame of reference of the program

Despite the aptitude for teaching that PAHO has always shown in its more than 80 years of existence, systematizing training in its own context and testing the potential of its different units has been no easy task, and the possibility of developing the program must be examined in light of three basic facts that may be regarded as triggers of the process and which at the same time are part of its orientation.

At the world level the first basic fact has to do with the efforts the World Health Organization (WHO) was making at the beginning of the Eighties to find strategies for attaining the goal of Health for All and specifically, in the situation that concerns us, with the call "to increase in the countries, in WHO, in bilateral and multilateral agencies, and in nongovernmental and voluntary agencies, the critical mass of leaders for Health for All."[11]

That proposal springs from the premise that the ambitious goal of Health for All will be unattainable without personnel who are deeply committed to its purposes and at the same time possess the knowledge and capabilities to accomplish those purposes.

Countless documents, and most particularly those about Health for All,[9] Primary Health Care,[10] and the World Strategies of Health for All,[13] assign a central role in achieving of the goal to international action. It is certain, however, that none of the theoretical baggage, experience, or above all the commitment required to address international health problems have been brought into processes of training health personnel in the service, education, or research areas, or are a primary concern of graduates in public health in our countries.

The leadership development initiative launched in 1985 by WHO[11] received a significant response from the Region of the Americas in extensive discussion of its meaning and implications as well as the development of three main lines of action. The first level was universities' involvement in an interdisciplinary approach to health; the second line was promotion and support of advanced education in public health, and the third was the focusing of efforts in PAHO itself on developing its International Health Program.

At the regional level, the program has found a particularly favorable situation caused by the implications of PAHO's mission, which was redefined by its then new Director and began to be implemented in 1983.

As part of that redefinition the new Director, Carlyle Guerra de Macedo,[2] spelled out and advocated the consideration and implementation of three basic components of PAHO's mission. The first was the management of knowledge, which required new ways of understanding the problems confronting health in the region and a search for appropriate solutions in each objective national situation. The second was mobilization of resources in each country for the benefit of all, and the third was the consideration of peace, understanding, and solidarity among peoples as so many additional dimensions of health. All this made it necessary to find new ways to address the development of health personnel.

In addition, that statement of PAHO's new mission was joined by a proposed quest for technical excellence, which was defined as beyond technical management, as enhancing the capability for understanding society, and most important of all, as including attitudes of understanding and solidarity.

In PAHO's Human Resources Development Program, historically charged with supporting regional efforts to train personnel in the public health field and develop social medicine in Latin America, experiences of varying duration have been undertaken over the last 20 years to make use of the potential of PAHO/WHO's doctrine of thought and action in developing health personnel.

In the Human Resources Development Program the proposal had reached a maturity that was reinforced and consolidated by trends of thought in the region and elsewhere in the world. PAHO therefore institutionalized the Training Program in International Health, launched it in 1985 as one of its actions to develop leadership in the Region of the Americas, and assigned its coordination to the Human Resources Development Program.

Proposals and objectives of the program

At the launching of the Training Program in International Health[5] also known as the International Health Residency,[3] PAHO set out to establish an internal program of training in international health for young professionals with master's degrees in public health who were interested in pursuing advanced studies and acquiring practical experience in this field. The purpose was defined as "to add to PAHO's own technical cooperation a component of high-level training for specialists who could devote themselves with an improved orientation to the coordination of international actions in the field of public health." Moreover, it was felt that the effort would be directed at facilitating technical cooperation among developing countries (TCDC) and at affording better utilization of or obtaining additional returns from plans of support to PAHO's member countries.

At the end of the program's first two years it was felt that its purposes should be defined more specifically on the basis of the experience acquired by both the participants, or "residents," and the staff members involved in the program.

The purpose of the program was then defined as "to promote leadership in international health and the development of technical cooperation in the countries of the region."[7]

To accomplish that purpose, PAHO devised a work-study program to attain the following objectives:

1. To acquire a deeper understanding a) of the health situation in the countries of the region and of its political, economic, social, and situational determinants at the local, subregional, regional, and international levels; b) of the approach to the fundamental health problems in the region, and c) of the options for transforming the health systems to meet the challenge of Health for All.
2. To learn about the role of PAHO and WHO in relation to the health problems of the countries, taking the experience of the residents as the basis for an analysis of technical cooperation in the health field.
3. To develop capabilities for analyzing, formulating, and evaluating technical cooperation programs in the health field.
4. To learn about the health policies adopted by the countries in the area of international cooperation, the goals adopted, and their implications for the organization of the sector.
5. To learn about the different agencies interacting in or contributing technically or financially to the development of the health sector in the countries of the hemisphere.

6. To develop a capability for mobilizing resources and formulating, executing, and evaluating projects.
7. To organize and critically review the scientific and technical knowledge bearing on the program's area of concentration.
8. To examine support programs at the regional and international levels and contribute to the design and performance of studies, options, and projects which would help solve the problems identified.
9. To promote communication and mutual support among the health workers of the hemisphere as part of a contribution to peace and solidarity among peoples.

Some features of the program

A characteristic feature of the program has been its dynamism, which has resulted in the generation of proposals and changes which have broadened its objectives beyond the initial proposals. Hence, on reviewing the development of the program and its preliminary results, it can be concluded that the experience is embedded in a field of study and practice in which there is much to be done and even more to be built.

The fact that the professional who joins this program has previously taken graduate training in public health and comes to it with experience in the health field, whether in service, teaching, or research, makes it easier for him or her to fit into a real process of study and analysis of and reflection on PAHO's technical cooperation process, its characteristics, doctrinal foundation, and interaction with other agencies. At the same time, the resident is able to delve more deeply into his or her own field of specialization and options for cooperation at the international level.

**The axis of the process into which
the participant is articulated**

This axis is PAHO's technical cooperation process itself, which in 11 months of work enables him or her to join in, interact with, and analyze a complete cycle of PAHO's work, from the formulation of policies through the analysis and formulation of strategies, plans, and program-budgets to their approval by PAHO's governing bodies.

For the participant or resident to be involved in the work of PAHO, he or she must first learn about the structure and functions of the agency, its historical development, and its interaction with other cooperation agencies. This knowledge is acquired in an initial period of orientation, which continues throughout the experience with participation in seminars, attendance at meetings of technical groups, committees, and advisory, governing, and executive bodies of PAHO. The most important activity, however, is interaction within the group of residents itself in its formal and informal activities.

In-depth study of the process of technical cooperation with the countries requires an intimate understanding of their health conditions, policies, and socioeconomic determinants, and of their modes of approach and action both nationally and internationally. It also requires knowledge of the health policies adopted by the countries in the sphere of international cooperation, the goals accepted and their implications for the organization of the sector, and the establishment of an adequate degree of comparability among the international policies and the dynamics of their development. This understanding, which PAHO furthers through activities that promote the study and analysis of these problems in the different units at headquarters, is enriched by the experience of working in different countries of the region and group visits to learn about the health systems of Canada and the United States.

PAHO exposes the resident to an understanding of the great challenges confronting health in the region as they are seen by its different in-house working groups and by those with whom the latter interact. But both in this field and in the interpretation and application that each resident will give to the doctrinal and strategic aspects that constitute mandates of PAHO, such as Health for All and Primary Health Care, each participant works out his or her own development, essential factors in which are his or her training, experience, prior commitment, and, even more important, the dynamic generated by the ongoing interaction within each group of residents.

Attendance at meetings of PAHO's highest governing bodies, even if only as an observer, gives the participant a feeling of how governments interact at the policy level, at which broad regional health guidelines and policies are approved. This experience is complemented by exposure to a broad range of technical and financial cooperation agencies, including those of bilateral and multilateral cooperation. When we speak of knowledge of these agencies we mean not just what is learned in an orientation or visit, but the study and understanding of their policies, their origins, and the dynamics of their financing, as well as the rules of the game that may permit appropriate use of their resources.

Instruction versus training

Perhaps the most important characteristic of the process we are examining is its capacity to transform. We have chosen to describe the program as one of training, and we think this term is valid in the understanding that it refers to involvement of the participant in a practice requiring an explanatory theory that generates a search for and production of knowledge that will enrich and generate proposals for that practice. Moreover, the process is profoundly reflective, for the participant is the subject of his or her training in a setting of collective development, that of his or her own group, in which growth has been generating changes in the subject and the group, and adding in turn to the theory and practice of new groups.

Articulation of the participant into a technical cooperation practice does not in itself guarantee the individual's transformation or the development of a commitment. Hence the program considers that the challenge is how to develop leadership along with a genuine commitment to the countries and to the health of their populations. This is why the dynamics of the process, group reflection, and the effort of the individual who is aware of his or her responsibility as a social subject are basic elements for ensuring the participants' adequate interaction in the different areas of the institution and favors their future placement.

Organization, coordination, and conduct of activities under the program

As previously noted, the axis of the program is the technical cooperation that PAHO offers to the countries. The program itself follows two main lines of development:

- A general one for the analysis of technical cooperation as a process that involves interdisciplinary aspects of health. All the activities in which all the participants join are coordinated and guided by the Human Resources Development Program.
- The other line, centered on continual application of technical cooperation to one area of concentration, is each resident's principal link with the coordination of the specific technical program.

These two lines of work constitute the response to the need for the development in each participant of an international vision of health and for the acquisition of a deeper understanding of his or her specific field. Specific areas are assigned on the basis of the candidate's own proposal and background and of the place that PAHO's technical units are able to make for him or her.

The distribution of time among the general and specific components is not rigid. Actually, 40% of the time has been allotted to general and 60% to specific activities. In practice the weight of the activities shifts with the resident's work, his or her articulation into the given unit, the potentiality of the specific field, and the permanent conflict between demanding intensive study which builds an overall view of the field of international health and technical cooperation in one specific area. Here, as in many objects of study and work, coincidences and contradictions arise between the general and the particular, and must be given special attention.

The scheduled activities fall into four fundamental areas or components:

1) Structure, function, and basic programs of PAHO/WHO, including analysis of programs and activities in the Country Offices.
2) Analysis of the health situation in the region.
3) Intensive study of the individual resident's specific area.
4) International cooperation, TCDC, financing and cooperation agencies, international health.

Summarizing very concisely, the program may be said to cover, the following activities, among others:

1) Orientation on the structure, functioning, and basic programs of PAHO.
2) Seminars on topics of basic and current interest in the health sector.
3) Specific projects in each participant's area of concentration.
4) Orientation visits to financing agencies, universities, foundations, and technical cooperation institutions concerned with the health sector.
5) Participation as an observer in meetings of the governing bodies of PAHO, special committees, and meetings of PAHO/WHO Country Representatives.
6) Participation in experiences relating to the areas of work of the participants in countries of the region selected for the purpose.
7) Preparation of reports on special studies or work done both at headquarters and in the countries, on occasion as a consultant.
8) Courses, seminars, and workshops in priority fields or to cover fields of knowledge in which reinforcement is needed.
9) Weekly working group sessions scheduled by the residents themselves.

As previously noted, these activities are organized in accordance with the cycles established by the Office of the Director of PAHO for the cooperation planning, programming, and evaluation system.

In its introductory first stage, the program emphasizes orientation activities, familiarization with PAHO and its basic programs, and activities that permit reflection on fundamental concepts which the participant will later study more intensively. In this stage the activities take place primarily at PAHO's headquarters, with sporadic visits to countries.

In the second stage, the number of activities dealing with theoretical and conceptual aspects diminishes and never takes up more than 20% of working time. Depending on the programs to which the residents are assigned, work in the countries is organized and defined with a time allotment that averages 30% and in some has reached 40% or more. The work the resident does in the countries to learn about and analyze the technical cooperation process and the activities involved in his or her specific project has been rated as highly valuable by both residents and PAHO and country officials.

Scheduling the visits requires coordination between the general coordination offices and the particular program and with PAHO's office in the country visited.

The final stage of the program concentrates the group at headquarters for group analysis, the completion of papers and reports, and intensified study in the individual's areas of greatest interest.

The physical premises of the program

The program is conducted in PAHO's operating premises, both at headquarters in Washington, D.C., and in the different countries of the Region of the Americas.

At the central level each participant has his or her individual working space in the technical unit or program to which he or she is assigned, and the residents have a room for their work as a group in the Health Manpower Development Program. The resident's involvement in the life of PAHO and the schedule of visits enables him or her to study and analyze other agencies and institutions of technical and financial cooperation with which PAHO interacts.

In the countries his or her articulation into PAHO's technical cooperation activities to which he or she is assigned exposes him or her directly to the health situation of the countries in the region and gives him or her an opportunity to analyze the modalities of the cooperation offered to those countries and the functions performed by the PAHO/WHO offices in the countries.

The program's participants, or residents

The process in which the resident becomes involved demands knowledge, experience, commitment, and a creative capacity to face challenges, not only as an individual but also in the group effort.

There have never been more than 10 participants in the program in any year. The first year started with six participants and benefited from the enriching participation of two Canadian professionals during the first six months. In the six years the program has been in operation, a total of 234 applications have been received, from which 56 candidates were selected. Fifty-two professionals have joined the program.

The importance of the selection process for the success of the program, especially the requirement for work in this field of commitment to social justice and equity, has been a subject of ongoing discussion among the different parties involved, including the residents themselves. It may well be asked how this quality is to be evaluated without intimate knowledge of the candidates. The challenge centers on how to ensure that candidates are chosen who are truly committed to the objectives of the program, as also how to provide mechanisms that will enable the process in which they join to stimulate and develop their future commitment and capacity for leadership.

The 52 candidates who have joined the program so far have come from 16 countries in the hemisphere, with the largest proportions hailing from Brazil, Argentina, Mexico and Ecuador, which have accounted for more than 50% of all participants (Table 1).

An acceptable sex ratio has been maintained, with 25 female participants (Table 2). As regards the professions of the participants, 73% (38) have been physicians and the remaining 27% have been members of other professions (Table 3), including some from the social area, who have brought essential enrichments to the groups.

Seventy-five percent (39) of the participants have held master's degrees in public health, and a smaller proportion master's degrees in social medicine, health administration, health economics, and international relations, among other fields (Table 4). The institutions in which most took those degrees were the School of Public Health of Buenos Aires; Hebrew University, Jerusalem, Israel; Havana University; the Xochimilco Unit of the Metropolitan Autonomous University of Mexico; Johns Hopkins University, and London University (Tables 5, 6).

Table 1
Nationality of Participants

Nationality	Number of Participants
Brazil	9
Argentina	8
Ecuador	5
Mexico	5
Bolivia	3
Colombia	3
Costa Rica	3
Peru	3
Uruguay	3
Cuba	2
Dominican Republic	2
El Salvador	2
Chile	1
Nicaragua	1
United States	1
Venezuela	1
TOTAL	52

Two Canadian professionals participated in the program for six months.

The exchange of experiences from their professional practice and the political, economic, social, and health situations in their own countries and the places they occupied in the international sphere are amplified by exchanges and analyses of experiences from their own training, which has provided an interesting instrument for the study of the graduate programs in public health in the different countries from which they come, most of which lack international health components.

Development of the program and its prospects

It is important to reiterate and emphasize that some of the most important aspects in the development of this program have been its dynamism, its enrichment with the experiences of each group, and the broadening of its prospects.

The program has undergone several analyses which have identified three stages in its development. These analyses have been made with the participation of actors representative of the different entities involved in the life of the institution.

The first stage was the period of organization, institutionalization, and launching of a one-year educational experience in a nonacademic agency. PAHO's decision to institutionalize it and the overcoming of resistances inside and outside PAHO required, at the directorial level, firm resolve and a conviction of the wider importance of the program. A group of young people without permanent employment ties was to be brought into PAHO and invited to become "the critical conscience of the institution," while at the same time developing a conscious commitment to its purposes for the benefit of their countries and the improvement of health conditions in the region.

The broadening of the program's focus—PAHO's technical cooperation—began with the first group of residents. The mere analysis of the historical development of PAHO itself, established in the setting of an inter-American system with highly concrete proposals for controlling quarantinable diseases and consolidated as a regional agency of a postwar specialized United Nations agency grounded on the fundamental principle that "the health of all peoples is fundamental to the attainment of peace and security and is dependent upon the fullest cooperation of individuals and States,"[12] has from the beginning enabled some to glimpse and others to strengthen a more inquiring, more penetrating vision for the study of other cooperation agencies and systems operating at the international level. Their annual evaluations as groups and as individuals have added content to the vision of health in the international context.

This emerges from an examination of the programming of the first years, which focused at the beginning on PAHO's structure and function, and gradually evolved into a seminar on international health and international cooperation in the health field at the beginning of the work of the 1988-1989 group; this seminar is difficult to organize and difficult to sustain because it involves not just the residents but the personnel of different units of PAHO.

Table 2
Sex of the Participants

Year	Men	Women	Total
1985-1986	3	3	6
1986-1987	4	5	9
1987-1988	5	5	10
1988-1989	3	4	7
1989-1990	6	4	10
1991	6	4	10
TOTAL	27	25	52

As more was learned about other cooperation institutions, their modes of operation, international developments, and most particularly, the operations of PAHO to which we referred at the beginning in its mission for understanding, peace, and solidarity as a new dimension of health, an interest built up in having a second stage of analysis and reflection.

The second stage was enriched by an analysis of the meaning of international health for the alumni of the first four classes. To their contributions were added an analysis of the teaching of international health in the schools of public health in the United States[1] in response to concerns awakened in the course of the residency itself. This stage arose from the need to call a pause in the program to evaluate what had been done, and its prospects, after having been repeatedly scrutinized in PAHO's governing bodies. This analysis was made by members of four classes who were invited to a meeting on "The Present Situation and Prospects of the International Health Field."[4]

The group addressed four basic topics: (1) the conceptualization of international health; (2) technical cooperation as a component of international health; (3) international health in the schools of public health of the United States, and (4) proposals for the development of international health.

Table 3
Professional Backgrounds of Participants

Year	M.D.	Other Professions	Total
1985-1986	5	1 Educator	6
1986-1987	8	1 Nurse	9
1987-1988	7	1 Dentist 1 Anthropologist 1 Sociologist	10
1988-1989	6	1 Veterinarian	7
1989-1990	6	1 Social Worker 1 Anthropologist 1 Nurse 1 Dentist	10
1991	6	1 Educator 1 Biologist 1 Dentist 1 Administrator	10
TOTAL	38	14	52

The group brought to this discussion its own way of looking at international health as a field of knowledge and practice still in development and discussion and with its own historical and social character, whose interpretation and practice depend on the specific historical setting, the ideological and social position and geopolitical agenda of the actor who works in the field, and it was considered necessary to become involved in an ongoing collective effort that would conjoin creative contributions and research of different actors   and persons associated with the subject of the meeting.

Table 4
Postgraduate Studies

Year	Master's in Public Health	Hospital Administration	Master's in Social Medicine	Other Master's Degree*	Total
1985-1986	4	0	1	1	6
1986-1987	6	1	2	0	9
1987-1988	9	0	1	0	10
1988-1989	4	0	2	1	7
1989-1990	9	0	0	1	10
1991	7	0	1	2	10
TOTAL	39	1	7	5	52

* Economy/Nutrition/Epidemiology/Health Sciences

Table 5
Place of Postgraduate Training

Year	Country of Origin	Other Latin American Country	United States	England	Israel
1985-1986	1	2	0	1	2
1986-1987	7	1	0	0	1
1987-1988	4	2	2	0	2
1988-1989	5	0	0	2	0
1989-1990	6	2	1	0	1
1991	7	1	2	0	0
TOTAL	30	8	5	3	6

Table 6

Institution in which Postgraduate Degree Taken*

Institution	Degree	City/Country	No.
University of Buenos Aires	M.A. in Public Health	Buenos Aires, Argentina	7
Havana University	M.A. in Public Health	Havana, Cuba	6
Hebrew University	M.A. in Public Health	Jerusalem, Israel	6
Metropolitan Autonomous University, Xochimilco Unit	M.A. in Social Medicine	Mexico City, Mexico	5
School of Hygiene and Tropical Medicine, Johns Hopkins University	M.A. in Public Health	Baltimore, Maryland, United States	5
School of Hygiene and Tropical Medicine, London University	M.A. in Public Health	London, England	3

* Lists only institutions with three or more participants at this writing.

This meeting was presented with the theories on which the notion of international health has been built historically, and it was decided to opt for a proposed approach to international health from two closely related viewpoints: on the one hand, international health as a segment of the field of international relations which can be identified in the sense of health as an international matter, and, on the other, consideration of international health as an expansion of the specific field of health, that is, the international dimension of health. The theoretical production presented to that meeting is another of the contributions of the International Health Program.

This second stage proposes a more open involvement of the program in the study of the field of international health. The next group actually pursued the subject deeply and built on technical cooperation in health as one of the areas of international health practices.

The advance in conceptualization of the field helped generate what we view as the onset of a third stage set off by the convening of this meeting of consultation, held jointly with the Governments of Canada and Quebec, on "International Health: A Field of Study and Professional Practice," in which we are disclosing the propositions, concerns, and some of the products developed by the program so far.

Subject to these prefatory considerations, we think PAHO's international health program may be examined through three basic aspects:
- Evaluation of the experience and production of each participant during his or her participation in the program.
- The results of the program itself as a collective endeavor.
- An assessment of the duties of each participant in the setting to which he or she has returned in his or her own country and/or the post he or she has been appointed to in the international sphere.

We have already referred in part to the first two points, especially as to the output produced by the residents individually and collectively as a result of ongoing reflection, and especially their contribution to a field of such enormous implications for and impact on the countries as that of international health, a field which is under both discussion and construction but whose practices link together a large number of health personnel, some aware and some unaware of their role and responsibility in that context.

Further study of international health should contribute to a recognition of the enormous responsibility imposed by work in that field, and of the need to develop technical excellence in the management of cooperation. That is not all, however: it is not just a matter of knowing the technical and financial resources worked with in the field and those that may be accessible, not just a matter of uncritical participation in that process, but a commitment, a responsibility, and above all else, solidarity and dedication to the work that the countries require to be done.

An individual's involvement in a cooperation exercise is in itself no guarantee that he or she will be transformed or develop a commitment. Uncritical involvement, in which the individual merely figures out how to be a "successful manager" but acquires no real commitment to the countries, would be truly frustrating. We consider that the dynamics of the process, group reflection, and the effort of an individual aware of his or her responsibility as a social being are essential to proper interaction of the participants with the different areas of work of the institution and will help improve his or her future placement in the field.

The program has been very clear that its aim is not to train individuals to enter the market of competition, or what Taussig[8] calls the scramble for grants. On the contrary, we are agreed that the individual must not just know the financing institutions and their policies and how to formulate a project, but above all else must know the impact and implications of aid, the best time to grant it, the responsibility to oversee its utilization, and the part played by the institutions. We would not want our residents to enter the labor market of experts who parade through the countries with no commitment and completely uninvolved with the country and the groups they are supposed and paid to help. This is why we repeat that the most important part of this articulation into the work of international health is technical excellence which includes involved commitment.

This is what the program has set out to do, and so far everything appears to indicate that exposure to and participation in this process has dispelled our concerns and doubts in the great majority of cases. The most important indicator for evaluating the results is the third element cited: the resident's placement in his or her own country or in some international post.

Information about the placement of a high percentage of the alumni in posts of management or high responsibility in ministries, universities, and international agencies is in itself a good indicator of the results of the program. But, beyond the contribution it may have made to the direct training of personnel and the production and dissemination of new knowledge, we think it should contribute to the introduction of new ideas in the field of international health in the training of health personnel of many countries, and in particular in that of the personnel of schools of public health, many of whom have given no thought to the enormous responsibility involved in releasing on a labor market that is increasingly internationalized, increasingly interdependent, increasingly in need of understanding and solidarity, personnel with no vision of the world in which they are to work and in many instances with no involvement in their own duties. To work for collective involvement in the search for new paths and new proposals is perhaps and has been the essential point of this program.

References

1. Godue, C.: La salud internacional: Un concepto en formación. Conference document, Montreal, January 1990.

2. Macedo, Carlyle G. de: La nueva misión. Address by the Director-elect of PAHO during the commemoration of the 80th anniversary of the Pan American Health Organization, Washington, D.C., 1982.

3. Pan American Health Organization. Residency in International Health. Directive No. 86-05, Washington, D.C., July, 1986.

4. Pan American Health Organization. "Reunión sobre la Situación Actual y Perspectivas del Campo de Salud Internacional." Eleven-page HSM report on a meeting from October 9 to 13, 1989, at the Pan American Health Organization, Washington, D.C.

5. Pan American Health Organization/World Health Organization. *Programa de Formación en Salud Internacional.* Subcomité de Planificación y Programación. En Propuesta de Líderes para Salud para Todos en el Año 2000/Salud Pública Internacional. Document SPP/3, March 1985.

6. Pan American Health Organization/World Health Organization. *Health Manpower Development Program. Health Manpower Development in the Context of International Technical Cooperation.* Washington, D.C., July, 1987. Mimeograph, 16 pages, with annex.

7. Pan American Health Organization/World Health Organization. *Residency in International Health.* Subcommittee on Planning and Programming, Executive Committee of the Directing Council. Document SPP10/6, Washington, D.C., April, 1988.

8. Taussig, M.: La nutrición, el desarrollo y la ayuda exterior: Un estudio de caso sobre atención de salud dirigida por Estados Unidos en una zona de plantación en Colombia. *In:* Vicente Navarro (ed.), *Salud e Imperialismo*, Mexico City, Siglo XXI, 1983, pp. 214-47.

9. World Health Organization. Technical Cooperation. 30th World Health Assembly, Geneva, May, 1977.

10. World Health Organization. Estrategia Mundial de Salud para Todos en el Año 2000. Serie Salud para Todos No. 3. Geneva, 1981.

11. World Health Organization. Proposed Programme Budget for the Functional Period 1986-1987, Geneva, 1984.

12. World Health Organization. Constitución de la Organización Mundial de la Salud. Documentos Básicos, 36 edición. Geneva, 1986.

13. World Health Organization/United Nations Children's Fund. *Atención Primaria de Salud*. Report on the International Conference on Primary Health Care, Alma Ata, USSR, September 1978.

International Dimensions of Health

Mario Rovere

Introduction

This paper can be regarded as the continuation of a dialogue initiated at the first meeting of the residency in international health organized by PAHO in 1985, its most recent precursor being the meeting on international health held in 1989.[1]

This meeting produced a conceptual approach that appeared to be consistent with the confluence of a number of empirical factors, such as the worldwide spread of communicable diseases and/or their causes, the expansion of the structure for explaining health-disease problems from individual countries to the international sphere, or the identification of health as a significant area in the field of international relations, with its own specific nature but linked to the larger whole containing it.

This conceptual approach has inspired two overlapping but distinguishable approaches to international health. The first of these identifies a certain segment of the sphere of international relations—conceived as a superstructure containing political, economic, military elements which governs the relations between nations—which has been called "health as an issue in international relations" (HIIR). The aim here is to analyze health-related regulations, rules, practices, and customs in the international arena and the flows of funds, goods, and services that circulate from one part of the planet to another, and to show how certain health actions have been turned into political actions (closing of frontiers), economic actions (quarantines), and military actions (blockades of medicines and medical inputs).

The other analytical approach developed in Latin America, using the viewpoint of national health systems, seeks to reveal international phenomena or processes that can help our understanding of the structure and operation of these systems and the dynamics of their reproduction and transformation. We have called this second line of inquiry the "international dimensions of health" (IDH) and it is on this area that this paper focuses.

Consequently, our initial workplan was as follows:

```
┌─────────────────────────────────────────────────────────────┐
│                                                               │
│                      Segment of the sphere of                 │
│                      international relations                  │
│                                                               │
│        International arena                                    │
│                                                               │
│                      Health as an issue in                   │
│                      international relations (HIIR)           │
│        International health:  ─────────────────────────────   │
│                                                               │
│                      International dimensions of health (IDH) │
│                                                               │
│        National arena                                        │
│                                                               │
│                      Analysis from the standpoint of          │
│                      national health systems                 │
│                                                               │
└─────────────────────────────────────────────────────────────┘
```

We will base our exploration of the IDH on this scheme, in the confidence that Ulysses Panisset's paper will deal with the first component, although we will not ignore the features the two perspectives share.

International dimensions of health (IDH):
a Latin American perspective

Our first (and not the smallest) difficulty was to define the potential offered by the IDH for throwing light on health in our countries: as we investigated the nature of our medical equipment, the knowledge provided by professional training curricula, health inputs, medicines, health and treatment practices, and the internationalization of the decisive factors in the health-disease process, it occurred to us that the question could be put another way, namely, what are the IDH in our countries?

Here we must mention the remark made by a Brazilian economist in the 1970s, who said: "The only thing Brazilian about our pharmaceutical industry is the smoke and noise made by the machines."

Postponing for the time being the search for a solution to our initial difficulty, we decided to go on to the next one: Supposing we were capable of defining the IDH, why would this be desirable since our investigation repeatedly brought us back to the theory of dependence and all the theoretical, political, and economic work done in Latin

America in the 1970s in light of this concept. This new doubt, however, soon yielded to the certainty that we did not want to make this study a protest song but rather a powerful analytical tool for understanding the nature of this elusive concept called international health. This would enable us to detect openings which would be essential for creating strategies that might give our countries greater freedom of action.

The third question we had to resolve was which standpoint, i.e. what coordinates and references, to adopt in writing this article, and it came to seem essential to state that this work was produced from within the representation of an intergovernmental health organization—as PAHO is—in a poor country with one of the worst health situations in the hemisphere. More important, the article was written at the beginning of 1991, a particularly auspicious year for the bold, since even in the worst case these reflections could only constitute another addition to the general confusion; but at the same time, 1991 was a year that brought such profound changes in worldwide economic, political, and ideological structures that virtually any event might quickly make our effort obsolete. Furthermore, the world had embarked on a new warlike adventure, whose impact was felt in every sphere of international relations, since it seems to sanction the right of military intervention in other countries (Panama, Iraq), which appears to be the real "basic principle" of the new international order.

The governments of Latin America began this decade only too well aware of the huge debts contracted during the time when they were dictatorships and ready to make significant changes in their economies and societies, which unquestionably are having an impact on the health of our peoples and the services available to them. It is worth noting here that at the beginning of the 1980s the relative insensitivity of the traditional indicators of health to the evident massive increase in poverty was regarded as paradoxical, but then the cholera epidemic broke out, and that seems to have removed all grounds for this perplexity.

Beset by all these doubts, we seemed to have two choices: the sensible one, namely to give up, and the alternative, made by those willing to risk everything in every theoretical venture. In practice, we decided to give up, but repeated appeals from Dr. María Isabel Rodrí- guez[2] kept bringing us back to the subject until it became evident that we were not going to be able to get out of this task so easily.

We therefore began to look for signs or traces that could provide some sort of approach to the IDH. The first notion that emerged was that the work ought to perform the service of making transparent something which had been concealed,[3] in other words, that the international dimensions of health and of the health service apparatus in our countries are as massive as they are invisible. To put this idea more clearly, the health services made available to our peoples are provided with knowledge, equipment, inputs, and standards which are predominantly imported, a fact about which people are very ignorant or to which nobody draws attention since it seems quite natural that this should be the case. Furthermore, the health conditions of the population are also determined by external factors operating in a curiously similar way in certain economic, political, social, and ecological processes in Latin America.

Why—and who?—should we bother with these observations? A modest question, and a rather belated one, but it arose in the following terms: if the epidemiological situations of our populations are specific, if the health-disease process is historically constructed in each separate society, if the very concept of disease is a cultural construction, and therefore different for each people, how is it possible that the health services and systems in all our countries have so many virtually identical features? In other words, if our realities are different and heterogenous, yet our organizations and forms of response are homogeneous, something is not working properly, and the study of the IDH may be able to discover what it is. In addition, analysis of the IDH might help to develop some original and innovating thinking as regards the health systems in our countries, thereby enabling them to adjust much better to the complexity and specific features of the societies in question and their health problems.

This prospect seemed somewhat unrealistic, however, until we brought analysis of the debt-crisis-adjustment sequence into the picture. What did the study of this notorious trio contribute? Basically, the consideration that the frontier of health service coverage in many countries in South America not only has not continued to expand, but has actually begun to retreat, partly owing to a decade of paralysis of investment, and partly to the clear signs of the dismantling of the so-called "welfare state", although many authors agree that such a state has never been achieved in Latin America.[4] Since the development implicit in copying the health service models of the developed countries can only be sustained in a context of constant expansion of investment, Latin America will only be able to improve its health situation if it can get away from the dominant service-provision models, which in practice condemn our countries to offer ever more complex, costly, and sophisticated services to an ever-decreasing number of people.

The need to organize our thinking regarding the IDH led us to a schematic presentation which, as generally happens with schemas, may oversimplify complex realities, involving the loss of some essential features. It seems useful at this stage of the analysis, however, to link together areas that are normally analyzed independently so as to organize these fields in a comprehensive way (Figure 1).

A Comprehensive IDH Analysis

The scheme refers to four basic components of the complex problems of health in a country, which are: the health of the population in question; the health service infrastructure, namely, the functioning and output of the entire social structure devoted to providing health services, which we will call the service model; the infrastructure for the generation and development of the productive factors in the country—obviously, this component will be larger or smaller according to the level of development, although it will depend, in a way that cannot be concealed, on essential "prior" factors which can only be supplied from outside; and finally, the determinants of national social and economic policies, whose effect is to define the area of what is possible for the other components.

We have accordingly indicated with arrows the general direction of the causality or determination (not determinism) of the components among themselves, "determination" being understood here as the capacity of a fact to establish the limits of the potential of other facts. However, in the belief that the spaces determined in this way include degrees of freedom that can be used in one direction or another, we have also indicated the general direction of the conditioning process, this being understood as the capacity of certain facts to impose conditions on the efficacy of others. The arrows shown as IDH indicate both determination and these conditioning factors. Merely by way of example, we could say that the arrival of the cholera vibrio in Latin America caused or "determined" the epidemic, but that the specific health conditions in each country governed or conditioned the epidemic "efficacy" of this factor.

Within the fields of influence, determination or conditioning grouped together under the name of IDH, and as a further refinement of this scheme, we identify five areas having a certain relative autonomy but being linked in a common theoretical framework which may serve as areas of research and policy formulation and for the design of action programs.

Problem area one: "Diseases do not respect frontiers", or the internationalization of risks

Given the evidence that health situations cannot be understood through closed analyses of individual populations, there is a need for an area of study that brings together research and actions on diseases that are communicable across frontiers either through vectors (malaria, yellow fever, dengue), or migrations whose origins may be economic (dams and large-scale engineering works), political (refugees), or military (armies of occupation), etc. Studies of cholera pandemics could be very significant in this area, as also would the analysis of other factors such as tourism or business trips (venereal diseases, AIDS, etc.).

International environmental problems such as pollution resulting from chemical, biological, or radioactive emissions into the atmosphere or waterways, deserve special emphasis. This field would permit the reconstruction of historical factors and the national and international agreements, commitments, and legislation that exist to neutralize, prevent, or compensate for outbreaks of disease. It could include panzootics having a health or economic impact (rabies, foot-and-mouth disease), as well as international action in the case of natural or deliberate catastrophes.[5]

It is clear that an epidemiology of an international (and consequently social) character could be a basic tool for research in this area and for the design of multinational control projects.

Problem area two: "Prescription for adjustment and biopolitics"

Since some distinguished economists have noted that gross domestic product per capita can be increased not only by raising productivity but also by reducing the number of people, it is necessary to investigate an area of some importance in the context of population problems, in what Foucault call "biopolitics", i.e., measures directly or indirectly targeting population control, including family planning programs and by extension those focusing on mothers and children, as well as the development of major projects in this area and the policies of donors.

This would involve a study of disagreements between countries with different policies on population growth and abortion, and their links with "women in development" programs. Another focus of attention would be the presence of private or religious NGOs implementing projects (in some cases beyond anybody else's control), especially in the poorest countries in the region, and a comparative analysis of the policies of the cooperation agencies in developed countries.

Although the population issue represents one of the main links between economics and health, a subarea that without question deserves investigation is the study of the numerous consequences of economic and political developments that are creating a dramatic social situation in Latin America. This situation, typified by the significant expansion in the number of people living below the poverty line, has called into question the models of the epidemiological transition and the supposedly irresistible improvement in health indicators (especially those linked to poverty) observed in the 1970s and at the beginning of the 1980s (see below, "adjustment for all in the year ... ").

Problem area three: "Exporting health service models"

This area covers the internationalization of health care models. It focuses on the "influence" of different models for providing services (basically management technologies), from hospital organization to the financing and management systems passed on via the courses, workshops, scholarships, and bibliographies, used by training schools and programs in public health, along with the conflicts, real or apparent, between administrative models and leadership models and the status of the development of "original thinking" in some countries in the region. It could also include an analysis of the spread of health service chains from the United States to some of the large cities in Latin America. Other issues would be the conflict between models of public health organization which is implicit in different concepts of primary care, the privatization of public hospital services and the role of different agencies in this area, an analysis of international marketing through such publications as *El Hospital*, and the nature of the infrastructure assistance provided by the major development banks.

Problem area four: "Science and technology"

This area involves studies on the production, dissemination, appropriation, utilization, and consumption of technologies and scientific knowledge of strategic value for the health sector. It would include an analysis of financing, the science and technology policies of different countries, the transfer of risky research projects to less developed countries, the problems of patents for medicines, the transfer of and dependence on inputs incorporating high technology, the policies and priorities of the large organizations financing health research and the nature of the comparative advantages our countries offer for this purpose, and the study of the imported raw materials that are essential for our domestic medicaments industries, including medical and health-related equipment and inputs.

Problem area five: "Universities, education, and health"

This area would include studies on the training and utilization of human resources in health, the "exporting" of training models, the flow of scientific information and instructional material, the role of the major foundations and Pan American and Latin American organizations in the area, agreements between universities in different countries to exchange faculty members or the development of entire programs for export to other countries, along with the migration of professionals, networks, and connections with their university of origin, flows of scholarships and those awarded them, national organizations that control the departures of scholarship holders and their different policies, and so on. It could include a comparative analysis of the assistance policies of the Organization of American States, International Labor Organization, United Nations Educational, Scientific, and Cultural Organization, PAHO/WHO, and similar agencies in this area.

Seeking linking themes: Adjustment for all in the year ...

An initial theme linking these problem areas could be the simultaneous introduction throughout almost the entire region of adjustment policies with an explicitly neoliberal orientation. Why Latin America's political systems are becoming increasingly homogenous, through the introduction of economic and social policies around which only five years ago there would have been no consensus whatever, is a question beyond the scope of this paper but one that deserves to be investigated.

Whatever the reason for this trend, the fact is that as a result of these policies, health in Latin America is not exactly enjoying its finest hour. After decades had been spent on the arduous construction of a public sector that had only just emerged from its philanthropic origins, and following the fairly generalized (relatively speaking) introduction in the more developed countries in the region of some form of social and health insurance, leading to some (rather uneven) improvements in health infrastructure and in certain health indicators, this progress seems to have ground to a halt and to be showing signs of going into reverse.

The fall of the communist regimes in Eastern Europe appears to have cut the ground from beneath those political projects of a more socially-oriented nature which seemed to be taking hold in the region in the previous decade. The so-called welfare state is denounced as responsible for fiscal deficits and inflation, while it is apparently no longer necessary for more extreme political projects to have a social base. As a result, and for the first time in our century, a common policy based on economic liberalism is being applied in most Latin American countries, without any need for military dictatorships.

The consequences for health are enormous because this policy, with its neodarwinist approach, has also singled out the media as another, simultaneous action area. This has led people to believe that although the social cost of adjustment is and will be huge, that does not matter since results down the line justify any sacrifice (it is worth remembering, in relation to the poorest countries of Latin America, that Roosevelt was criticized by some economists for creating jobs to pull the United States out of the Depression; they argued that the market could solve the crisis, to which he answered, "I'm sure it could, but by then we will all be dead").

The health of the peoples of Latin America is threatened by adjustment policies on the following fronts, among others:
1. **Economic.** Since the most important social policy is economic policy, an economic policy based on concentrating wealth in the highest-income groups increases the number of families living in

poverty, and critical poverty at that. Skewing the social structure towards the upper quintile results in the provision to this quintile of top-quality services (including health services) of international caliber, and the abandonment of the lower quintiles to their own devices. Multiple linkages can be identified between poverty and health, all of them negative.

2. **The State**. Under the liberal economic policy which has now taken over, the state must be dismantled as a regulator and producer, without even any acknowledgement of the services it provided by sustaining the pool of labor for the market. All public enterprises (even profitable ones) will now be sold off as inefficient, the welfare state will give way to the "ill-fare" state, as Eduardo Bustelo has called it, and when public services can no longer be maintained, new forms of welfare will be revived which, though touted as modern, will in fact reflect a return to the practices prevailing at the beginning of the century.

3. **Social security**. Since the true variables for adjusting policy in order to restore the rate of return are a fall in real wages, loss of labor market stability, reduction of indirect remuneration, and destruction of labor unions, social security must be dismantled or cut to its lowest level. This is achieved by reducing contributions as a result of the expansion of the informal sector and unemployment and of the decline in real wages of the contributors, accompanied in some countries by partial privatization for major contributors, which destroys the solidarity of the system.

4. **Cultural**. This policy also calls for the destruction of solidarity and the promotion of individualistic attitudes and behavior since it is based on achieving governability by either destroying participatory bodies or rendering them powerless, a process which is undermining representative institutions and the organization of health services in many Latin American countries.

The expansion of the medical-industrial complex

As the second broad theme of this work, we will argue that one of the organizing principles for analyzing the field of the IDH is the expansion of the medical-industrial complex (MIC), in other words, that the expansion of the markets of the MIC can explain a great deal regarding the homogeneity, already referred to, of the health service model in Latin America. Is it possible, however, to discuss the MIC concept without overstating its influence?

The medical-industrial complex is in practice nothing more than a collection of companies which, either right from the time they were established or since the expansion of their operations into new markets, have been producing goods that form inputs or working tools for the production process in the health sector.

Originally these companies produced for the domestic markets in their own countries. They then expanded into international markets and in some cases, having analyzed their comparative advantages, have internationalized their production processes in all the ways used by other kinds of industries (creation of subsidiaries, affiliated national companies, etc.).

What is new in this production process is the progressive loss of leadership by the health sector, which these companies began by serving and which nowadays they use, to the point where its role has become merely that of a marketer of expensive products.

In the health context, concern is often expressed in various countries in Latin America about the decline in the professional status of pharmacists, whose solid social status has within only a few decades diminished as they have become nothing more than rather ill-defined retailers. But if we look more carefully, is the position of a doctor or laboratory technician any different? Isn't it perhaps just a question of time?

This change in the control of the work process is superbly illustrated by Fernández de Castro:[6]

> The hen eats corn; the subject of the verb to eat is the hen. The farmer raises hens; the subject of the action of raising hens is the farmer. The hen lays eggs, and the farmer produces eggs. In the sentences in which the farmer is the subject, the hen as subject has disappeared, although these sentences describe actions by the farmer that include the physical process whereby the hen eats corn and lays eggs; the complete and complex process of producing eggs, performed by the farmer, includes the productive consumption of corn by the hen and also the wonderful transformation of the corn into eggs that occurs in the biological laboratory that is the hen. The farmer gets all the credit and benefits of this process, not because he is the subject of the physical actions that are performed, but because he is the subject of a different relationship that precedes that process, namely the relationship between him and the corn and between him and the hen: a relationship of appropriation, occupation, and power, a subject/object relationship.

Reading this, we cannot help asking: Are doctors and other health professionals the farmer or the hen? From the way the producers of technology and consumption goods for the health sector talk, it would seem definitely the latter.

On this point, let us look at a text that helps greatly to understand the thinking of "the farmers." I refer to the magazine *El Hospital*, which claims to reach 14,000 key readers in Latin America as the marketing magazine of the MIC.

The Welch Allyn company's attitude is revealed in a feature article which is a kind of advertisement:

> By the time that George Blowers, a veteran sales manager for Welch Allyn, was sent to Central and South America in 1965 to explore the possibilities of greater penetration of the market, Welch Allyn had already made fiber optics the wave of the future for medical diagnosis.
>
> In 1963 they had developed the first handheld diagnostic instrument utilizing fiber optic light; it used specially treated glass fibers and a very small source of light which transmitted a cool, intense light ideal for purposes of medical diagnosis. Blowers made a big impression in his visits to hospitals and clinics to demonstrate the new source of light. Although these fibers had already been seen in the United States, they were virtually unknown in Latin America, says Blowers. "I was holding a bunch of fibers fastened together at one end and I shined a small flashlight through them so that the tip of each fiber was turned into a tiny electric lamp." As Blowers remembers it, "the effect was astonishing: people gathered round inquisitively like moths drawn to a flame."[7]

Reading this, one cannot help being reminded of the description given by Christopher Columbus, almost 500 years earlier, of his first meeting with the "natives" of the new continent.

If we accept the hypothesis that major changes are occurring in the work process, including loss of control by health workers who have been changed from subjects to objects of the process (from farmers into hens), then it is also very possible that the entire crisis in the Latin American university system, which Tedesco[8] called the "devaluation of traditional educational standards"—which in practice means a steep decline in the quality of professional training—may be an absolutely inseparable element in this deteriorating situation. In the same sense, the widespread dissemination of positivist attitudes in the training of health professionals and the absence (even the rejection) of any social awareness may be facilitating the unselective incorporation of these professionals into the health services.

In the example of the pharmacists cited above, what knowledge is required to participate in the process of selling drugs? Something rather similar is happening with doctors, who at one time designed their own instruments, whereas nowadays they are often unaware either of the nature of the chemicals they are prescribing (which they know only by their fantastic market names) or of the scientific basis for the diagnostic technology or treatment they are using or prescribing; more serious still, they have lost control of the production of new knowledge, which nowadays takes place elsewhere. This fact is not mitigated by their occasional participation in some therapeutic test designed and financed by laboratories, and so it is not surprising that it is now these laboratories that are supporting the scientific superstructure (congresses, meetings, publications) in most of our countries.

Nonetheless, the expanding capacity of the medical-industrial complex is still not well known in most Latin American countries, where there is great ignorance of the major changes occurring in this area in the developed world; consequently there is no ongoing analysis of the repercussions of this phenomenon on our countries.

As a result, the traditional study of the chemical companies that produce medicines, although still very useful in terms of introducing health personnel to the economic dimensions of their profession, is now inadequate if it lacks any analysis of the profound qualitative changes brought about by the MIC.

In his book *The Medical Industrial Complex*, Stanley Wohl analyzes just these qualitative changes and points out that the process began as far back as the end of the 1950s through the application of capital, which came from outside the medical profession, to creating companies to provide networks of final services, by buying up and merging previously existing services. "Frist and other medical colleagues took the unusual, and as it turned out, historically significant step of selling shares in their hospital in order to raise capital," Wohl writes.[9]

In the same author's opinion, 1965 was a key year in this little-noticed process since it was then that the U.S. Congress approved the two major health insurance programs now protecting the poor and the elderly in the United States, namely, Medicare and Medicaid. This simultaneously created an enormous pool of inelastic demand (largely insensitive to prices) which has since led to the buying and selling of shares in health service companies, and mergers, on a huge scale. It was these developments that led Paul Starr to emphasize the industrial characteristics that medicine is currently acquiring in the United States:

Unless there is a radical change in economic and political conditions in the United States, the last two decades of the twentieth century will see a decline in the resources and autonomy of many doctors, voluntary hospitals and medical schools; two current developments are foreshadowing the future, namely the rapid increase in the number of doctors and the constant search for some kind of control over the growth of medical costs.[10]

In the January 5, 1990 issue of its magazine *American Medical News*, the American Medical Association uses headlines such as "Medical Practice Changes as Business Issues Gain Ground," "Antitrust Concerns Spread from Boardroom to Exam Room," "MDs' Patients: Where is the Trust? High Costs, Technology Drive Wedge in Relationship."

The signs of recession, loss of control, and multiplying regulations and pressures seem to indicate that the American Medical Association, probably one of the most successful professional organizations in history, understands but is not accepting without a fight the "farmer or hen" challenge.

Meanwhile, the vast majority of health professionals in Latin America are unaware of these issues and almost entirely ignorant of any relationship that might exist between the war which is going on in the health sector in the United States and the present and future situation of the national health systems in our various countries. In 1984, Wohl was already discussing the exportation by the major chains of complete services to Mexico City and São Paulo, and it is probably only the current crisis that has so far prevented such chains from expanding in the same way as the McDonalds, Sheratons and Kentucky Fried Chickens (a major shareholder in one of the large health service chains).

But if the expansion of these chains in Latin America is only beginning, the spread of medical technology and inputs with high value added has been rapid over the last 10 years, in conjunction with the notable expansion of the pharmaceutical industry. In discussing medical technology we must bear in mind the other important change highlighted by Wohl, namely that the industrial giants have entered the market in strength; consequently it is not surprising to see names such as Philips, Toshiba, or Kodak dominating and modernizing the advertisements in the magazine *El Hospital*. Wohl also refers in his book to the strong presence of General Electric, Hewlett-Packard, Sears, and IBM in the health market.

Their involvement is very significant since it is changing the rules of the game; most traditional suppliers were generally family firms, with very different kinds of marketing systems.

To sum up, this paper has sought to draw attention to the existence of a hidden, or barely visible, dimension of our national health systems, which behind their outward appearances depend to a significant and growing extent on an international medical-industrial complex.

"'We have noticed that the nations of Latin America are developing economically,' says [Lew] Allyn, vice president of Welch Allyn and general manager of the company's medical division. Welch Allyn, according to him, has found found excellent opportunities to do business in a region that regards health as a basic right extended by national authorities to the entire population"[11] (a curious view of the right to health).

Conclusion

"International dimensions of health," as one of the approaches to an analysis of international health, can provide a basis for a more comprehensive interpretation of what is going on with regard to health in our countries.

Our purpose in this paper was to answer certain questions, such as, what are the international dimensions of health, how can they be used to analyze international health, and what are their possible components and principal linkages? The purposes of this exercise are to define a field that will enhance our understanding, promote research, and gain greater freedom of action in health and the health care of the peoples of Latin America.

The multiple dimensions of the field of health, its steady internationalization, the understanding of global phenomena, the growing mismatch between health service infrastructure and the health needs of populations, the decline in living (and health) standards of increasingly large segments of these populations, the focus on expensive services for elites and the qualitative and quantitative reduction in services provided by the state, the crisis in social security stemming from the wage containment policy, which has been made a favorite adjustment tool—these seem to be main features of the current situation in most of Latin America.

Consequently, it is essential for our countries to reconsider the international dimensions of health and study various alternatives in depth in order to build national capacity and develop our own approaches to health in Latin America. The decline in living standards in our continent makes it impossible to postpone this task any longer.

References

1. Final Report of the Consultative Meeting on "Conceptual Development of International Health." Washington, D.C., PAHO, October 1989.

2. Coordinator of the PAHO/WHO Training Program in International Health and an organizer of the Quebec meeting.

3. For further analysis of the strategic sense of the concepts of transparency and opacity, see Mario Testa's "Pensamiento estratégico y lógica de programación," Buenos Aires, PAHO, 1989.

4. E.g., Ugo Pipitone, *El capitalismo que cambia*, Mexico City, Era, 1986.

5. See Mario Rovere's "Salud internacional," PAHO mimeo, Washington, D.C., presented to the Consultative Meeting on "Conceptual Development of International Health."

6. Fernández de Castro, Ignacio. *Sistema de enseñanza y democracia*. Madrid, *Siglo XXI*, 1980. Page 27.

7. Emily Morrison, "Welch Allyn en el cuidado de la salud en América Latina," *El Hospital* (Confluence, Pennsylvania, USA) 46(1):4 (February/March 1990).

8. Juan Carlos Tedesco, *El desafío educativo: Calidad y democracia*, Buenos Aires, Gel, 1987, page 52.

9. Stanley Wohl. *The Medical Industrial Complex*. New York, Harmony Books, 1984. Page 7.

10. Paul Starr. *The social transformation of American medicine*. New York, Basic Books, 1982.

11. Emily Morrison, *op. cit.*, page 14.

Reflections on Health as an International Issue[1]

Ulysses B. Panisset

The succession of surprises and radical transformations in national and international structures during 1991 have unleashed a period whose principal characteristic will be instability. Instead of raising new issues, this period of instability will cause old problems which remain unresolved to resurface again and again.

As a cruel illustration of the resurgence of old problems the Persian Gulf War exploded, unearthing conflicts over artificial boundaries that were buried since the beginning of the century under a light dusting of sand and petrodollars. In Central Europe the ingrained interests of different social groups are erupting in ethnic and nationalistic confrontations.

In Latin America, despite all the developmentalist rhetoric of the Sixties and Seventies, the gap between the living conditions of our people and those of people in the technologically advanced nations continues to increase as the years go by. As a reflection of this regional reality, the ever increasing concentration of income widens the already gaping inequity between the rich and poor.

In all these events, in an increasingly interconnected world, it is possible to find direct and indirect repercussions on the health of people. One day we hear that cholera has claimed three victims in Peru. The next we learn that it is affecting more than 55,000 people. The following week cholera crosses national boundaries, legally and illegally, contaminating a whole region plagued by similar social problems.[2]

In a world integrated by sophisticated means of communication, health problems take on an international dimension. Old problems and the debates about them are rehashed and even given new slogans. Results, however, are inferior to the real and possible capacity humankind has for addressing those problems. Yet it is not enough to give the impression that the health-disease is process increasingly internationalized. Solutions must also be internationalized.

To attain the goal of finding common solutions, one has to devise theoretical instruments and mechanisms for action that support more effective and beneficial health initiatives. The contradiction between the persistence of old problems and their damaging effects upon the health of people and the constant changes in fundamental realms of our societies forces us to frequent and mutable conjectures. It also obliges us to undertake a theoretical effort—an attempt to better understand the rhythm and pulsations of the close of this century—targeted to nurturing our healthy actions at the international level.

We shall begin by discussing our conceptual proposition for international health in its more explicit realms—national and international. Rovere suggests analyzing the "international dimension of health" within the national realm. Health in the international realm—or "health as an international issue" exists as a "segment of the vast field of international relations" and is the aim of this article.[3]

The dynamic relationship between health and disease generates repercussions that go beyond its local, national or even regional boundaries. International health—which encompasses the complex network of state and private systems, international agencies, social issues, economics, production, markets, services, as well as the health-disease process itself—does not exist in a void of its own. It is an integral part of the equally intricate field of international relations, which is dedicated to building theoretical landmarks in a changing world.

In addition to the international dimension that already shapes health within each individual nation-state—which nevertheless retains specific qualities in each locality—collective health is without doubt an international issue.

Health-related issues affect countries in both directions in relation to their boundaries. Just as it is impossible to treat the health-disease process as if it took place solely within national boundaries, it is impossible to understand the nature of health issues in the international realm without reference to its national expressions. Despite their different manifestations, the two analytic vantage points—the "international dimension of health" in the national realm and "health as an international issue" in the international arena—form an intricate dialectic relationship. The decision to analyze each dimension separately at this meeting is due to conceptual needs. It is the overlapping of the two realms that determines the overall result, however.

The main purpose of the following reflections is to explore some aspects of the distinct forms in which issues deriving from the health-disease process express themselves in the international realm, that is, the relations among nation-states, their institutions and their peoples.

The complexity of the theme "health as an international issue" calls for instruments and methods of analysis that go beyond those traditionally applied to the study of the local repercussions of health-disease phenomena. As a segment of international relations, international health's theoretical and pragmatic underpinnings should search for inspiration in those of international relations.

In our world of accelerating changes, it is necessary not only to study but to reorient international cooperation on health-related issues, particularly technical cooperation among countries. Furthermore, new methodologies and mechanisms are needed to improve international technical cooperation in the health sector. The current lack of an existing, clearly delineated international health theory allows us to venture into this evolving field of study. I will explore a series of questions and reflections here that I believe are central to the objective of developing a perspective of health as an international issue.

Is international health a political issue for governments and private actors?

How does the health sector reflect the rapid transformations occurring in the current international political arena? Does health somehow have an impact on international relations?

Notwithstanding the conflicts and transformations of our era (high technology, increased competitiveness, large commercial blocks, political-ideological changes, etc.), is it possible to envision cooperation among nations in the health field?

Does the necessity, opportunity, and viability of developing a Latin American perspective on international health exist?

In addition to the lack of a coherent theory, a further limitation on the debate regarding health as an international issue is that even those who use the historical-structural paradigm of the subject in their analysis do not address international health as dialectically related to the process of health and disease. Rather, they view it as an entirely separate subject. In other words, they reduce a complex interaction to a simple instrument for comparing health systems or policies, isolated from the context and broader concept of health. Another problem related to the aforementioned is the traditional treatment of international health as an isolated discipline and not as an influential variable in all considerations of the health-disease process.

Rovere tries to make the concept of international health more precise and objective. For him, international health is:

> A cross-section of the field of international relations that through the exchange of knowledge, information, financing, investments, technology (in products and management), and political influence tends to improve the health and living conditions of populations within the limits that the national interests of the involved nations impose.[4]

We seek to examine another facet of the limits imposed by national interests: those imposed on the health situation of the less powerful countries by the central, dominant nation-states, and their consequences for cooperation in health.

The health sector—seen as a small part of the larger whole—does not determine international policy. It does influence that policy, however, and health is an integral part of international conflicts, with both domestic and international repercussions.

It is therefore important to understand the diverse dimensions that contribute to the health-disease process on an international level.

The first step towards grasping these concepts is to examine the dimensions of the relations between nations. To truly comprehend the multiple dimensions and meanings of health, and international health, one has to assess the context of the quality and results of the relations among nations. The domestic and international historical, ideological, political, and economic contexts must be taken into account.[5]

The study of and work in international health requires a historical perspective of the health-disease process. This is the key to deciphering how the health systems of different countries developed and how the health-disease process of each country is interrelated with that of other countries.

Health interaction on an international scale is not a novel idea. During the quincentennial of the arrival of Columbus in the Americas, it is relevant to remember the age-old controversy over the illnesses and other calamities that invaded the American hemisphere with the European colonizers. To illustrate these hoary discussions, it is sufficient to mention the heated arguments about whether syphilis was introduced to the Americas by the colonizers or spread in Europe after the return of the first conquerors.

As a theoretical possibility, international health is not new either. Thomas Malthus could be said to be one of the first international health theorists. In his "Essay on the Principle of Population as it Affects the Future Improvement of Society," published at the end of the 18th century, Malthus considers disease, starvation, and war as means to guarantee world resources only for the fittest survivors. His cynical view of social problems still finds enthusiastic supporters in world politics, with drastic consequences for the health of millions.

An international approach to health can be found in authors as diverse as Hobson, Engels, Lenin, Choucri, and North who emphasize relationships between population increase, world demand for resources and technologies, the need for new markets, and conflicts that threaten peace.[6]

Practically all dimensions (cultural, ethnic-national, demographic, epidemiological, ecological, etc.) that have a direct or indirect bearing on health in the national arena cause an international chain of reaction, especially in today's world. But we will concentrate our discussion on three dimensions—ideological, political, and economic—which we consider the most appropriate for underlining the consequences of health as an international issue.

International health, understood as a part or segment of international relations, is an important arena for ideological battles. Health is used by competing countries to promote or discredit different economic and state models. Additionally, health is a field that clearly reflects the definition of internal priorities and policies pursued by government and society, and even the very organization of health services to address those priorities.

Despite governmental rhetoric and the efforts of health ministries, health promotion is not a real priority in most of Latin America. This can be seen in the scant and disorganized allocation of resources to that area, which compounds long-standing social inequalities. Further evidence is the slow improvement of health indicators in the region. The fundamental decisions governing the health sector are generally made by economics ministries which, in these times of epidemic neoliberalism, base their policies on the market and the concerns of international banks.

The nature of the state—its ideological dimension—is what shapes both national and international health policies. When a state is capitalist a private corporation's executives can influence the health system toward maximizing profits. In other words, the dominant ideology is what ultimately determines the principal health policies of a nation-state. Since ideology also defines a nation-state's relations with other countries, it does so in the health field as well.

Braillard states that the fragmentation of the study of international relations is "characterized by the absence of a paradigm and by the fact that there exist various general explanatory models confronting each other, various concepts of the object."[7]

Different theories of international relations are mainly as attempts to explain the doctrines underlying the action of countries dominating the international scene. They are theories in so far as they explain a conjunction of political facts determined by the nation-state doctrine of action. These "explanatory models" are concomitantly doctrines in the sense that they orient governmental policy according to the beliefs and objectives of the dominant national ideology. The doctrines of international relations therefore develop from the state's ideological and conceptual stamp and its political practices in the international arena.

Apart from whether we view international relations as an autonomous discipline or as an area of political science, its conceptual bases are indisputably exercised in the political field or in the political relations between nation-states. The variety of social determinants involved in international health, and the multidisciplinary nature of the subject, require that this subject be addressed primarily in the social science field, especially politics.

As an economic sector, health has specific characteristics that differentiate it from other parts of the economy. In the health sector, the mutual benefits entailed in the cooperation between countries—especially at the most advanced level of regional integration—are more easily perceived than they are in other areas. The reciprocal nature of the benefits is clearer. Diplomacy, geopolitical elements, and economic relations, among other factors, determine relationships between nations on the political level as well as on the international health level. Health has a marginal influence on international relations in some cases, however.

The relative importance of health as an instrument of diplomacy can be illustrated by several examples. The Pan American Health Organization-sponsored "Health as a Bridge to Peace" in Central America is one of the expressions of the influence international health might have in keeping doors open to negotiations between countries. It served as an indication of the possibility of negotiations about at least one indisputable issue—health—until the institutionalization of diplomatic mediation in Esquipulas.[8]

Commenting on the "Health as a Bridge to Peace" initiative, Carlyle Guerra de Macedo stated that: "We believe that health transcends political divisions. We believe that not only can it do so, but it has often been a key factor in promoting dialogue, in fomenting solidarity, and in contributing to peace among peoples and among nations."[9]

Another example of the health issue's ability to influence dialogues between countries is the case of improved commercial relations between Brazil and Cuba. Cuba exchanged vaccines for Brazilian products ranging from frozen chicken to automobiles, so solving part of the trade balance gap that favors Brazil and improving overall relations between the two countries.

Despite its singular characteristics and humanitarian dimension, international health cannot be examined in isolation from the manipulation and management of conflicts that take place in the international arena.

The ideological, political, and economic actions and mechanisms of nation-states in international relations (doctrines, strategies, alliances, cooperation, foreign aid, bellicose actions, conflicts) as well as the actions of transnational corporations (international trade, cartels, joint-ventures, strategic alliances, consortia, etc.), reverberate with ripple effects in the health field. The government of a nation-state that puts priority in its production efforts on exports has a foreign policy that is governed by the exigencies of international commerce in technologies, goods, and services. Health technologies, their products, and services are no exception in such an export-oriented economy.

The case of Japan is obvious. Since 1958 the Japanese government has invested money in "cooperation" efforts designed to benefit Japan either by financing the importation of Japanese capital goods or by developing natural resources which are later exported to it.[10]

As Samarasinghe points out: "In Sri Lanka the Japanese hospital equipment supplied through grant aid is replacing such equipment traditionally supplied by European manufacturers. Japan obviously is creating a durable market for its medical equipment through aid."[11]

The Brazilian Cooperation Agency (ABC) of that country's Ministry of Foreign Relations attempts to open and consolidate new markets through international cooperation, but does so with less direct involvement by Brazilian business. In addition to distributing student scholarships and grants, and cooperating with international organizations, ABC spends seed money to develop health cooperation projects.

Although not fully accepted by the mainstream of Brazil's foreign relations ministry (Itamaraty) and its highly professional diplomatic corps, ABC represents a new development among bilateral cooperation agencies. It was designed to channel private and public resources towards cooperative ventures in the third world. The interesting and dynamic work of ABC should serve as an example to agencies with greater resources. In keeping with the export promotion policy of Brazil, however, ABC acts primarily in areas where Brazilian enterprises are developing engineering services (for example, dam and road construction in Central Africa) or where there is a potential market for Brazilian products.

Cuba stands in a unique position in terms of international cooperation in health. It is a country that accords health national priority and uses it as a basis for its foreign policy toward other developing countries.

Due to the political decision to develop a sophisticated domestic health system and promoting "internationalism" and "solidarity toward the third world," Cuba is probably the most militant country regarding international health activities. Today around 3,000 Cuban health workers, more than half of whom are doctors, work voluntarily in 26 third world countries.[12] The Cuban experience shows that international cooperation in health may generate returns to the donor country. Recent developments suggest that Cuba, pressed by its worst economic crisis ever, now profits from the reputation it earned through international health cooperation by exporting health technologies, products, and services.[13]

In an opposite approach, a state that engages in global intervention based on the doctrine of realism and the policy of containment of adverse ideologies tries to control the health-disease process in relation to its own pretensions and global geopolitical interests. For "realists," a military presence in specific areas of geographical conflict is often perceived as a better policy for ensuring stability than aid, cooperation, and development.

The paradigm of "realism" dominated the study of international relations in the United States from the 1940s to the end of the 1960s. Its theoretical and doctrinal bases continue to underlie current time-specific outputs of North American foreign policy decision making.

Realism springs from Thucydides who, in his analysis of the Peloponnesian War, characterized international politics as the relationship between "power, impersonal forces, and grand leaders." Other antecedents of realism are found in Machiavelli's analysis of the relations between Italian states during the 16th century, as well as in authors as different as Hobbes, Hegel, and Weber. The old "realists" have in common with their 20th-century counterparts the idea that the principal characteristic of international politics is a struggle for power.[14]

Contemporary realist theoreticians (Niebuhr, Spykman, Morgenthau, Kennan, Kissinger, etc.) hold, with relatively few differences among them, that nation-states are the fundamental actors in international politics. The elites of the state have as a priority the design and execution of strategies whose goal is to guarantee or expand interests that ensure national security. For the realists, "self-help" and the use of force are the rights of a nation in defense of its national objectives and security.

The clearest applications of realist concepts are in the military field. Realists believe that if the international arena is inherently conflictive and anarchic, external threats justify the use of national strength against nation-states that represent a threat.

Another proposition of realism is that domestic policy can be clearly separated from foreign policy. The facts demonstrate that at least in the area of health-related issues, however, this premise is false. The epidemic consumption of narcotics is obviously one of the gravest current public health problems. It is an example of an area in which international health dimensions in the national realm (domestic policy) combine with the question of health as an issue in international policy making.

In a fairly revealing article on the application of realist doctrine to this specific health issue, Bruce Bagley analyzes the fallacy of North American domestic and foreign policy in combatting drug trafficking. Bagley seeks to explain the reasons for the failure of the "drug war" policies of the last 10 years as precisely a result of the adoption of the realist paradigm in the strategy for confronting the international drug trade.[15]

The North American doctrine for combatting the drug traffic, which Reagan called a national security issue in 1982, affected five Latin American countries directly—Bolivia, Colombia, Mexico, Peru, and later Panama. Without consulting the countries involved, the U.S. Congress supported the President by approving laws to increase the budget for repression and eradication activities in the producing countries and against drug-trafficking intermediaries. Nevertheless, drugs continued to penetrate the North American territory.

According to Bagley, the realist perspective holds that the United States has a right and a duty to carry out laws and maintain international order to eliminate instability. Realists therefore believe that the United States should force less-powerful nation-states to stop drug production and smuggling, thus guaranteeing North American security as well as the stability of the international system. When applied to the "war on drugs," the realist position also promotes unilateral force, as in the case of economic sanctions and military interventions.

The application of the realist paradigm to international health could, among other calamities, lead to the inversion of a priority that appears to be given to a particular domestic/international health problem. During the invasion of Panama, for instance, the real health threat represented by epidemic cocaine consumption in the United States served as an excuse for a military action with geopolitical—not health—objectives which killed a large number of civilians. To confront the narcotics trafficking problem we do not need unilateral actions, but rather the cooperation of all the countries involved in consuming, producing, or serving as intermediaries in drug trading. Most of all, long-term domestic and international strategies, as well as the recovery of economic growth in the region, are requisites for controlling the production and international smuggling of narcotics.

The neorealist propositions of Waltz, Kindermann, Gilpin, and others emerge in North American academic circles as alternatives to the realist proposal. Despite their profound differences, which we will not analyze in detail, the two currents and their variations hold that cooperation among nations based on "interdependence" is possible.

At this time, as newly thriving democracies in Latin America adopt neoliberal concepts as paradigms for national economic adjustment and international policies, it is worthwhile characterizing the contemporary "liberal" theoretical trends in international relations. With roots in 19th-century economic liberalism, neoliberal functionalist institutionalism appeared in international relations theory after World War II as a response to realism.[16]

The primary tenets of neoliberal functionalist institutionalism can be characterized by the theory of "functional integration" (Mitrany), which defends the leadership of international organizations in relations between nations. At the end of the 1950s and through most of the 1960s neofunctionalism emerged as developed by Haas, Schmitter, Lindberg, and others who espoused regional integration through free trade associations. Neofunctionalists highlighted the leading role of labor unions, political parties, trade associations, and supranational bureaucracies in cooperation between countries. In the 1970s and 1980s, Nye, Keohane, and Oye developed theories of economic interdependence, singling out the role of "multinational corporations and transnational and transgovernmental coalitions."[17]

It is true that powerful modern states generate "multiple channels of access," consistent with the neoliberal interdependence theorists, impeding a central government monopoly over foreign policy. However, the neoliberals try to ignore the fact that although these actors have their own agendas, most of them share in common an ideology of domination over the whole of society which unifies them and produces a common foreign policy out of their distinct actions.

Multiple issues and interrelations in the international sphere call for the creation of specialized international institutions. Contrary to what interdependency theorists such as Keohane and Oye postulate, however, that the role of international bodies is circumscribed by the limits imposed by their principal financial supporters and power brokers.

The manner in which each school in the international relations field addresses questions of "interdependence" and the need for cooperation is distinct. The realists accept dependent relations between nations as inevitable. Moreover, the application of their basic concepts to foreign policy tends to reinforce the acceptance and maintenance—even through military action—of the current power structure. The result of the application of realism in the health field is thus to maintain inequality.

The neorealists work with similar concepts, but do so through a window that tries to understand more clearly the needs, possibilities, and conditions under which conflict and cooperation occur. Neoliberals of all shades ignore fundamental questions related to the distribution of power and the division of the world into central, peripheral, and semi-peripheral nations. On the positive side, however, they accept the existence and participation of various other actors in addition to governments in the definition of international policy. It appears to us that this understanding is fundamental to working towards cooperation in health.

Neorealists, neoliberals, and others speak of interdependence as a modern phenomenon, generated in an interconnected world economy. "Interdependence" became a fashionable word to describe growing trade among countries and the impact of revolutionary communications technology on the development of the international economy.

The neorealist Knorr, states, however, that "power, influence, and interdependence" are inextricably linked. Two or more states may be in conflict over some issues yet cooperate in other areas: "When [states] cooperate, they benefit from the creation of new values, material and nonmaterial. When they are in conflict, they attempt to gain values at each other's expense. In either case, they are interdependent."[18]

Countries depend of each other to promote health and avoid the propagation of disease. But would it be true to assert that the basis for cooperation between countries in health or in any other economic sector is "interdependency"?

Gilpin discusses the "highly ambiguous" concept of market or economic interdependence. He uses the term "interdependence" to mean a "mutual albeit not equal dependence."[19]

Cardoso and others who adopt the historical-structural perspective of dependency relations argue that interdependency between a country in the vanguard of the technological revolution and a country in the process of technological and industrial development is similar to the relationship existing between a banker and a future client. It is obvious that a technologically advanced nation needs the markets, resources, labor, and materials of other nations with the goal of guaranteeing its development. In this sense there exists some level of interdependence, but the quality of the two dependencies is distinct. The historical-structural perspective appears to us an adequate instrument to analyze the flow of health-related capital goods, consumption products, technologies, and services toward Latin America and other third-world countries.[20]

Explaining a dynamic situation of accelerating interactions between sovereign nations in the health areas as mere "interdependence" appears essentially incorrect to us, or at least only a partial explanation of the problem. The term "interaction" better characterizes the unequal exchange existing between countries' economies than the term "interdependence." To understand how international health phenomena manifest themselves, one must understand the actual pattern of capitalist expansion and the international division of labor among central, peripheral, and semi-peripheral countries. Elling, for instance, utilizes a theory of world systems which suggests a direct relationship between the nature of the state, its ideological and economic system, and the consequent results in international health. Later on, in discussing the aspects of international health cooperation, we will try to analyze aspects of the impact of dependency relationships between countries in such cooperation.[21]

In analyzing the possibilities of interactions and various forms of cooperation among countries in the health area, the following question arises: Is cooperation in health a means of affirming interdependence or of assuring dependence?

The actual relationships of exchange between countries in the region reflect qualitative differences in the terms and conditions under which the exchange takes place. In keeping with our drug-trafficking example, a country's international health activities can be used as an instrument of diplomacy and cooperation as well as one of domination.

The economic integration process now taking place in subregions of Latin America and the Caribbean, however, open doors for the development of real interdependent relations deriving from common needs. At least one can expect the increase of interactions among countries, with profound repercussions in the health area. The existence of real interdependence, however, will obviously be decided independently from the health sector.

One can formally consider sovereignty and national identity as characteristics of the modern state. But sovereignty and national identity exist in relation to the capacity of a state to develop and exercise its power in the international arena. Similarly, a country's health situation reflects its capacity to develop at the national and international level, since it depends on domestic determinants as well as innumerable variables determined internationally.

The myth and the appearance of interdependence can conceal the fact that any relationship between nations presupposes the existence of some level of conflict and the necessity of its resolution. Stein states that:

International cooperation and conflict are inextricably joined. Both are omnipresent in world politics, as they are in many other forms of social and biological relations. Both reflect purposive calculated behavior in an interdependent world, and both emerge from the interaction of an array of situational factors ... competitive and conflictual relations can underlie concerted, cooperative ones.... Outcomes of international cooperation and conflict emerge as a result of states' strategic choices, which include both cooperation and conflict as strategies.[22]

In this statement Stein, a neorealist, admits the conflictual dimension of "interdependency." Any act of cooperation between two or more countries presupposes conflict. The understanding of this condition disarms illusions and facilitates the negotiation of mutually beneficial agreements. Furthermore, Stein alerts against concealing aspects of "coercion, power, and conflict" involved in cooperation among countries:

A focus on cooperation alone is equally problematic. Some economists recognize that their discipline focuses on mutually beneficial exchange and that the efficiency of the market masks a great deal of the coercion, power, and conflict that attend market exchanges.... Even cooperative interactions have conflictual and competitive elements.[23]

A nation-state can promote cooperative actions with a lesser degree of its own interest in health than in military issues or frontier disputes, for instance. However, in case these cooperative health actions include trade in medical equipment, pharmaceutical and immunobiological products, or other highly valued health-related products, the degree of that very interest rises, as protective measures commanded by the governments of most technologically advanced countries show.

International trade in goods, services, and health technology also expresses clearly the conflicts and disputes in international relations and their intersection with international health. Health technology is implicated in commercial disputes and important conflicts over technology transfer. As an illustration, we can cite the debates within GATT over pharmaceutical and biotechnological patents and specific disputes between the Brazilian pharmaceutical industry and that in the United States, with the U.S. Commerce Department placing commercial sanctions on Brazil.

According to Albert Hirschman, the power to interrupt commercial and financial relations with any country is the causal origin of the power that a country acquires over others.

In the economic arena, one can note various situations of real coercion in disputes between countries and their repercussions on health.[24]

The "new dependency" of Latin America on central countries is primarily characterized by the exportation of capital in the form of interest payments on external debt. Thus it is necessary to deepen studies of the impact of Latin American external debt and economic adjustment policies on the health of our peoples.

Our habitat encompasses the global population with unequally distributed vital resources. The international distribution of such resources is directly related to the possibility of peace and the health conditions of the people. It should therefore be one of the principle aspects analyzed from the international health perspective.

Health can be a fundamental stimulus in promoting development, both as representative of general living conditions as well as a vital economic sector. Approximately 7% of the gross national product of the Latin American countries is health-related. A significant proportion of the labor force is directly or indirectly involved in the production of medical equipment or the provision of health services.

As an important economic sector, health services and the products related to them such as medical equipment, pharmaceutical products, and various technologies constitute a worldwide international market in labor, services, technology, and products totaling close to a trillion dollars.

The international market in human health-related products is estimated at $180 billion for medications and $70 billion for medical equipment and hospitals. Biotechnology epitomizes the modern expanding and accelerating market. It has been forecasted that it will expand to $1 trillion annually before the year 2,000, a huge chunk of it dedicated to health.

It is necessary but not enough only to study the impact or adaptation of new health technologies to living conditions in Latin America. It is equally essential to identify the impact of this market on the development of the region.

Latin America includes 8% of the world's population, produces 5% of the gross world product, and consumes 3% of the medications and medical equipment produced on the planet. In order for us to better grasp the magnitude of the Latin American market, Costa Rica alone consumes around $100 million of medical equipment and hospital materials annually. MERCOSUR, the planned common market embracing Argentina, Brazil, Paraguay, and Uruguay, encompasses 190 million people. Even considering the exclusion from that market of the more than half the subregional population living in poverty, MERCOSUR stills represent a market of significant dimensions, especially in the health field.

The region is still experiencing a decade characterized by a decline in the majority of the population's quality of life and by economic stagnation, however. In the short term, a recovery of production is unlikely. In different degrees and with different policies, the nations will continue in the 1990s adjusting themselves to the problems that affected them severely in the 1980s.

Regional blocs for economic integration and international health

The scientific and technological revolution transformed age-old geopolitical concepts. Control of scientific and technological development acquired even more relevance than direct control of physical territories. Dougherty and Pfaltzgraff summarize Aron's view about the issue: "Technological innovations modify previously held spatial concepts, including the strategic value of geographical positions and the economic importance of certain natural and human resources."[25]

In the health sector, just as in the rest of the economy, technological innovation accelerated. Transnationalization of markets and inducement of demand and artificial consumption in the health area have "transformed the relations between nations, accentuating regional economic differences and provoking a geopolitical reorganization."[26]

The international geopolitical reorganization, based on the new actors of technological development, is heading in the direction of consolidating integrated regional blocs. Within these blocs the unequal division of power and labor persists. Although unequally distributed, such blocs promote potential benefits for all integrated countries.

Among the most striking examples of newly integrated regional blocs is Europe, which is strengthening its economic-technological prowess through the process of integrating the European Economic Community by 1992. Another example is the South Pacific where there are few formal integration agreements. Instead, commercial and technological exchange is based on a rigid horizontal division of labor with large Japanese capital investments.

Formerly socialist countries are enduring painful adjustments to fit settled blocs. In addition to ideological ruptures, one of the reasons that led to the decay of the Mutual Support Council of the socialist countries, was the need of the Central European countries to look for new production methods in capitalist economies, paying with hard currency.

While these new processes of regional integration are being defined with greater clarity, Latin America cannot squander effort or time on integration rhetoric. The Southern Cone, stimulated by the advance of the democratic process, is looking for its own routes with the signing of the MERCOSUR protocols and its plan to create a convertible currency and form a common market by January 1995.

Contrary to the proposals made by the functional integrationalists of the 1950s and 1960s, the participation of diverse social sectors in the integration process is today increasing. Private enterprises, universities, research centers, and many more are involved in the integration of the Southern Cone.

The possibility of Latin American economic integration represents the most important hope for ending the current crisis in the region. The Pan American Health Organization (PAHO) and all organizations in the health sector should be prepared to reinforce this trend toward regional development.

Regional integration by itself, however, does not represent equal relations between unequal partners. Regional integration may also signify a new form of control by "more independent countries" of "less independent countries." Within each participating country, especially in Latin America, not everyone benefits directly from economic integration policies. The health of vulnerable sectors of the population will require close monitoring.

In integration efforts, health has to be perceived by policy makers as an issue influenced by the process of lessening barriers and as an important economic sector which can boost integration and requires common regulation. In the North American Free Trade Agreement (NAFTA), which is currently being negotiated by the United States, Mexico, and Canada, health and environmental concerns have surfaced as key arbitration and regulation problems.

Whereas Europe only recently included health issues in its negotiations, Latin America has an opportunity to introduce health from the outset of the integration process. PAHO shows positive signs of promoting health within Latin American integration processes, and is participating in initiatives such as the Convenio Hipólito Unanue, ABREMEX (regional cooperation in pharmaceutical), SIREVA (cooperation in vaccines), and CONVERGENCE (cooperation in health technology) and through subregional initiatives (Central America, Southern Cone, Caribbean, Andean Group, NAFTA).

The current economic crisis has a double contradictory effect on technical cooperation between countries. On the one hand, it complicates channeling resources for cooperation. On the other, however, it obligates countries to unite their efforts to save scarce resources. This in turn opens new opportunities of cooperation between countries with similar problems.

Cooperation among countries:
The primary network for international health

Technical cooperation among countries (TCC) is a decisive instrument for overcoming the existing gap between Latin America and the countries in the vanguard of technological renovation. In addition, exchanges among the Latin American countries permit improving their national capacities while enhancing their bargaining position with the more developed countries.

Grieco defines international cooperation as "the voluntary adjustment by states of their policies so that they manage their differences and reach some mutually beneficial outcome."[27]

He emphasizes that the principal characteristics of this concept of international cooperation are willingness, defining the state by a common objective, and a long-term relation with the "establishment and operation of an international regime in the issue area in which joint action is undertaken." As a basic condition for successful cooperation, he suggests "the acceptance and development by governments of common rules."[28]

With the goal of identifying methods of protecting cooperative activities, we must ask ourselves the meaning of the concept of willingness to cooperate. The person who volunteers to fight because it is the only option to avoid starving to death is not like one who does it for principles, ideals, or even money. The former's negotiating condition, strategic objectives, and capacity to act are different from those of the latter. In a cooperative venture as well, a common objective may camouflage a secret agenda. A technologically advanced country may have obscure interests in the health market of a less developed country starving for new technology. The interaction between the two countries may reflect different but not necessarily incompatible goals. The common rules of a cooperation process, however, may be distorted or interpreted in different ways by two or more partners.

Stein states that "even mutual altruism need not resolve incongruent interests." On the other hand, altruism and solidarity can exist and persist in collaboration agreements if they are conceptualized as the capacity to make decisions and implement agreements which include different degrees of benefit for both parties. Concessions will have to be made concerning some issues. In the ultimate analysis, altruism and solidarity between countries, even in the health field, coexist with their perception of their own short- and long-term interests.[29]

The number of participants is a condition that, according to the neoliberals, influences the outlook on perspective cooperation. Oye states that "the prospects for cooperation diminish as the number of players increases."[30] This statement is not totally applicable to the health field, however. In spite of certain national peculiarities, the similarity between the problems of and solutions to the health situation in Latin America, as well as the proven possibilities of jointly attacking them, demonstrate the viability of intersubregional and interregional cooperation agreements. In some situations where specifics prevail over generalities, bilateral and trilateral accords can clearly be pursued.

We also agree with the neofunctionalist statement that the advance of democracy favors cooperation between nations. This assumption is consistent with the thinking underlying MERCOSUR and the prospect of future Southern Cone integration.

According to the neofunctionalists, an additional condition for cooperation is the size of potential benefits. This too seems obvious to us: that the magnitude of the gains for our peoples from cooperation in the health area is a sufficient reason to strive for it.

There have traditionally been both subtle and open traps in economic negotiations between countries. The neoliberal institutionalists, in an attempt to eliminate this problem, believe that circumstances exist which enable the success of cooperation between countries. Despite their weaknesses in defining different forms of coercion and power struggle, they espouse the sound position that international bodies can act to prevent fallouts in cooperative activities. In this case, we agree with the institutionalists. The reality of the possibilities of cooperation in health between countries whose degree of cooperation varies requires the participation of a third, more impartial partner in the venture. Despite its limitations, PAHO meets all the requirements for performing this role.

When negotiated in isolation from other economic issues, health issues face prejudices on the part of authorities mediating economic integration. Health is often cast aside or postponed as a social issue to be tackled later. To alter the low priority accorded health in this situation, strategies must be designed to permit the sector itself to intervene in decision making, while opening potential avenues to facilitate the integration process. The participation of the private sector usually helps promote the economic aspects of health by creating an area for discussing health problems that stem from the integration process.

To promote health as an international negotiation issue, PAHO and other United Nations agencies rely on a well-suited instrument called "technical cooperation between developing countries" (TCDC), whose potential for the region in health has not been completely explored. Proof of the lack of development of TCDC projects in Latin America is the area of biotechnology, which currently represents a market of $1.6 billion annually for Argentina, Brazil, and Mexico alone. Yet only Argentina and Brazil have joined efforts in this area, for an initial amount of only $2 million.

Traditional technical cooperation by international agencies with countries has its own specific demands. PAHO could increase its contribution in the international health area enormously by looking more aggressively for a development strategy which employs TCDC as its principal instrument of action and promotion for integration and health.

Cooperation among Developing Countries is a catalyst for both Latin American integration and regional development. TCDC does not exclude cooperation with technologically advanced countries, however. On the contrary, such cooperation is necessary and indispensable, if it is done within the limits of solidarity and for the mutual benefit of the involved parties. Nor do we propose that Latin America be transformed into a grandly autarkic region. Quite the opposite: the region must adapt to the competitiveness of other regionally integrated blocs by increasing its negotiation capability in the development and acquisition of new health technology.

A practical test of altruism and good will of a technologically developed country in relation to the Latin American nations would be precisely its willingness to finance TCDC activities as well as to transfer new technologies. The apparent naivete of such a statement is counterbalanced by searching for acceptable benefits to donor countries also, and combining them with the cooperation efforts negotiated through TCDC.

We must look for different modalities and mechanisms of commercial cooperation such as joint-ventures, consortiums between private enterprises and research centers, strategic alliances, and other innovative conceptions. Latin America can look for new opportunities for negotiation while still respecting its own interests.

The role of PAHO in cooperation between the countries in Latin America

Earlier we mentioned PAHO's role as an intermediary in the opportunities for health cooperation between countries. PAHO has a mandate and a historic opportunity to examine the joint process of international health without the risks of lesser specific interests.

So that PAHO may perform its work as a stimulator of cooperation more efficiently, it must promote studies of its own international health policies. The daily workings of multilateral, international organizations such as PAHO and the World Health Organization (WHO), promote a tacit, unwritten concept of international health. This de facto concept risks confusing international health with this daily practice or, more precisely, with the traditional instruments utilized by the organization in technical cooperation. The same biases present in graduate courses and the discipline of international health also manifest themselves in the case of international health organizations. In both cases the broader strategic vision of health as the fruit of distinct national and international determinants sometimes is reduced to the utilization—or even to the rhetoric of the utilization—of the instruments of technical cooperation. At PAHO, health cooperation is often reduced to technical cooperation practices between countries in highly specialized areas in addition to rhetoric about cooperation between countries, which in reality is achieved only infrequently.

The temptation to reduce the practice of international health to the implementation of limited aspects of technical cooperation, or to substitute a strategic objective for a working instrument, hides from view an enormous variety of factors in the international arena which directly or indirectly affect the health-disease process. The result of this way of working is to reduce the institution's capacity and potential field of action.

The reduced attention given to questions related to the health sector's international trade and its consequences for people's health reveals the typical biases of the functionalists and neofunctionalists towards integration. During the 1950s and 1960s they believed that regional integration should occur primarily through international agencies and their technical experts. They forgot the vital extent of the conflicts involved, as well as the group of actors whose national and transnational interests affect any integration process.

Those who believed in interdependency and other modern functionalists, meanwhile, identified the participation of multiple actors beyond the central government in international politics as a positive aspect. These other actors—political parties, labor unions, scientific institutions, etc.—increase their roles as democracy advances. The expansion of capitalism stimulates the growth of national and transnational entrepreneurs and commercial associations. To the degree that health is not a priority matter on the foreign policy agenda of most governments, various other actors acquire greater weight in sectorial decision making within the international health environment.[31]

PAHO recently began to assess the actual extent of the impact of the health market in the Americas. The recent project, Convergence of Technical Cooperation for the Development of Health Technology in the Latin American and Caribbean Countries, represents a significant advance in the perception of demands for new forms of cooperation in health in the region. Organized by PAHO, the United Nations Development Program, the Latin American Economic System (SELA), Ministries of Health and Foreign Relations, and various private actors, the CONVERGENCE project seeks to reinforce the regional integration strategy by coordinating the cooperation activities of the governmental, academic, and private sectors. Among its other characteristics, CONVERGENCE promotes cooperation among countries in the crucial areas of information, human resource development, health technology development policies, and international trade. One of its key objectives is to develop a specific methodology for TCDC in health.

PAHO operates within the same geographic universe as the major international creditor of the region (the United States) and the major debtor (Brazil). It encompasses nation-states with extremely antagonistic systems such as the United States and Cuba. PAHO hence needs to continue to develop and perfect a greater variety of instruments for analysis and action.

PAHO must respond to the growing challenges of the direct and indirect impact on health of the regional and international economic situation. In order to perfect and orient its practices when faced with great ideological diversity, it is necessary for PAHO to study and understand its own policies of international health and their repercussions.

It is necessary to conceptualize and work on all direct and indirect relations of exchange between countries which have an impact on the health of the people on the following levels:

1. The economy, including commercial flows of goods and services, financial resources, the external debt, the flow of capital to the central countries, the impact of economic adjustment, integrated economic blocs, protectionism, activities of international cartels, technology transfer, industries, services, infrastructure, etc.

2. Policies including technical cooperation in health, legislation, regulations, patents and standards, bioethics, agreements, policies of scientific and technological development, integration policies, environmental policies, armed conflicts, military blockades that include food and health goods, displacement of people due to war or economic crisis, etc.

3. Biology and epidemiology, including pandemics such as AIDS, environmental contamination and other man-made disasters, natural disasters, immunization, malnutrition, etc.

4. Cultural aspects, including habits and customs, architecture and health, lifestyles, etc.

It is reasonable to state that PAHO has already begun significant efforts to separate itself from the limited concept of international health. These include studies and novel initiatives such as "Health as a Bridge to Peace," recognizing bellicose international conflicts as a fundamental question in health, the impact of external debt and adjustment programs on health, proposals to study the dimensions of cooperation and international technology trade in the health sector, and through other unique programs mentioned previously, such as CONVERGENCE. With its International Health Program, PAHO forms human resources with both a national and a Latin American perspective.

PAHO's practice, organized from distinct and sometimes contradictory theories and ideological conceptions, offers the possibility of understanding the magnitude of international determinants of health to the degree that it manages to involve the diverse actors who work directly in the vast domain of international health.

Despite the constant efforts of Ministries of Health and PAHO's country representatives to promote the improvement of collective health, in the international sphere a series of important events occur independently of the direct actions of health authorities. Most negotiations and cooperation efforts in health take place primarily through contact between individuals, private enterprises, NGOs, and other institutions. A study we conducted of opportunities for cooperation between countries in the region demonstrated that the state health management subsector did not participate in the planning, negotiations toward, or even the administration of any of the bilateral accords concluded between Argentina, Brazil, Mexico, and Cuba on science and technology. In the case of Argentina and Brazil, health —included in the biotechnology protocol— was included in the accord as defined by the ministers of science and technology and of foreign relations. This phenomenon is not limited to Latin America. Health was not included in the Treaty of Rome of the European Economic Community.[32]

A greater effort is therefore needed by the countries, and PAHO needs to design and develop new cooperation strategies to establish an influential presence for its "Health for All" policies in the international health economic sector. To increase PAHO's participation in the international health process, its technical expertise and the breadth of disciplines and instruments of international relations must be improved. The work of channeling and administering the new basis for cooperation between Latin American countries requires perfecting the professionalization of the various areas of international health as well as more precise concepts and strategies.

Final observations

The frequent calls of PAHO and WHO for support of Health For All by the Year 2,000 contrast with the stagnation and even regression of some of the health indicators of the countries on the road to development. The economic crisis and its tragic social effects, as well as inadequate relations between countries, are enormous obstacles to achieving Health For All.

Only a concerted joining of efforts by all of Latin America with other countries, particularly those with similar problems, can overcome the lost time. Health should be one of the priority axes of integration and mutual support that transcends the conventional initiatives.

I believe that an international health policy emanates from many countries and regions. It is unwritten and is limited in its conceptualization, but it is acted upon by various actors. This brings us back to the question: Is it possible to speak of a Latin American perspective on international health?

Charles Godue pointed to the confused practice of several North American universities, which see international health as the health of underdevelopment. In spite of running the risk of reinforcing the same confusion, I believe that Latin Americans can develop a regional perspective to defend and promote health in the region which involves various actors in governments, universities, and the private sectors in different countries. The underdevelopment of the health of our peoples demands a search for common policies and actions within a regional perspective to improve living conditions in the entire region.

References

1. This article originated from fruitful discussions with residents in different generations of the International Health Program of the Pan American Health Organization, especially with Mario Rovere, Charles Godue, and Patricio Márquez, as well as from the persistence of María Isabel Rodríguez in developing a school of Latin American analysts attempting to understand health as a means to achieve social justice, peace, and better coexistence among different peoples. The support of Jorge Peña-Mohr in the organization of CONVERGENCE, a PAHO project for technical cooperation among countries, also stimulated many of the reflections hereafter. The guidance and patience of Dr. Riordan Roett, director of Latin American Studies at Johns Hopkins University's School of Advanced International Studies in Washington, D.C. in teaching foreign policy to a physician encouraged ventures in this intricate subject.

2. Even an observer who wants to forget social issues and reduces health to its simplest biological concept has to conclude that old diseases, easily preventable with the existing scientific and technological arsenal, recrudesce again and again.

3. Mario Rovere, *Aportes para la discusión sobre el campo de salud internacional*, PAHO/WHO unpublished mimeograph, 1990, p. 5.

4. Mario Rovere, *op. cit.*, p. 5. Translated from Spanish.

5. "Health sector" is defined here as an economic sector which includes industries, services, agriculture, and trade. More broadly, we include in the terms "health" and "health sector" what is usually called the "health system" (both governmental and private), as well as political and social relations involved in the health-disease process.

6. Although not mentioning health specifically, Dougherty and Pfaltzgraff, in analyzing environmental theories, comment on the different approaches of the writers mentioned in relation to population increase, resource distribution, social justice, and peace—all related to the health situation of populations. See James Dougherty and Robert Pfaltzgraff, Jr., *Contending theories of international relations: A comprehensive survey* (New York: Harper & Row, 1990), pp. 54-5.

7. Philippe Braillard, The social sciences and the study of international relations, *Internat Soc Sci J* 36(4):631 (1984); cited in Dougherty and Pfaltzgraf, Jr., *op. cit.*, p. 540.

8. Examining inequities in the world's distribution of medical doctors, Pust points out different between Cuba and the United States government in their international health aid efforts and mentions the possibility of health functioning as a foreign policy instrument. See R. E. Pust, Abundance of physicians and international health, *JAMA* 252(3):385 (1984).

9. Prologue to *Salud un puente para la paz en Centro América y Panamá*, Washington, D.C., Pan American Health Organization, 1989.

10. Saburo Okita. Japan's growing role for development financing. *In:* Michael R. Reich and Elji Marui (eds.), *International cooperation for health* (Dover, Massachusetts, Auburn House, 1989.), p. 364.

11. The market and long-lasting profit are guaranteed by maintenance and replacement costs. See S. W. R. de A. Samarasinghe, Japanese and U.S. health assistance to Sri Lanka, in: Michael R. Reich and Elji Marui (eds.), *op. cit.*, p. 112.

12. Donna Rich, Cuban internationalism: A humanitarian foreign policy, in: P. Brenner, et al. (eds.), *The Cuba reader: The making of a revolutionary society* (New York, Grove Press, 1989), p. 407. For an in-depth analysis of Cuba's international health policies, see Julie Feinsilver, Cuba as a world medical power: The politics of symbolism, *Lat Am Research Rev* 24:2 (1989).

13. For a comprehensive study of the current international health policies of Cuba, see Julie M. Feinsilver, *Will Cuba's wonder drugs lead to political and economic wonders? Capitalizing on biotechnology and medical exports*, a paper presented at the Latin American Studies Association 1991 annual meeting in Arlington, Virginia.

14. See J. Dougherty and R. Pfaltzgraff, *op. cit.*, pp. 90-135.

15. Bruce M. Bagley. Dateline drug wars. Colombia: The wrong strategy. *Foreign Policy* Winter 1989/1990, pp. 154-71.

16. The terms "liberal" and "neoliberal" are used here not in the American sense of interventionist government, but in that of the neoclassical school of economic thinking which praises controlled government spending and the relative absence of government regulation.

17. Joseph M. Grieco, *Cooperation among nations: Europe, America, and non-tariff barriers to trade* (Ithaca, New York, Cornell University Press, 1990), pp. 4-7. See also Dougherty and Pfaltzgraff, *op. cit.*, pp. 119-123.

18. Klaus Knorr, *The power of nations: The political economy of international relations* (New York, Basic Books, 1975), p. 3.; cited in Dougherty and Pfaltzgraff, *op. cit.*, p. 85.

19. Robert Gilpin, *The political economy of international relations* (Princeton, New Jersey, Princeton University Press, 1987), pp. 17-18.

20. Gereffi's study of the pharmaceutical industry and third- world countries' dependency clearly illustrates the strength of historic-structural instruments of analysis in explaining international commercial and industrial flows in the health sector. See Gary Gereffi, *Industria farmacéutica y dependencia en el tercer mundo* (Mexico City, Fondo de Cultura Económica, 1986).

21. Ray Elling. The capitalist world system and international health. *Int J Health Serv* 11(1):21-51 (1971).

22. Arthur A. Stein, *Why nations cooperate: Circumstance and choice in international relations* (Ithaca, New York, Cornell University Press, 1990), pp. 172-3.

23. Arthur A. Stein, *op. cit.*, p. 173.

24. Albert Hirschman, *National power and the structure of foreign trade* (Berkeley, University of California Press, 1945), p. 16; cited in Robert Gilpin, *op. cit.*, p. 23.

25. Dougherty and Pfaltzgraff, *op. cit.*, p. 115.

26. Jacques Marcovitch, "O novo contexto mundial e a gestão da pesquisa," paper presented at PAHO/WHO's Seminar on Scientific Policy and Technology in the Health Sector, Mexico City, 1989.

27. Joseph M. Grieco, *op. cit.*, p. 22.

28. Joseph M. Grieco, *op. cit*, p. 22.

29. Stein, *op. cit.*, p. 167, note 51. The case of Cuba, mentioned before, also serves as an example of altruism combined with national interest. For a formal analysis of altruism in a negotiating process, Stein suggests consulting Norman Frohlic, "Self-interest or altruism: What difference?," *J Conflict Resolution* 18:55-73 (1974) and Bruce D. Fitzgerald, "Self interest or altruism: Corrections and extensions," *J Conflict Resolution* 19:492-79 (1975).

30. Kenneth A. Oye, "Explaining cooperation under anarchy: Hypotheses and strategies," *World Politics* 38:18 (October 1985); cited in Grieco, *op. cit.*, p. 151.

31. In the health area, these actors are in the private services, products, and technology subsector, universities, research and development centers, foundations, other nongovernmental organizations, and state and provincial governments.

32. Ulysses B. Panisset. *Cooperación técnica entre países (CTP/CTPD) para el desarrollo tecnológico en salud: Posibilidades de cooperación entre Argentina, Brasil, México y Cuba.* Unpublished 145-page HSP/HDT document, PAHO/WHO, February 1990.

Training in International Health: A Canadian Perspective

Vic Neufeld

In the world community of nations, Canada has made a relatively small but not insignificant contribution to international development. This is expressed in the transfer of funds (official development assistance), in the work of individuals and institutions, and in the development of ideas and new knowledge. In the last several years there has been an increasing interest among Canadian universities and other institutions in the field of international health. A feature of this process has been the collaborative nature of discussions, planning, and project implementation.

This paper has three objectives:

1. To summarize current Canadian activities in international health;
2. To describe a collaborative training initiative: the Canadian University Program in International Health; and
3. To make some additional observations on the conceptual basis of the "field" of international health, in part arising out of the Canadian experience.

International health activities in Canada

This section briefly summarizes Canada's recent and current activities at two levels, national and institutional. It focuses on activities that are relevant to training in international health.

National activities. Several national organizations and networks have a particular interest in the field of health in the context of international development. Four organizations are described below, and a comment is included regarding collaboration among these groups.

1. The Canadian Society for International Health (CSIH). Originally a Division of Tropical Medicine of the Canadian Public Health Association (CPHA), this society was incorporated in 1977 as the Canadian Society of Tropical Medicine and International Health (and an affiliate of the CPHA). As the society evolved, its name was changed in 1989 to the Canadian Society for International Health, which has a division of tropical medicine. The CSIH is committed to promoting international health and development. It is made up principally of individuals from many different professional backgrounds who work in federal, provincial, and local governments, universities, nongovernmental organizations (NGOs), and other international agencies. The current membership of almost 500 individuals has recently been engaged in a review of the Society's mission and strategic plan. The CSIH has identified three focus areas for its activities during the 1990s: communication, education, and advocacy. Related activities include educational and research awards, conferences and workshops, study consultations, and publications.

In the area of training, the CSIH is responsible for managing the International Health Exchange Program (IHEP). Initiated in 1983 with funding by the International Development Research Centre (IDRC), this program is now funded by the Canadian International Development Agency (CIDA). Its goal is "to provide a well-structured educational exchange program between Canadian and developing country institutions." The aim is to increase the pool of Canadian health professionals aware of and interested in international health in order to meet the growing demand in Canada and abroad for qualified international health professionals. More than 340 health science students have participated in the program, usually through "electives" as part of their health professions education. Spending a minimum of 8 to 10 weeks, participating students conduct projects, with the guidance of developing country supervisors. Priority is given to projects that enable students to interact with communities in rural areas.

2. *The Canadian Public Health Association and its International Health Secretariat.* The Canadian Public Health Association (CPHA) was incorporated in 1912 as a nonprofit national organization, committed to the improvement and maintenance of personal and community health in Canada and around the world. It represents a special health resource in four general areas: health programs, liaison/advocacy, publishing, and events (conferences, workshops, study tours). CPHA's International Health Secretariat cooperates with public health associations in countries around the world through a variety of projects targeted on extending and strengthening primary health care. These activities provide an opportunity for Canadian community health workers to learn of innovative approaches to primary health care in developing countries and to facilitate an exchange of information and mutual support between Canadians and their international (principally third-world) counterparts. In the Latin American region, several CPHA-initiated projects involve training of community health workers (Chile), occupational health workers (Bolivia), and environmental health workers (the Caribbean).

3. *The Association of Universities and Colleges of Canada (AUCC).* This association of Canada's 89 universities and university-level colleges serves as a voice for these institutions on the national and the

international scene.   It has an International Division which provides information concerning international cooperation in higher education. For several years, the AUCC, in collaboration with the CSIH, has provided an International Health Communication Service. The main expression of this service is the newsletter *Synergy*, a bilingual quarterly which provides information in the broad field of international health for Canadian and overseas readers. Recently an online service has been added, using the BitNet electronic network which is used by all Canadian universities. The AUCC has also collaborated with other Canadian organizations in the development of a clearinghouse and database of Canadian international health information.

4. Canadian University Consortium for Health in Development (CUCHID). Increasingly over the last several years, Canadian universities have collaborated in the field of international health and development. In 1988, seventeen universities formed a consortium with the mission of "strengthen[ing] Canadian academic capacity for contributing to the solution of important problems in developing countries, and to bring together Canadian and developing country university resources in this process."

Several distinctive features characterize this consortium, which has now grown to include 30 institutions. The members are institutions (rather than individuals), with the understanding that, when linked with developing country institutions, an international collaborative arrangement provides access to a broad range of expertise, and in turn facilitates mutual learning; the intent is to strengthen academic capacity in Canada, including graduate level education and scholarly research and analysis in the field of health in development. The consortium focusses on a small number of key areas reflecting a commitment to improving health outcomes in the world's most disadvantaged communities. These features are operationalized through working groups. A training group is developing a collaborative graduate program (see below); another group is developing a national clearinghouse and database on Canadian involvement in international health; a "scientific forum" working group plans events to facilitate critical analysis of Canada's involvement in health and development; some "theme groups" have been formed to focus the resources of the Canadian academic community on specific problems, such as "health, nutrition and structural adjustment", and "institutional capacity strengthening." CUCHID shares a secretariat with the CSIH and collaborates with it in several working groups.

Increasingly, the national organizations described above, recognizing that each has specific areas of interest and strength, are ensuring communication with the others and are engaging in collaborative and conjoint initiatives.

Institutional activities. Several Canadian universities are active in the field of international health; included are specific training activities. A few examples are briefly presented to illustrate the range of current activities. In addition to these examples, several other universities conduct courses, seminars, and workshops in various aspects of international health.

1. *The University of Calgary (Alberta).* In April 1988, the CIDA announced the establishment of a "centers of excellence" program to strengthen the capacity of Canadian universities to make outstanding contributions to international development. Among the first to receive the award, the University of Calgary is working with Asian partners to conduct research in community-based participatory development, and to conduct courses in this area. Health, in the context of development, is included. This project (the Canada Asia Partnership for Education and Research in Rural Community-based Development) is conducting courses dealing with community-based participatory development in several countries: Thailand, the Philippines, Nepal, and Canada.

2. *Queen's University (Kingston, Ontario).* As another example of the CIDA centers of excellence program, the Queen's University Centre for the Development of Community-based Programs for the Physically Disabled will help communities in developing countries gain expertise in assisting the disabled and their families. The project consortium includes institutions in Indonesia and India, as well as elsewhere in Canada. Both research and education will be featured in this new venture. It is expected that the skills acquired will strengthen community-based rehabilitation in the various undergraduate and graduate education programs of the participating institutions.

3. *McMaster University (Hamilton, Ontario).* Since 1982, this university has been a Centre for Research and Training within the International Clinical Epidemiology Network (INCLEN) funded by the Rockefeller Foundation. The goal of INCLEN is to strengthen the health research capacity of universities in the developing world, through the establishment of "clinical epidemiology units."[2] Each year approximately 10 young university faculty members from developing countries enroll in a master's degree program in "Design, Measurement, and Evaluation" to prepare themselves to conduct research on important health problems in their own countries.

The Canadian university program
in international health

From its inception in 1988, a key objective of the Canadian University Consortium for Health in Development (CUCHID) as been "to provide training opportunities for Canadians and developing country colleagues in health and development, with a particular emphasis on preparing young health professionals for careers in the international health field." At present there is no single Canadian university with sufficient capacity to provide in-depth training in this field. With the inauguration of CUCHID, it seemed possible to develop a national training capacity which involved a number of universities in both Canada and developing countries. A working group led by Dr. Richard McLean, of McGill University, was assembled to explore this concept. Two complementary activities are underway. Under the leadership of Dr. Kay Wotton, of the University of Manitoba, an introductory set of training modules in "International Health and Development" have been prepared and are now ready for testing. Two 11-day workshops will be conducted, one in Canada and the other in a developing country (probably Tanzania). Up to 30 participants in each workshop will participate in these initial workshops. The modules are designed for health professionals and individuals from related fields who have an interest in international health but little systematic understanding of key concepts in health and development. This module series will likely serve as a basic foundation course for the larger program described below.

On a somewhat larger scale, six Canadian universities are designing a collaborative graduate program in international health; the universities are Calgary, Dalhousie, Laval, Manitoba, McGill, and McMaster. The program will be called the "Canadian University Program in International Health." The proposed program has two objectives: (1) to strengthen the capacity of Canadian universities to conduct research and provide training in international health; and (2) to strengthen the capacities of universities, governments, and NGOs in developing countries to conduct research and provide training in international health.

The program is being designed for individuals who already have their basic training and professional qualifications in one of the relevant (usually health) professions. The focus will be on the development of generic competencies which are required for work in this field. The knowledge base is fairly broadly defined and includes:
- the principles of disease patterns, dynamics, risks, and solutions relevant to developing countries;
- the political, economic, and social dimensions of health;

- the process of enhancing the participation of women in health and development;
- the history and dynamics of health development in developing countries;
- principles of managing and financing health development, and
- mechanisms of skill transfer between health personnel and the community.

The skills include capacities to monitor and evaluate health programs in developing countries; plan and implement sustainable health education, effective health services, and community-based development; skills to update and maintain competence in the field; collaborative skills for intersectorial teamwork, and creative problem solving in a variety of situations.

Each participating institution is currently providing an inventory of strengths and available resources (people, library resources, and others) to participate in the program. Specific developing-country universities which already have links with Canadian universities are being invited to join this international training network. A database of available resources and current expertise is being created. The proposal has been submitted to the IDRC for initial funding. It is anticipated that the first students can be enrolled sometime in 1992.

Special mention should be made of the important role of the IDRC. This agency was founded by the Government of Canada in 1970 and has the goal of promoting research by and for developing countries. There are four major sectors: agriculture, health sciences, social sciences, and information sciences. Within the Health Sciences Division are three areas: health and the environment, health and the community, and health systems. The IDRC is committed to fostering links between the Canadian academic community and counterparts in developing countries. With this in mind, the IDRC has supported the development of CUCHID in general and the training initiatives described above in particular.

**Some further observations on
training in international health**

Two further considerations are presented in this section. The first is concerned with a definition of the field of international health. Secondly, there have been recent important developments globally regarding health research for development. These have important implications for current and future international health training programs.

Toward a definition of international health. In designing training programs in international health, questions appropriately arise about its framework, elements, and boundaries, both as a field of study and as an area of professional practice. Proposed below is a definition of international health which is offered as a conceptual framework, with the intention of stimulating further discussion and achieving a clearer understanding among colleagues who are interested in this field of study and practice. A five-element definition is proposed.

1. *Health as a focus.* Beginning with the commonly accepted definition of health, stated originally in the 1978 Declaration of Alma-Ata, with some later refinements, *health* as a concept within the broader field of "development" has much utility. It can be measured using a set of specific indicators. Health is valued by individuals and communities, and is understood as an idea. There is a close interdependent relationship between health and "wealth" (economic status). And there is increasing understanding that health is a product of a broad set of determinants, only one of which is the system of health services.

2. *A defined population (usually a country) as the main unit of analysis.* The word "international" implies a bias toward the idea that nations represent the starting point for discussion and understanding. Countries have names, geographic boundaries, systems of political jurisdiction, and populations; thus they represent the simple basis for national, and therefore international, study. To provide more flexibility, however, it is proposed that any defined population could be identified as the unit of analysis. With a given country, the "unit" of interest could be a geo-political entity (such as a state, province, or region), or several countries could be grouped together for analysis on the basis of their geographic proximity or some other feature (such as a common colonial history; for example, the French-speaking islands of the Caribbean). Or the population of interest could be some other defined group within a general population such as women, children, the poor, or the aged.

3. *Comparison across countries (or other populations).* The term "international" also implies consideration of two or more countries. The point here is the act of comparison—looking specifically for similarities and differences—and making systematic observations about the facts (assessment), the explanations for similarities and contrasts (analysis), and the effects of specific interventions as applied to a defined population (action).

4. *Evidence-based decision making.* Using the practice of clinical medicine as an analogy, awareness has been growing for several years that medical practitioners need to know how to determine whether their clinical decisions are based on strong scientific evidence (the principle of

validity) and whether a proposed clinical decision is relevant to the patient and clinical problem at hand (the principle of applicability).

It is proposed that the same kind of analysis and action used in decision making about the health of *individuals* be used in making decisions about the health of *populations*. Thus we need to learn to ask: What is the scientific basis for a proposed new policy or for a decision to allocate resources that will affect the health of populations, or for a specific public health "intervention."

5. *A foundation of "values."* Finally, it is proposed that underlying all our efforts (both study and practice) in the field of international health is a set of values. These are not restricted to the health sector and, in fact, are derived from the broader experience of international development. As a starting point for further discussion, two specific values are proposed as fundamental to the study and practice of international health. The first is *equity*: a commitment to this principle immediately draws our attention to the poorest nations and populations, which also demonstrate the least favorable set of health indicators. The second proposed value is *mutual benefit*: the idea that we all, individually and nationally, have something to learn from and contribute to each other; this construct provides the strongest basis for true cooperation and partnership.

As an accompanying caveat to this proposed definition of international health, there need be no contradiction between strong values and strong science (evidence). In fact, the two elements can be mutually supportive. A commitment to equity in health can lead to rigorous scientific analysis of differences in health outcomes, why they exist, and what actions can narrow the gap.

Health research for development. In 1987, sixteen sponsoring agencies formed a Commission on Health Research for Development, with the mandate to study and make recommendations on how research might improve the health and well-being of the people of the developing world. The commission released its report in February 1990 at the Karolinska Institute's Nobel Conference in Stockholm, with the participation of over 90 representatives from developing and developed countries, United Nations agencies, development agencies, private foundations, community organizations, and academic institutions.[1] The Conference endorsed the Commission's four major recommendations, especially the concept of Essential National Health Research (ENHR). The work of the Commission and its principle recommendations are important considerations for any proposed training program in international health.

The Commission envisaged a pluralistic, worldwide health research system nurturing national scientific groups linked together in networks, to address both national and global health problems, and made the following recommendations:

- All countries should vigorously undertake Essential National Health Research (ENHR) to accelerate health action in diverse national and community settings and ensure that resources available for health achieve maximum results. Health research should not be limited to the health sector, but should also examine the health impact of development in other sectors as well as socioeconomic determinants of health. Countries should adopt and support a long-term strategy of building and sustaining their research capacity.
- The national efforts of developing countries should be joined with efforts in industrialized countries in international partnerships which mobilize and focus the world's scientific skills on the highest priority health problems.
- Larger and more sustained financial support for research from international sources should be mobilized to supplement investments by developing countries. Development assistance agencies should increase their program aid to research and commit at least 5% of all health project aid to ENHR and research capacity building. External agencies should allow greater latitude to developing country research institutions and make long-term commitments of at least 10 years for institutional capacity building.
- An international mechanism should be established to promote financial and technical support for research on health problems in developing countries and to monitor progress.

Together these recommendations would mobilize the power of research to enable developing countries to strengthen health action and discover new and more effective means to deal with unsolved health problems. EHNR will strengthen the ability, and the resolve, of developing countries to meet the needs of the most disadvantaged and accelerate progress towards the fundamental goal of equity in health. The Commission disbanded in late 1990, but as a followup a Task Force on Health Research for Development has been formed, with a secretariat based in Geneva. Its goals, over a defined period of two years, include:

- promoting, facilitating, and supporting ENHR in countries that wish to undertake it;
- developing and evaluating options for longer term mechanisms for supporting ENHR;
- promoting synergism between research on global health problems and ENHR.

The Task Force is working with more than 20 countries wishing to begin the ENHR process. Close links have been established with the major United Nations agencies and with a group of international networks which are already working in the field of health research and development. A monograph describing the ENHR process and analyzing ENHR experiences will be published in 1991. A periodic newsletter, *ENHR Forum*, provides up-to-date information about this important and growing international movement.

A concluding comment

In a recent book, Ivan Head, the former president of IDRC, has made an important argument for all nations, particularly industrialized societies (using Canada as a prime example), to consider. He asserts that not only is international action based on the "mutual benefit" principle desirable, it is mandatory, because all nations share a "mutual vulnerability."[3] A quotation from the book's jacket provides a suitable introduction to this argument:

> Industrialized countries have long assumed that their superior economic performance, scientific accomplishments, and military prowess guarantee them a high degree of invulnerability to events in the developing countries. *This assumption is fatally flawed.* As populations in the developing countries burgeon, so have environmental deterioration, economic uncertainty, social turbulence, and political instability—all with consequences increasingly overflowing into the industrialized world.

In his conclusions, Head states that our current generation is the first ever to recognize that the global environmental balance is fragile, that continued imbalances will inevitably lead to irreversible effects, that certain actions (for example, nuclear war) are unacceptable, and that we have the knowledge for positive action—if we can overcome human indifference. He proposes some general strategies, all based on the principles of pluralism, consultation, coherence, consensus, compassion, and cooperation. These strategies include asking basic questions, creating a climate of openness, looking for specific opportunities (to overcome artificial impediments and to provide people with a "fair chance"), reformulating our personal and institutional social contracts, and reflecting on the lessons of history, both past and recent (for example, wars can no longer be won).

This analysis of our current international situation and others like it provide an important basis for considerations about how the field of international health can contribute to a desirable world order.

References

1.   Commission on Health Research for Development.   *Health research: Essential link to equity in development*. Oxford, Oxford University Press, 1990.

2.   Halstead, S. B., P. Tugwell, and K. J. Bennett. The International Clinical Epidemiology Network (INCLEN):   A progress report.   *J Clin Epidemiol* 44(6):579-589 (1991).

3.   Head, Ivan L. *On a hinge of history: The mutual vulnerability of South and North*. Toronto, University of Toronto Press, 1991.

Conceptual Bases for Education and Research in International Health[1]

Julio Frenk
Fernando Chacón

Introduction

International health is becoming increasingly important as a result of the growing complexity of international relations and their impact on health and health systems, and of the implications of the latter for those relations. The interactions between international relations and health create a need to develop and consolidate an academic and intellectual tradition that will provide support for the generation of knowledge and a foundation for its practical applications.

Conceptual and strategic changes are occurring in international health that must be taken into account in order to ensure completeness and consistency in the scope, approach, and emphasis of education programs, research projects, and health activities, whether national, bilateral, or multilateral.

This paper identifies these conceptual and strategic changes and proposes core definitions, the scope of the field, and the disciplinary basis of the "new" international health; it also describes the background, institutional location, objectives, strategies, and programs underpinning the operations of the International Studies Unit is Public Health (UEISP) in Mexico.

Specifically, we propose a transition to a new notion and practice of international health, which is guiding the education and research activities being undertaken by UEISP.

The term "transition" is used in two senses: first, to indicate the great changes occurring in the health sector at the present time, and second and consequently, to indicate the emergence of a paradigm of international health. In this sense, the transition in international health refers to the series of complex, interrelated changes taking place both in the dynamics of international relations and in health conditions and systems worldwide.

---

[1]A preliminary version of this work was presented as a paper in the Distinguished Lectures in International Health series organized by the School of Public Health at the University of North Carolina in Chapel Hill on February 12, 1991.

Background

The emergence of international health as a field of study and sphere of action was a consequence of developments in international relations from the middle of the last century onward. International trade, as the principal cause of the spread of infectious diseases along trade routes, led to bilateral and multilateral action to contain epidemics through the introduction of quarantine measures.[3,18,19] An example of such action is the establishment of the Egyptian Quarantine Council, which was created more as a response to commercial considerations than out of concern for public health as far back as 1831.[5]

The ever-increasing importance of international health derives mainly from the growing complexity of international economic, political, and social relations, which in its turn entails changes in the epidemiological profiles of populations and alterations in health systems.

Indeed, the rise of new economic, political, and military blocs, the liberalization of international trade, the financial adjustments associated with the internationalization of capital, the international division of labor and production, the changing balance of power between capitalist and socialist production systems, and international conflicts are all directly affecting the economic, political, and social variables in each country: health must therefore necessarily be affected too, being as it is the point at which the biological and the social, the individual and the community, and social and economic policy all converge.[10]

Meanwhile, the natural spread of disease knows no frontiers or geopolitical boundaries, a fact which also affects international relationships by opening up or intensifying new fields for cooperation or conflict among members of the international community, and as a result influencing the economic, political, and social relations between states. The cholera epidemic in Peru is a pertinent example of how a national health problem becomes an issue transcending national boundaries and affecting international relations.

These connections between international relations and public health underscore the need to construct theoretical and conceptual frameworks to make the field of international health more consistent as regards its scope of education and research programs and services.

The theoretical framework for approaches to international health has hitherto tended to analyze international health phenomena without any precise delimitation of their scope or of the field of study, and according to particular perceptions and interests. Indeed, international health has been regarded as a field of professional study and practice which the developed countries have encouraged in order to promote and justify their activities and interventions in the health problems of the developing countries.[1,2,7]

This situation challenges us to develop and consolidate a vigorous academic and intellectual tradition of international health as the foundation for efforts to generate knowledge and guide its practical applications. The development of this field of study[4] can be based on the following four elements:[9,10,13]

1. A conceptual base that enables the scope of international health education, research, and action to be established and demarcated, the ultimate objective being a precise definition of international health, and more specifically, the *new* international health so as to distinguish it from the traditional uses of the term.

2. A production base that facilitates the generation of a body of knowledge by providing substantive content for the field through the conjunction of groups of institutions to bring together a critical mass and density of researchers.

3. A reproduction base that ensures the consolidation and continuity of an intellectual discipline—and hence the construction of a true tradition—in three principal ways:

    (a) the design and development of education programs to train new researchers and practitioners,

    (b) the creation or consolidation of publications to disseminate the results of research, and

    (c) the establishment of academic and professional associations among institutions with common interests to exchange ideas and promote and project international health issues.

4. A utilization base enabling knowledge to be expressed in two kinds of products: (a) technological developments, including new organizational schemes, and (b) decision making based on the results of research.

In brief, this field of knowledge must be given a conceptual base that meets the needs of all countries and which therefore avoids forms of information linked to the purposes of each country or region. At the same time there is an urgent need to promote a production base through the constitution of multidisciplinary and multicentric working groups which are interested in this burgeoning field, and to create the conditions for ensuring the reproduction of knowledge, by training and developing researchers and practitioners, disseminating research results, combining efforts, exchanging experiences and ideas, and linking up the interests of institutions in both the developed and developing countries.

Only with these conceptual and production bases and this reproduction effort can a foundation be created for utilizing the knowledge thus generated to study and solve health problems that transcend national frontiers and affect more than one country.

From this standpoint, international health is undergoing significant conceptual and strategic changes which must be taken into consideration to ensure completeness and consistency in the scope, approach, and emphasis of education programs, research projects, and health activities, whether national, bilateral, or multilateral.

The new international health

The way in which international health is conceived as a field of knowledge and professional practice must reflect ongoing realignments in the international community. Consequently, the traditional focus of international health has undergone conceptual and strategic changes that must necessarily be taken into account in the conceptualization, production, reproduction, and utilization of the new international health. Table 1 summarizes some of the most representative changes which have occurred in relation to the scope, focus, and emphasis of international health.

Thus, the new international health regards health problems as issues that are the responsibility of all countries, without regard to their level of development; it rejects the view that these problems are only the concern of the developing countries. Taylor recognizes this concern by observing that "the most mature motivation [in international health activities] is to recognize the reality that health problems anywhere in the world are the responsibility of us all.... Many of the unsolved problems of health care are shared by both developed and underdeveloped countries."[21]

The reasons for this new scope of international health, in light of worldwide concern about health problems, the damaging effects on health, and the anachronism of national frontiers in this context, are well stated by Soberón:

> Throughout the history of mankind it is possible to find examples of diseases which, originating in a specific geographical location, then spread through a process of dissemination which, given certain ecological, climatological, geophysical, and even cultural conditions, enables them to sweep across all the artificial geopolitical boundaries that men impose on governmental jurisdictions. Leprosy, the plague, tuberculosis, yellow fever, malaria, and now AIDS are examples of the fact that diseases have no frontiers.[20]

The new international health recognizes the economic, political, and social diversity among countries as well as the specific features of their populations and problems, thus rejecting the obsolete view of the homogeneity of the developing countries. This recognition is an important condition for promoting true development.

As Crandon says in evaluating the project in Bolivia: "We inherently lack respect for the non-Western, the non-scientific.... It can be argued that our programs often remain inherently ethnocentric."[6] This is confirmed by Foster:

> It was generally assumed that "scientific" medicine, both preventive and curative, would work equally well everywhere... A hygiene model that had proven effective in the American South [United States] failed when applied in a different sociocultural setting.[8]

The international dimension of health requires close collaboration among countries in order to tackle together health problems that affect all nations. As examples of this kind of problem, Gellert mentions global warming, the disappearance of the ozone layer, the dumping of toxic and radioactive wastes, the deteriorating quality of air and water, and the AIDS epidemic, among others.[16] These problems need bilateral and multilateral action if they are to be contained and solved.

Likewise, the notion that the relationship between the developing and developed countries is one of dependence is replaced by the notion of the interdependence of the two groups. Interdependence in economic, environmental, and demographic matters is having a growing impact on world health conditions.[15] The replacement of the concept of dependence entails changes at the negotiating table in the sense that each group of countries must look on the other as an ally in the development process.

While the traditional international health was concerned with technical assistance from developed countries to developing countries in the provision of health services, the new international health emphasizes cooperation and collaboration in education, research, and health services. This new approach to international health requires innovative collaboration procedures. International health should not be seen as a one-way process of providing technical assistance, but must be based on a relationship of technical cooperation which will bring benefits to both parties.[21]

Finally, the new international health is conceived in terms of the epidemiological transition and changes in health care systems,[14] rejecting the reductionist emphasis on controlling communicable diseases and primitive health systems.

The epidemiological transition refers to changes in the frequency, size, and distribution of the health conditions of a particular community in the long term, expressed in patterns of disease, incapacity, and death.

Table 1. Conceptual and Strategic Changes
in International Health

Nature of the Changes	Traditional International Health	New International Health
SCOPE	Health problems affecting developing countries	Health problems affecting all countries
APPROACH	Homogeneity of the developing countries	Diversity among and within developing countries
	Unilateral measures	Bilateral and multilateral measures
	Concept of dependence	Concept of interdependence
	Assistance for the provision of health services	Cooperation in education, research, and health services
EMPHASIS	Control of communicable diseases	Epidemiological transition
	Primitive health services	Transition of health services

The transition of health systems, in turn, is related to changes in the patterns of organized social responses, expressed in the ways in which health systems are structured to provide services.[14] There is a close link between the two transitions. The changes in the epidemiological profile of the population require alterations in the organization and operations of health services so that they are consistent with the epidemiological reality of which they are part.[12] International health must emphasize these transitions so as to be able to respond adequately to the growing complexity of health conditions and actions transcending national borders.

Basic definitions

On the basis of these changes, which support the new concept of international health, we can approach the definition of international health as a field of knowledge and an instrument for action.

Like public health, international health is defined in terms of the level of its analysis of populations;[11] its distinguishing feature is the type of population, which consists of the members of the international community: nations (populations with their own territorial and cultural identity); states (as the political organization of nations); international organizations; economic, political, and military blocs and public and private organizations, whether for profit or non-profit.

As a field for research, international health may be regarded as the interdisciplinary study of the range of phenomena, links, actions, and interactions in the health-disease process that occur among the members, and in the territories, of the international community. This definition includes the effects of international economic, political, and social relations in health, the repercussions of health on these relations, and the health conditions and actions that transcend the boundaries of a single country.

As a field for action, international health can be defined as the systematic effort to identify health conditions and to organize responses among the members of the international community, including the formulation of international policies and technical cooperation to identify health needs and mobilize the resources required to meet those needs.

The sphere of international health

International health education, research, and practice all share the same sphere of action. As the three-dimensional matrix in Figure 1 indicates, this consists of the subjects of analysis (health conditions and responses), application areas (populations, problems, and programs), and levels of analysis (national, bilateral, and multilateral).

Hence the development of human resources, the generation of knowledge, and action on real problems are all focused on the health conditions of the population and on organizing responses that transcend the frontiers of any single country, from a national, bilateral, or multilateral perspective.

Fig. 1. The Sphere of International Health

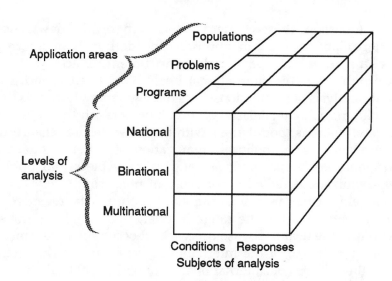

The application areas of international health are numerous: specific groups (for example, mothers and children, adolescents, the elderly, migrants, peasants, the rural or urban population), concrete problems (for example, drug addiction, environmental pollution, malnutrition), and specific programs (epidemiological surveillance, health inspections, immunization, health education). For example, the problem of environmental pollution in a frontier zone may be a matter for study and bilateral action to reduce the harm being caused to the health of the child population. On the basis of the subjects and levels of analysis and the application areas, the following issues can be identified as major areas for education, research, and action purposes: international health policies and strategies, international technical and financial cooperation, international health regulation, frontier region health, international migration and health, international trade and health, transfer of environmental risks, technology transfer, and the drug traffic and drug addiction, among others.

Disciplinary base

Education and research in the area of international health problems must call on different disciplines in both the social sciences and health sciences in order to treat the subjects of analysis and application areas with scientific rigor and consistency.

The multifaceted nature of international health problems and programs requires a knowledge of the social sciences.[17] Among these social science disciplines, international relations and associated areas such as political geography, international economics, international law, and diplomatic history are particularly important. It is worth noting that this integration of disciplines represents an additional step beyond what has already been achieved by public health, which brings together disciplines such as epidemiology, demography, economics, sociology, the administrative sciences, law, and ethics.[11]

Consequently, international health becomes the point at which the social science disciplines, including international relations, and the health sciences, especially those directly linked to public health, converge. The body of knowledge and the theoretical and conceptual framework of international relations provides the foundation for an understanding of the dynamics of the international community in terms of the economic, political, social, and ideological issues that affect interactions among countries. Public health provides the theoretical, methodological, and technical tools for tackling the study of the consequences of these interactions in terms of health conditions and the organization and operation of health services.

The International Studies Unit in Public Health

The internationalization of health causes, conditions, and responses calls for the consolidation of a vigorous academic and pragmatic tradition in international health. UEISP represents an interinstitutional effort in the training of human resources, research, advice, and practice in health needs and actions that transcend national frontiers and affect two or more countries.

The mission of the International Studies Unit in Public Health in Mexico is to help consolidate an authentic academic and empirical tradition in international health through the development of the necessary conceptual, production, reproduction, and utilization bases.

Given the new concept of international health, UEISP has developed as a response to the need to train specialists, undertake research on health needs and responses that transcend national frontiers, and influence practices in this field. UEISP likewise aims to promote international technical cooperation in the areas of health education, research, and services.

Background and institutional location

UEISP was established in 1988 as a joint program of the National Institute for Public Health (INSP), the Autonomous National University of Mexico (UNAM), the Department of International Affairs in the Secretariat of Health, and the Representation of the Pan American Health Organization in Mexico (PAHO-Mexico). The concerted efforts of these institutions are helping consolidate UEISP's scientific, technical, and operational infrastructure so that it can fulfill its mission.

UEISP is located within the INSP, which consists of the Mexican School of Public Health, the Center for Public Health Research, and the Center for Infectious Disease Research. This location provides an institutional base offering great potential for developing the field, involving as it does 147 fulltime teachers and researchers working on 61 research projects in various problems of public health, and offering nine graduate programs, including the Doctorate in Public Health.

UNAM, with its comprehensive range of activities, tradition of excellence and experience in training human resources and in research, supports UEISP through the University Health Research Program, which has a multidisciplinary and international perspective.

The Secretariat of Health, well aware of Mexico's priority health problems, available resources, the status of action strategies, and the performance of programs, is a crucial factor in identifying priorities and determining the relevance and feasibility of international health programs and projects.

PAHO-Mexico, as an international organization, provides experience in the planning and execution of international health programs; UEISP's activities benefit from its analysis of the planning, scope, and limitations of such programs. In addition, this organization has a vast amount of relevant information for comparative research into health needs and systems.

Furthermore, Mexico is an appropriate, available, and accessible setting for the development of educational, research, and advisory programs in international health issues. Its geographical position and intermediate stage of social and economic development make it a point of convergence between developing countries and developed countries. In addition, given its economic situation and the similarities of customs and language with other Latin American countries, Mexico offers favorable conditions, both in terms of costs and cultural aspects, for the establishment of programs involving the participation of foreign students and researchers.

Objectives and strategies

The general objectives of UEISP are, on the one hand, to promote the conceptual development and academic consolidation of international health as a field of instruction, research, advice, and action in public health and, on the other, to promote international cooperation in education, research, and technical assistance projects among the Unit's constituent Mexican institutions and foreign universities, governments of developing and developed countries, and international organizations.

UEISP helps to achieve these objectives by training and developing high-level human resources in the field of international health through formal courses and continuing education; it stimulates research, preferably of a multicentric nature, on the phenomena of the health-disease process and health actions transcending the frontiers of a single country; it promotes technical advice to agencies providing health services and to higher education institutions, both Mexican and foreign, in the fields of public health and international health; and it sponsors academic events and disseminates their results in order to facilitate the exchange of ideas and experiences.

These activities link teaching and research to the practical field of health services, strengthen the learning-teaching process, and generate information for decision makers, thus contributing to a better understanding of international health phenomena and to the solution of the problems involved in providing health services on a bilateral and multilateral basis.

UEISP's strategies for establishing the right conditions for achieving its objectives are:

Interinstitutional collaboration. One of the basic elements in the attainment of UEISP's objectives, and implicit in its mission, is close collaboration among the participating institutions. This strategy enables information to be exchanged and services to be improved, thereby facilitating the planning and execution of joint programs and projects.

Intrainstitutional collaboration. UEISP's links with the various constituent academic entities of both the INSP and the UNAM enhance the performance of its activities, making it self-sufficient in human resources and infrastructure, permitting efficient utilization of institutional resources, and exploiting the benefits deriving from joint efforts to achieve common objectives.

Consolidation of multidisciplinary working groups. Teaching, research and advice in the area of international health require an interdisciplinary focus which permits a comprehensive approach to the problems to be taught or investigated. Consequently, the establishment of multidisciplinary working groups ensures that collective efforts produce better results, while also promoting the individual development of group members. These groups consist of teachers and researchers at the participating institutions.

Research/teaching/service integration. This strategy is regarded as an essential element whereby the process of identifying international health needs and the study and application of bilateral and multilateral programs generate knowledge that provides feedback for the design and evaluation of study plans and programs and the training and development of human resources, in line with the operating needs of the health services.

Mobilization of external resources. The feasibility of special teaching, research, and advisory projects depends largely on the external resources made available. In this sense the collaboration and financial support of national and international organizations and foundations is a prerequisite for the development of UEISP. As a result, serious attention is being given to the mobilization and management of external resources.

Programs and projects

UEISP's objectives are embodied in two programs, one academic and the other involving international technical cooperation.

The academic program involves three main lines of work or action areas: conceptual development of international health, training of human resources in international health, and research in international health.

The conceptual development of international health as a field of study within public health is regarded as the cornerstone of UEISP's activities, in the sense that it provides a basis for the content of the study programs and makes it possible to demarcate research topics and define the professional sphere of the specialist in the area.

UEISP therefore arranges activities designed to be opportunities for the study, analysis, and discussion of problems in the field of international health and to help identify certain common factors which will encourage the participants to set up cooperative projects, thereby promoting the development of international health as a field of knowledge and practice within public health.

In the education context, the academic program, in conjunction with the Mexican School of Public Health, helps to train and develop human resources by planning and giving formal and continuing education courses in the field of international health, and to provide and consolidate the appropriate human and physical infrastructure in the participating institutions so as to offer opportunities for completing career requirements and preparing master's and doctoral theses to Mexican and foreign students who are interested in linking their training with international health.

There are two aspects of research in international health: first, research that focuses on the phenomena of the health-sickness process and the health actions that transcend the frontiers of a single country, and second, comparative analyses of health needs and systems among different countries and regions.

Consequently, UEISP promotes the planning and execution of research projects, preferably multicentric, which study international health phenomena from both perspectives. The working groups consist of researchers from the institutions that comprise the Unit.

As regards the future of UEISP, as part of the 1990/1998 Development Plan, it is intended to introduce in 1994 a focus on international health in the Master of Science degree and, in 1998, to include an area of specialization in international health in the Doctorate of Public Health, both offered by the Mexican School of Public Health. Similarly, once the production and reproduction bases have been consolidated, there are plans to include a line of research on international health in the INSP.

For its part, the International Technical Cooperation Program basically includes activities designed to strengthen the academic links of the INSP and UNAM with other institutions of higher education, ministries of health in developing and developed countries, and international organizations. Action areas for advice and consulting services are the training and development of human resources in public health and related disciplines, research in public health, and the provision of health services.

Under the International Technical Cooperation Program, exchanges of teachers and researchers among institutions belonging to the INSP and foreign universities are taking place so as to advance specific teaching, research, and advisory projects.

One of the strategic projects making an important contribution to fulfilling UEISP's mission is its coordination, in the capacity of Technical Secretariat, of the Latin American Network for Promoting the Management of Health Systems, financed by the W. K. Kellogg Foundation. The Network currently consists of the health administration programs at the National School of Public Health at the Oswaldo Cruz Foundation, Rio de Janeiro, Brazil; the Mexican School of Public Health at the National Institute of Public Health, Cuernavaca, Mexico; the Getulio Vargas Foundation, São Paulo, Brazil; the Central American Institute of Public Administration, San José, Costa Rica; the Javeriana Pontifical University, Bogotá, Colombia; the University of Chile, Santiago; the Cayetano Heredia Peruvian University, Lima; and the University del Valle, Cali, Colombia. The central objective of the Network is to strengthen the management of health systems by exchanging information and experiences, complementing services, and undertaking specific projects in the areas of multicentric teaching and research, nontraditional teaching models, and instructor exchanges.

Conclusions

There is an ever-increasing need for international health, as a field of knowledge within public health, to construct theoretical and conceptual frameworks enabling it to analyze changes in the international community which affect the health of populations. At the same time, it is essential to intensify the study of the consequences of health conditions on economic, political, and social relations at the international level.

International health as a field of knowledge and action area has experienced conceptual and strategic changes in its scope, approach, and emphasis; these changes require reconsideration of educational programs and lines of research and of the bases for formulating policies and programs at the national, bilateral and multilateral level.

One example of the efforts to consolidate an academic tradition in international health is the creation of the International Studies Unit in Public Health in Mexico. The nature and character of UEISP are evidence of an effort at interinstitutional coordination to plan, organize, and execute activities that help promote and protect international health, both in the education and research areas and in the provision of health services.

Indeed, a start has been made on a serious, consistent process of conceptualizing this field of knowledge; a critical mass and density of researchers interested in international health has been identified; and a solid foundation has been established for training human resources, publishing and disseminating information and bringing together an important group of Mexican and foreign academic institutions which are both capable of and committed to efforts to improve the health levels of their populations.

Much still remains to be done. These achievements must generate knowledge and be reflected in concrete measures and procedures designed to provide feedback for the formulation of policies to help solve the health problems affecting two or more countries.

The experience of UEISP enables us to conclude that the development of local institutions, supported and complemented by international networks or partnerships, is an effective and efficient strategy for consolidating the production, reproduction, and utilization bases of international health. If local institutions are strengthened in this way, the continuity of this effort can be ensured through multicentric teaching and research. Cooperation in the field of health can provide an example of concrete achievements in our shared search for a better future for mankind.

Acknowledgements

The authors are grateful to Sagar C. Jain and Octavio Gómez D. for their valuable suggestions.

References

1. Barry, M., and J. Frank. Departments of medicine and international health. *Am J Med* 80:1019-1021 (1986).

2. Berliner, H., and C. Regan. Multinational operations of U.S. for-profit hospital chains: trends and implications. *Am J Pub Health* 77(10):1280-1284 (1987).

3. Biraud, Y. The international control of epidemics. *Br Med J* 1950(May 6):1046-1050.

4. Bourdieu, P. Algunas propiedades de los campos. Lecture at the Ecole Normale Superior, Paris, 1976. Cited in: H. Mercer, La medicina social en debate, *Cuadernos Medico-Sociales* 42:5-13 (1987).

5. Buchanan, G. S. International cooperation in public health: its achievements and prospects. *Lancet* 1934(May 5):935-942.

6. Crandon, L. Grass roots, herbs, promotors and preventions: A re-evaluation of contemporary international health care planning. The Bolivian case. *Soc Sci Med* 17(17):1281-1289 (1983).

7. Elling, R. The capitalist world-system and international health. *Int J Health Serv* 11(1):21-51 (1981).

8. Foster, G. World Health Organization behavioral science research: Problems and prospects. *Soc Sci Med* 24(9):709-717 (1987).

9. Frenk, J. La investigación en salud pública: Una nueva realidad. *Gac Med Mex* 124:155-156 (1988).

10. Frenk, J. La nueva salud pública. Study prepared for the Pan American Health Organization. Cuernavaca, Mexico, 1991.

11. Frenk, J., J. L. Bobadilla, J. Sepúlveda, J. Rosenthal, and E. Ruelas. A conceptual model for public health research. *Bull Pan Am Health Organ* 22(1):60-71 (1988).

12. Frenk, J., J. L. Bobadilla, J. Sepúlveda, and M. López-Cervantes. Health transition in middle-income countries: New challenges for health care. *Health Pol Planning* 4(1):29-39 (1989).

13. Frenk, J., and L. Durán. Investigación en sistemas de salud: Estado del arte en México y perspectivas de desarrollo. *Ciencia* 41:15-25 (1990).

14. Frenk, J., T. Frejka, J. L. Bobadilla, C. Stern, J. Sepúlveda, and M. Jose. The epidemiologic transition in Latin America. International Population Conference, New Delhi. Liege, Belgium, International Union for the Scientific Study of Population, 1989. Vol. 1, pp. 419-31.

15. Gellert, G. Global health interdependence and the international physician's movement. *JAMA* 264(5):610-613 (1990).

16. Gellert, G., A. Neumann, and R. Gordon. The obsolescence of distinct domestic and international health sectors. *J Pub Health Pol* 1989;Winter:421-424.

17. Giovannini, M., and A. Brownlee. The contribution of social science to international health training. *Soc Sci Med* 16:957-964 (1982).

18. Howard-Jones, N. Origins of international health work. *Br Med J* 1950(May 6):1032-1037.

19. Seah, S. K. K. Canada and international health. *Can Med Assoc J* 115:377-378 (1976).

20. Soberón, G., C. Valdes, and O. de Caso. La salud sin fronteras y las fronteras de la salud. *Salud Pública Mex* 31(6):813-822 (1989).

21. Taylor, C. Changing patterns in international health: motivation and relationships. *Am J Pub Health* 69(8):803-808 (1979).

International Health and Latin American Integration (Outline of Proposed Program in International Health)

Eleutério Rodrigues Neto
Ivo Ferreira Brito
Alina Maria de A. Souza

Introduction

The purpose of these working notes is to discuss a proposed program in international health to be carried out by the Public Health Studies Unit (Núcleo de Estudos em Saúde Pública, or NESP) and associated institutions in Brazil. The subject in question is of vital importance to the countries in the region since current world developments and recent changes in health institutions, in the context of state reforms and adjustment policies, indicate the need for cooperation and the execution of joint activities overcome poverty and the impasse resulting from the crisis in the economic development model adopted in the region.

The rapidity of international change and the uncertainties in the process of worldwide economic and social integration are redefining the relationships and roles of the countries of Latin America. The traditional foreign policy pursued hitherto requires radical changes, with a view to restoring the technical skills that lead to economic development. Although the international outlook may be unfavorable in terms of resource flows, the process of institutional reform and the blossoming of democracy in the region are facilitating regional economic integration, technical cooperation, and the establishment of common markets.

Health is one of the areas regarded as strategic for the resumption of economic development. Macedo, for example, expresses this idea as follows:

> ... a major role in the development process is being claimed for health, on the basis of evidence that health can be a positive factor for development, while at the same time it must also be one of development's basic objectives. Redefining health and efforts to improve it in this way is also to recognize that health can no longer be the exclusive responsibility of the sector's institutions and professionals, but must be appropriated as a concern of the society as a whole, including the so-called productive sectors linked to capital and labor, and the various agencies and interests of the government, including parliaments, international action, and individuals, families, and communities.[1]

In this sense, health becomes a strategic element in Latin American integration, vitally important to overcoming regional and subregional blockages so that economic development with equity can be resumed.

In this paper we shall discuss the general aspects of international health in the context of changes in international relations. The first section provides a framework, the second discusses health and Latin American integration as interdependent factors, and the third considers the internationalization of health, processes linked to the new international division of labor, and internal adjustments in the regional economies. The fourth section spells out the main lines of research, training, and technical cooperation under the program, and the fifth considers the institutional bases and relations that must comprise it.

International health: Framework

International health is a multifaceted field of knowledge. Many authors approach the concept from different viewpoints and employ distinct theoretical frameworks.[2] In general terms it might be said that international health is defined by two substantive elements: (a) it is part of the field of international relations, here considered as a system of power relationships; and (b) it belongs to the domain of economics, given its significant participation in the new international division of labor. These two elements presuppose two other features of the international context which must be considered: economic interdependence and asymmetric international relationships in terms of economic development and external debt.

The changes that occurred in the world economy and international relations during the 1980s have raised new problems for an understanding of the configuration and correlation of forces in the world economic system. The parameters of the model established at Bretton Woods in July 1944, which established the International Bank for Reconstruction and Development (IBRD) and the International Monetary Fund (IMF), were profoundly altered by the crisis ushered in by the oil shock in 1973. The main features of the changes in the world scene can be summarized as follows:

- A growing trend to multipolarity among economic centers, intensified by the weakening of the policy of detente and the progressive dispersion of economic power among the industrial countries, along with a marked diversification of economic structures in Eastern European countries;

- The end of the expansionist phase in the industrial countries and the start of a period of instability and uncertainty, against the background of a trend toward chronic inflation, aggravated by the crisis of the 1970s;
- A decline in the growth rate of the western economies and disequilibrium in the balance of payments in almost all the industrialized countries except Japan;
- An intensified process of economic interdependence among all countries, driven by the growing expansion of trade, international financial markets, and the activities of multinational companies.

These developments are significantly altering the pattern of health-related issues in the international context. The Alma Ata conference, for example, which adopted the goal of health for all by the year 2000, was held in a rather unfavorable international context. The points made in the letter of principles regarding the expansion of primary care and the development of simplified technologies in the area of health services are in keeping with an approach that stresses the asymmetry between rich and poor countries. The expansion of coverage and basic health actions in the underdeveloped and developing countries strengthen social inequities and the contradictions among classes in these regions.

The asymmetric relationship mentioned above and the internationalization of some health sectors are increasing the disparities between northern and southern countries. This internationalization ranges from industrial sectors (production of pharmaceutical and immunobiological products, blood derivatives, etc.) to service sectors via private insurance and group health companies.

In addition, questions such as the movement of populations across frontiers, the fight against endemic and communicable diseases, and the drug traffic problem are becoming the focus of actions transcending national boundaries and are not the exclusive concern of the poor countries.

The transfer from the north to the south of industrial plants harmful both to the environment and to health was the result of three factors: (a) internationalization of the economy and industrial flexibility, (b) the high cost of labor in the central countries, and (c) the emergence of new social forces demanding greater control over polluting industries. Meanwhile this transfer of industrial plants found favorable conditions in the peripheral countries: obsolete health and environmental legislation, tax incentives, and the low capacity of local social groups to exert pressure and control. However, what supposedly began as a transfer of problems from the center to the periphery in the 1980s took the form of the internationalization of the economy and the increasing mobility of populations across frontiers.

Economic integration of national markets was the response of the central countries to the impasse resulting from the world economic crisis. The recession of the 1980s mobilized the industrialized nations in the European Community to take measures to correct the distortions in the economic and commercial relations among its member countries. The purpose of economic integration is to revive economic growth and increase labor productivity, on the basis of a model of multilateral cooperation that emphasizes the interdependence of different areas of the economy and society. It must be pointed out that many problems still remain to be overcome, including those relating to the resurgence of national and ethnic conflicts, immigrant flows, and more recently, the deterioration of the social and economic structures in the countries of Eastern Europe.

The spread of internal national conflicts and the reorganization of regional economic blocs, through the process of integration, are shifting the center of gravity of international relations. This process in turn makes it possible to identify a whole range of international circuits in the areas of energy, food, industry, technology, trade, finance and even health. The access of different countries to these circuits no longer depends on their position in a homogeneous international hierarchy, but on their role and decision-making capacity in relation to the interests in play in each of the above-mentioned areas, and on greater reciprocity in relations between the center and the periphery.[3] In this sense, health is sure to become an issue in the agendas and processes of economic integration and technical cooperation in the decade now beginning.

It is important to stress that the process of economic integration is not free from international and sectoral conflict. The growth of nongovernmental institutions (NGOs) active at the international level is making the process of making decisions even more complicated. NGOs are, however, safeguarding the community's role in decision-making at the international level, through the use of more informal, democratic solidarity networks. The activities of NGOs are based on a new kind of thinking that emphasizes the autonomy and direct participation of those involved, thus influencing the decision-making process and forms of lifestyle in modern society.[4] In such situations, the overlapping and interaction of the various spheres, in unstable contexts, is becoming increasingly unpredictable. But not all these organizations can be regarded as neutral vis-à-vis international economic interests. The activity of regulatory organizations in the area of demography, for example, has been both authoritarian and conservative.

Economic integration in Latin America: Health and development

The adjustments made by the industrialized countries to correct the distortions in their development model were reflected in the peripheral countries. The external debt and its service intensified the internal crisis in the countries of the region. The redemocratization of these countries and the impasse resulting from their integration into the new international division of labor have significantly changed the relations between them and the countries exercising international hegemony.

The economic growth that occurred between 1950 and 1970 as a result of the effects of comparative advantages in the expansion of exports changed the structure and composition of industrial plants and national markets in the region. The 1980s were not kind to the economies of Latin America, however; what has become known as the "Lost Decade" is clearly reflected in the numbers. In the 1970s growth averaged 4% a year, while in the following decade, between 1980 and 1986, it fell to 2% a year on average, according to GATT data.[5] The deterioration in living conditions worsened as a result of structural adjustment measures and neoliberal economic programs that sought to counter the impact of the fiscal crisis by reducing state expenditure on social programs. The transfer of resources abroad reached approximately 25% of the region's gross product, as indicated in Table 1.

Table 1
Latin America: Transfer of Resources
(millions of US$)

Year	Capital Inflows	Remittances and Interest	Transfer of Resources
1980	29.7	18.2	11.5
1981	37.6	27.2	10.4
1982	20.4	38.8	-18.4
1983	3.0	34.4	-31.4
1984	9.3	36.3	-27.0
1985	3.3	34.8	-31.5
1986	8.7	30.5	-21.8
1987*	14.4	30.1	-15.7

Source: United Nations Economic Commission for Latin America and the Caribbean, *Preliminary Report on the Latin American Economy, 1987.*

(*) Estimated

This situation was aggravated by the fact that world prices of primary products, the basis of Latin America's exports, were declining. Another factor contributing to the crisis was that, as a result of international competition, the central countries adopted restrictive and protectionist measures, contrary to the liberal Bretton Woods principles. Meanwhile, internal adjustments and the adoption of deflationary economic policies to counter the crisis affected the living standards of the populations concerned and the services provided to them. The cuts in the financing of social services and the reduction in private expenditure in the health sector adversely affected the lowest-income groups, thereby widening social inequalities.[6] Table 2 shows changes in central government health expenditure for the countries of Latin America and the Caribbean. Figure 1 gives an idea of the regressive effects of the Brazilian Government's fiscal policy on the basic basket of goods, using as a reference the turnover tax (ICM).

Table 2
Central Government Expenditure on Health
in Latin America and the Caribbean, 1970-1988
(1988 dollars)

Year/Country	1970	1975	1980	1985	1987
Argentina	10.36	13.73	17.55	13.89	22.91
Bahamas			242.59	311.35	333.82
Barbados	110.36	149.34	245.13	207.59	230.58
Bolivia	6.8	8.94	16.83	3.4	
Brazil	18.89	24.63	32.34	6.51	
Chile	43.93	45.1	49.01	57.66	
Colombia		9.96	11.75		
Costa Rica	7.22	21.37	36.01	7.64	6.75
Dominican Republic		23.4	33.23	7.71	
Ecuador	4.14	10.94	28.58	27.26	
El Salvador	10.75	13.76	17.22	15.22	
Guatemala		10.25	25.6	10.79	
Guyana	25.86	27.08	44.46	29.17	21.45
Haiti	2.41	3.48	3.13	3.3	
Honduras	11.24	10.32	13.37	17.22	19.29
Jamaica	50.59	61.98	61.5	36.39	
Mexico	42.69	56.47	62.66	41.31	31.42
Nicaragua*	8	18.96	50.2	94.13	
Panama	37.97	42.85	40.41	43.43	
Paraguay	3.42	3.37	5.75	11.95	6.24
Peru	14.61	16.23	18.38	13.44	
Suriname		86.09	16.26		
Trinidad and Tobago		68.01	116.63	196.04	178.24
Uruguay		23.75	34.22	23.95	
Venezuela	53.52	56.13	48.63	44.1	

*Estimates from 1980 onwards probably reflect very unrealistic exchange rates.
Source: Based on Data from the Inter-American Development Bank.

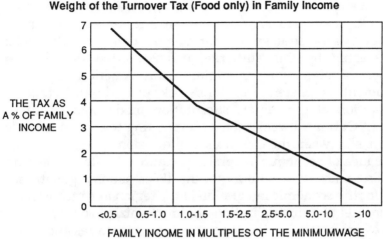

Fig. 1
Weight of the Turnover Tax (Food only) in Family Income

THE TAX AS A % OF FAMILY INCOME

FAMILY INCOME IN MULTIPLES OF THE MINIMUMWAGE

The ongoing institutional reforms and the changes in the role of the state point up the need for a more flexible external policy which redefines the economic integration of the countries in the region on new, less residual, and functional bases.

The divergences regarding proposals for integration in the region center on three basic issues: (a) internationalization of national markets as against the model of self-sustained development; the emphasis here is on the participation and integration of the region in the context of the reconstruction of the central economies, and focuses on the import substitution model; (b) the international rivalry between the two economic superpowers in the post-war period (Cold War) and the appearance of national independence movements in Africa and Asia; in this situation, the external policy of the Latin American countries was based on close adherence to the foreign policy of the United States; and (c) the reordering of the world economy, the impact of technological changes, and the rise of military regimes in a number of countries: this situation exacerbated intraregional problems and led to a diversification of relations with the central countries, at the same time giving rise to the adoption of the doctrine of national security and military cooperation.

In the past, discussions of economic integration in Latin America were based on the industrialization and import substitution model, involving the adoption of a foreign policy that was nationalist in outlook and expression and maintained a low profile in relation to international alliances. The developmental phase saw a return to earlier attitudes, with the adoption of a pragmatic policy for the integration of national markets as foreign capital began to flow in. The rise of authoritarian regimes in a number of countries in the region altered the foreign policy framework, leading to an emphasis on internal security and military cooperation as the strategy for affirming the defense of the region. The hiatus created by this authoritarianism affected decisions and the directions of plans for integrating Latin American markets. The development of bilateral relations took place in the context of the intensification of the import substitution model and of international relations. Current developments are pointing toward greater flexibility in relations between the countries in the region.

The idea of economic integration acquired a different significance in the 1970s. Since the beginning of the 1960s national governments had argued for the economic integration of the region as a means of achieving a higher level of industrialization and modernizing society. While these measures promoted the development of infrastructures and an industrial base oriented toward producing consumption goods, they also produced a decline in the living standards of the population. The difficulties and problems resulting from this belated industrialization led national governments to adopt more specific measures in the area of international relations, designed to improve commercial, technical, and scientific relations among the countries of the hemisphere. The response of the Latin American countries to the policy adopted by the United states at the Bogotá Conference focused on the need to extend cooperation to areas other than military matters. It was at this time that the initiative was taken to establish a cooperation program, then called Operation Panamerica and extending to the economic and social field.

During the 1980s, which saw the revival of democracy in Latin America and a widening of the international economic crisis, the approach to regional integration changed. The discussion was no longer couched in terms of the model of self-sustained development or the model of national security adopted by the military regimes, but was based on a modern approach giving priority to integrating the region with a view to bringing about an economic transformation with equity, and the adoption of a geopolitical and security policy emphasizing intraregional relationships and mutual cooperation.

The starting point for this scenario must be the need for a more competitive economy, the objective being to transform the current pattern of social inequality by mobilizing different decision-making instruments at both the national and international level.

In this sense, the experience of cooperation among the Andean countries and the recent establishment of a common market among the

Southern Cone countries (MERCOSUL) are initiatives of vital importance for the development of policies and cooperation in the area of health. The Andean countries' experience with the establishment of Andean Cooperation for Health (CAS), and the cooperation among Central American countries against the background of their struggle for peace and human rights, are examples that must be evaluated in light of the process of economic integration; in fact, integration should be extended beyond its specifically economic features. The democratic issue is of fundamental importance here in terms of policy harmonization and the correction of possible internal distortions. Many analysts agree that the greatest obstacle to implementing integration is instability in the national economies of the larger countries.

From this standpoint, the scope of integration can be expanded to permit the development of cooperation and multilateral agreements in different sectors of the economy. Seen in this light, health becomes one of the priority areas for consolidating a common market in the region. Among actions for consideration in the years ahead are the coordination and definition of common policies in the area of the production of medicines and basic inputs, immunobiological products, and services. In this context we should emphasize the efforts being made by PAHO/WHO vis-à-vis national governments to reduce conflicts of interest in the field of external relations by breaking with the authoritarian approaches of an earlier period and articulating the desirability of, and procedures for, health, development and integration with equity.[7] The experience already acquired in the economic area, which led to the creation of the United Nations Economic Commission for Latin America and the Caribbean (ECLAC) and other regional organizations, should promote the development of other areas so that we arrive at a more comprehensive notion of integration and create a common market in the region.

The internationalization of health

The health sector in Latin America is undergoing profound changes, in both its structure and institutional configuration. The reform of the state and the ongoing return to democracy, in the context of a worldwide economic crisis of unprecedented severity, have made it necessary to reconsider the provision of social services and their financing. In general terms, it could be said that the model prevailing in the region consisted of a two-tier health care structure: curative treatment provided on an individual basis, basically in the private sector, and preventive medicine oriented to the majority of the population and generally financed from public funds.

The growth of private and individually-focused medical assistance centered on the medical-hospital complex was reinforced in the 1970s by financing through social security systems. The Brazilian model, for example, was financed from the social insurance system. This expansion of the private sector was detrimental to public health activities. Public expenditure on health fell significantly in the 1980s as a result of structural adjustment measures, whose impact can be seen in the health indicators for the region. Many countries are seeing an increase in their social debt to the majority of the population, and a significant number of diseases that had been regarded as eradicated in the previous decade have returned to stay. The recent cholera epidemic in Peru and the rise in the number of malaria cases in the region confirm the deterioration in health conditions in Latin America. The growing impoverishment of the population, the increase in unemployment, and the expansion of the informal sector of the labor market are aggravating the nutritional status of the low-income groups in urban areas.

The incorporation of modern technology in the health sector has not been accompanied by investments in specialized human resources. There is a profound mismatch between the technological resources available and the training of personnel to operate these instruments. Meanwhile, the technology that has been absorbed, almost all of it controlled by multinationals, is reproducing on a larger scale the inequalities between the countries of the center and those of the periphery.

The internationalization of the health sector, given the developments referred to above, is now a reality. This process was the result of the development of the medical-industrial complex, particularly the incorporation of the technical progress ushered in by the third industrial revolution and the expansion of finance capital via health insurance. Meanwhile, the intensification of the economic crisis, migratory flows, and the implementation of major industrial and agricultural projects—construction of dams, highways, mining operations, etc.—make it essential to have better information regarding their social impact on the population.

It is apparent that the health sector, confronted by the internationalization of health, has not been able to establish an institutional base for promoting regional integration and cooperation. Innumerable difficulties remain to be overcome, among which the inequalities among countries in the region should be emphasized. The success of an appropriate policy for integration in the area of health for purposes of bringing about productive change with equity therefore depends on making arrangements and agreements among the various government agencies operating in the health sector, altering the kinds of activities undertaken by regional institutions and organizations, and turning them into forums for debate on integration and the establishment of a common market.

Having considered these issues, the University of Brasília's NESP is preparing proposals for a program in international health, to be carried out in conjunction with other academic institutions, with a view to training strategic personnel and generating information in the area so as to facilitate the process of integrating the Latin American economies and improving the instruments of technical cooperation that already exist.

Program objectives

• To create an interinstitutional group to formulate a program in international health so as to train strategic personnel[8] at the decision-making level, promote technical cooperation, undertake research, and disseminate knowledge in this area.

• To develop institutional arrangements and instruments that will facilitate the integration of the health sector in the context of establishing a common market in the region, with a view to productive change and to improving the population's quality of life.

• To promote technical and scientific cooperation in the area of health as part of the process of regional economic integration, by participating actively in decision making and the formulation of policies of international scope, with priority being given to joint projects in: (a) science and technology; (b) training of human resources; (c) epidemiology and issues related to the environment; (d) health surveillance of foodstuffs, medicines, and blood derivatives; (e) the management, planning, and administration of health services.

**Main lines of the development of research,
training of human resources,
and technical cooperation**

The main lines of the program are the training of human resources, development of research, and technical cooperation.

The training of strategic personnel is designed to produce specialists to make decisions in national and international organizations and formulate policies and programs that promote regional integration in the area of health. The program therefore proposes to offer specialization courses of international scope to take up the kinds of issues that will be investigated as part of the research activities. The establishment of a master's degree program in international health is one of the activities to be undertaken in the medium term.

Preparing personnel who will focus on the objectives mentioned above is of vital importance to national governments and also meets the requests of international agencies, especially as regards the preparation and implementation of international projects.

Holding seminars on specific subjects represents a more flexible way of updating information on and discussing relevant issues in response to short-term requests, and also offers opportunities for deepening our knowledge of conceptual issues.

Technological research and development are important for developing a critical mass in this area. Recent experience in the technological area in the establishment of "incubators" in the universities for transferring technology to the industrial sector could be extended across the region through technical cooperation arrangements and mechanisms among universities and companies. The same is true of the establishment of university health systems, which could be incorporated in national and regional systems through bilateral or multilateral cooperation. Intraregional technology transfers are another important factor in economic integration and health sector autonomy. The machinery for these linkages could be built on the scientific and technological councils of the international multilateral organizations, such as the Latin American Biological Sciences Network (LAMBIO), the Microbiological Resource Centers (MIRCEN), the UNDP/UNIDO/UNESCO Latin America Regional Biotechnology Program, and such other linkages as could be arranged. Existing experiences could motivate efforts in other useful areas such as hospital maintenance and equipment, medicines, vaccines, and blood derivatives.

We can suggest a number of lines of research that could help promote scientific and technological development in the region. Among these are:

• Production of data on institutional resources in science and technology, procedures for regional linkages, and technical cooperation in the area of health.

• Discussion of problems relating to patents and technology transfer in the context of regional economic integration.

• Comparative epidemiologic studies on the international dynamics of the principal endemic and epidemic problems.

• Development of quality control instruments in the circulation of products (medicines, cosmetics, foodstuffs, toxic products used in agriculture, etc.) in the international market, especially in Latin America, in light of the policy of eliminating customs barriers. Finally, there is technical cooperation as a special field to promote regional integration in the area of health. Institutional needs for cooperation must be identified and arrangements for meeting them defined. Cooperation may take place between national and international institutions, between national institutions and nongovernmental organizations, and between NGOs engaged in regionwide operations, through bilateral and multilateral agreements or even via the formation of informal cooperation networks.

Institutional bases of the program

NESP has existed for five years, is administratively part of the Faculty of Health Sciences of the University of Brasília, and is linked programmatically to the Center of Advanced Multidisciplinary Studies (CEAM) at the same university.

NESP was created to fill what had hitherto been a gap in the capital of Brazil and the center-west region of the country in relation to teaching and research in community health. With a technical team made up of professionals in many fields—doctors, nurses, sociologists, economists, dentists, anthropologists, social assistants, and nutritionists—NESP has over the last five years gained wide experience in the areas of personnel training and technical cooperation in response to the needs of the region and Brazil as a whole as a result of the changes occurring in the health sector in Brazil. In this context, it is worth stressing NESP's experience with training courses geared to national and regional health sector directors in a number of critical areas, especially those involving the training of human resources, health planning, medicines, and health surveillance. It has also regularly offered a course on specialization in public health, the only one of its kind in this field, in Brasília.

NESP's location in Brasília gives it a number of special advantages, such as its proximity to the central bodies in Brazil's health system, the National Congress, international organizations and the government's external relations agencies, as well as the headquarters of the diplomatic representations in Brazil.

Consequently, there are certain natural areas for NESP's activities, such as technical cooperation with the Ministry of Health, the Ministry of External Affairs, and the Legislative Advisory and Studies Office, as well as the international aspects of health issues, whether handled by international organizations or in the context of bilateral relations.

NESP has already accumulated wide experience in such areas as legislative advice and technical cooperation on health policies with the National Congress and Ministry of Health, respectively, and in liaising with PAHO/WHO. The same circumstances of location led to the establishment in the University of Brasília of a department of international relations offering a graduate program in this area; in addition, it has for the last five years also offered a doctoral program in the area of comparative public policies as a joint undertaking of the Department of Sociology and Political Science and the Latin American School of Social Sciences (FLACSO).

In this context of ongoing interinstitutional relations, we propose more substantive linkages between the the University of Brasília's NESP, FLACSO, PAHO/WHO, the National School of Public Health and Oswaldo Cruz Foundation, and the Institute of Advanced Studies at the University of São Paulo, so that these institutions can act together to develop the international health program.

References

1. Macedo, Carlyle Guerra de. Salud en desarrollo: Nuevas alternativas para la integración regional en América. INTAL 164:2 (January-February 1991).

2. See the papers by Mario Rovere, "Dimensiones internacionales de la salud" [International dimensions of health], and Charles Godue, "La salud internacional: Un concepto en formación" [International health: A concept in formation], presented at the seminar-workshop on "International Health: A Field of Professional Study and Practice," at Quebec in March 1991.

3. See the article by Luciano Tomassini, "La cambiante inserción internacional de América Latina en la década de los ochenta" [The changing international position of Latin America in the 1980s], in *Pensamiento Iberoamericano*, No. 13 (January/June 1988), and Celso Lafer's article, "Dilemas da América Latina num mundo em transformação" [Latin American dilemmas in a changing world], in *Lua Nova, Revista de Cultura e Política* (São Paulo), No. 18 (August 1989).

4. See Jürgen Habermas, "A nova intransparência: A crise do estado de bem-estar social e o esgotamento das energias utópicas" [The new nonttransparency: The crisis of the welfare state and the exhaustion of utopian energies], in *Novos Estudos Cebrap* (São Paulo), No. 18 (September 1987). One of the most significant examples of the growth of collective action independent of the state in the area of health was the establishment

of international networks to fight AIDS, bringing together health professionals, groups of homosexuals, etc.

5. See Roberto Bouzas, "América Latina en la economía internacional: Los desafíos de una década perdida" [Latin America in the international economy: The challenges of a lost decade], in *Pensamiento Iberoamericano*, No. 13 (January-June 1988).

6. See André C. Medici, "Saúde e crise na América Latina" [Health and the crisis in Latin America—the social and political impact of adjustment], in *Revista de Administração Pública* (Rio de Janeiro) 23(3) (May/July 1989).

7. See the United Nations Economic Commission for Latin America and the Caribbean's *Transformación productiva con equidad* [Productive transformation with equity], Santiago, ECLAC, 1990.

8. Strategic personnel are those working at higher levels in state and international organizations in formulating policies, executing actions of a decisive long-term nature, and participating in the establishment of multilateral cooperation arrangements.

International Health: Approaches to Concepts and Practices

Paulo Marchiori Buss

Introduction

This is a very timely meeting, aiming as it does to exchange experiences and approaches to concepts and practices in the field of international health.

Recent worldwide political and economic developments are pointing the way to significant changes in international relations and to a reordering of the connections and alliances between countries and regional blocks.

It would be difficult for the field of health to remain unaffected by these worldwide geopolitical and economic changes, given the high level of dependence of the health of populations on the economic, social, political, and cultural processes prevailing in whatever national or international contexts health issues are examined.

Our view of international health is basically a function of our understanding of what health is, the health/sickness process in society, and of the principles that should govern relations between nations.

I therefore decided to organize this presentation in two sections:

• An analysis and interpretation of a world in transformation as this century draws to a close;

• a view of the health/sickness process and of health organizations, as determining what I understand international health to be in conceptual terms as a field of study and practice and as an area for political action.

A changing world

As we reach the threshold of the twenty-first century we are witnessing formidable, worldwide economic and political changes. The internationalization of the world economy, the questioning of the modern nation state, and the widening of the enormous social disparities between nations and between social classes within nations are the most obvious signs of the processes now at work in the world.

The establishment of economic and political blocs such as a united Europe, the so-called Asian bloc, and the North American bloc is reordering world relations and having significant repercussions on the life of the populations of national states.

Meanwhile, a number of ethnic groups in Eastern Europe, the Middle East, Latin America, and Africa are demanding political autonomy within nation states.

These reaffirmations of ethnic and cultural identity, ideals of life, and the rights of citizenship are creating a great diversity of interests and conflicts running counter to the trend toward the establishment of supranational blocs in various parts of world.

The most obvious sign of the globalizing of the economy is the existence of multinational companies representing powerful economic interests and operating in different countries and market sectors. The multinationals' interests frequently conflict with those of national states, and at the very least with those of the working classes in the various countries in which they operate.

Paradoxically, when we speak of a world in transformation, we are referring to a world in which intolerable differences and imbalances are actually increasing. Political and cultural differences among countries are understandable since they are attributable to events during their individual histories and their interactions with other nations. But the most striking feature of current events is the worsening of inequality, especially in the economic and social spheres.

When we refer to a world in transformation, from Latin America to Africa, we are talking about the widening gulf between the rich and poor, between a rich world that is becoming richer and a poor world that is becoming poorer, with all the consequences that this entails.

Specifically as regards Latin America (and the third world in general), the international division of production has assigned that region the role of supplier of certain raw materials and agricultural products whose international prices are subject to manipulation, with the tragic consequences that one might expect: geometric expansion of external debt to finance imports and a nascent industrialization and modernization of infrastructure; a brutal degree of income concentration in the hands of the "new captains of industry", i.e., that section of the national bourgeoisie that has allied itself with international capital; intensified concentration of land ownership in the hands of agroexport companies, and the migration of large sections of the rural population to medium and large cities and metropolitan regions, with predictable consequences for living conditions and health.

The import substitution strategy recommended in the 1960s, which was to be implemented by industrialization, has become fragmented; industrial sectors were established in some Latin America countries, but they did not constitute a real, modern, competitive industrial base or create a domestic market able to sustain the process. On the contrary, the dispossessed masses have increased, and unemployment and underemployment have isolated workers, women, and children from the market and society. In Brazil, for example, income concentration was beating all records at the end of the 1980s, with 1% of the economically active population receiving 15.5% of total national remuneration from labor, while the poorest 10% received only 0.7%. Likewise, while the richest 5% received 38.4% of national income, the poorest 80% received only 9.6%.[5]

During the 1980s the already poor region of Latin America was a net exporter of striking amounts of capital, representing increasing proportions of gross domestic product, to the rich countries in the form of debt service obligations. Thus an internal economic process producing profound social inequalities was compounded by the hemorrhage of resources generated in the region.

The total debt of the developing world is more than US$1 trillion. In most countries annual payments of interest and principal exceed flows of new external funds, absorbing some 25% (if not more) of the export receipts of the developing countries.[10]

Meanwhile, over the last 10 years the real prices of the principal commodities produced by the developing world have fallen some 30%.[10]

Brazil alone paid its creditors—official and private banks—the remarkable sum of US$101.7 billion between 1983 and 1988. Even more astonishing is the fact that during that period Brazil's external debt actually increased from US$85.4 billion to US$112.7 billion. This absurdity is mostly attributable to floating rate loans, on which the interest payable, thanks to the policy adopted by the U.S. Treasury to finance its own deficits, rose from 6% a year to 8%, 12%, 15%, and even a maximum of 16% during the period.[2] Similar situations occurred in Mexico, Argentina, and Venezuela.

Yet at the same time these countries had no funds to finance basic sanitation (water and sewerage) or education, for example, or health services for tens of millions of people in major urban centers, victims of the perverse international division of production that imposes on certain countries monocultures for export and "dirty," polluting, second-rank industries.

Are these not "pathogenic processes" which should be strongly denounced at the international level? Should international health not be concerned about them? The serious economic crisis in the developing countries, along with political events in many parts of the world, such as Eastern Europe, is exacerbating a phenomenon that is having wide-ranging social, economic, political, cultural, and health-related repercussions, namely, migrations among countries and even within countries.

This mobility of populations not only brings with it the spread of diseases and pathogenic agents but also has serious consequences for health systems in the countries concerned, which makes it a pertinent issue for the field of international health.

Meanwhile, according to the World Food Council of the United Nations,[1] world food production as a whole has increased at an annual rate of around 3.2%, while world population has risen approximately 2.1% a year. Furthermore, the current grain reserve is the largest ever known. All the large food-exporting countries, such as the USA, European Community, Canada, Australia, Brazil, and Argentina increased their food production in almost every year of the past decade, the major exception being the Soviet Union. Other large countries, such as China and India, have substantial grain reserves, as on a smaller scale do various areas of South America, Asia, and the Indian subregion.

These economic data are closely linked to the issue of health, since we are well aware of the serious food and nutrition problems affecting hundreds of millions of people in very many countries around the world. In Southeast Asia there are more than 50 million malnourished children, despite the food surplus in that region. In Latin America there are 25 million malnourished children, although our region has become the largest food exporter in the world after the United States.[10]

One in three Africans suffers from hunger, according to the Food and Agriculture Organization, which also denounces the fact that the number of malnourished persons in Africa rose 27% during the 1980s.[1]

What a strange "world in transformation" this is, incapable, despite the relative abundance of food, of feeding the highest species in the so-called "food chain" and the animal kingdom!

The same pages in the newspapers that tell us about military expenditure in the Gulf War (and which were justifying the arms industry) bring us the tragic news of the devastation caused by famine and misery: In the province of Manica, in the center of Mozambique, more than 500,000 risk dying of hunger as a result of the worst drought in 40 years, which has destroyed most of the harvest.[6] Maybe the resources that were spent on a few "hours of bombing" in the Gulf War could resolve the problems of that group forever. The developing world spends some 30% more on the military than on education and health combined. Recent cuts in government expenditure have also fallen most heavily on health and education.[11]

The World Bank, in its World Development Report for 1990, whose basic theme was poverty, notes that one billion people live below the poverty line in developing countries; in other words, they earn less than US$370 per head per year.[12]

A review of the literature also indicates that the best strategy for reducing poverty quickly and on a large scale should have two elements: economic growth that ensures the productive use of the labor of the poorest groups *under acceptable safety conditions*, and the provision of basic social services, including *health and sanitation*, to those earning less than US$370 a year. The World Bank's report also warns that although national policies are critical to reducing poverty, *this will not occur without international assistance*.

It therefore seems indisputable that health conditions worldwide will not change significantly until the economic gulf separating the poor countries from the rich countries is closed. Certain small advances may be made in particular areas by expanding access to certain health technologies through the generalized use of oral rehydration or certain vaccines. But global improvement in health conditions will only occur when human wealth is more equitably divided among countries and, within countries, among social classes and groups.

International health: some questions about concepts and practices

The concept of international health has been applied in different contexts according to the views of authors or institutions about the health/sickness process, society, and international relations.

This is very apparent when one examines the concepts and practice of international health found in textbooks and scientific articles, or the programs of academic institutions, international agencies of countries, or multilateral organizations.

Biological reductionism of the health/sickness process is responsible for many concepts and practices that give pride of place to "tropical diseases" as the focus of the production of knowledge or of teaching, assistance, and action programs. In an entirely opposite camp are those notions that identify international health exclusively with the area of law and the international health code. Still other concepts, leading to educational and research activities and action programs, reduce international health to technical cooperation and assistance among countries or among institutions in different countries, or to courses in public health attended by students from different countries.

Another current connotation identifies international health with underdeveloped countries and with poor, marginal groups who are *destined* to suffer from diseases. We already know with certainty that there is no mechanical, necessary relationship between the level of economic development and community health conditions, which thus contradicts the pathological inevitability of "average poverty." Rather, the determining factor is the social relations of production prevailing in the society.[7]

There are evidently, other viewpoints and frameworks resulting in specific views and approaches to the problem of international health. The survey by Godue[4] contains an interesting summary of a number of interpretations which quickly reveal the attitude and technical-scientific posture of the institutions and authors studied.

Perhaps international health covers all this and much more as well. One basic question pertains to the standpoint from which the problems and practices of agencies and individual actors in the area of international health are examined.

Most of the "donor" countries, agencies, and individuals providing cooperation and action programs and education clearly "simplify," in general terms, the realities in the so-called underdeveloped countries "receiving" these actions. In practice, "tropical reductionism," i.e., a particular view of the "unhealthy tropics" and the programs generally proposed as a result, conceals an enormous ignorance of the complexity and challenges of Latin American and African societies. Immersed in economic considerations, discussed briefly in the previous section, many of these protagonists are expressing the "epidemiological transition" so well described by Omran[8] at the beginning of the 1980s and more recently elaborated in concrete economic and social terms, e.g., for Mexico by Frenk, Bobadilla, and others[3] and for Brazil by Possas,[9] to mention but two examples.

The complexity of their health systems, which are real "Belíndias"—i.e. a mixture of Belgium and India, a term coined by the well-known Brazilian economist Edmar Bacha—containing, paradoxically, both the problems of underdevelopment and those resulting from industrialization and urbanization, represents an incomprehensible challenge to the simplistic concepts of many agencies and actors.

For these are enormous health systems, with critical problems in all sectors and components, ranging from the logistics of the operation of simple local services to the most difficult and intricate challenges in the area of financing and involving dimensions different from those more traditionally associated with international health.

It may even be essential for Latin American teachers and researchers to work in the faculties and agencies of the developed countries in the region, a process which should be recommended and encouraged so as to ensure greater attention to issues and programs oriented toward Latin America.

The very nature of the health/sickness process, understood as a social and historical process, with its concepts and theoretical and methodological features so well expressed in the Latin American concept of social medicine,[1] has been given very little attention in international health programs of any kind.

This same current of thought in social medicine has pointed to inequities in social relationships as undeniable pathogenic and anti-ethical factors. In addition, we are all well aware how iniquitous are the political and economic relations between the developed and underdeveloped countries. Political and economic processes are having a decisive impact on individuals and the environment. For example, when a country prevents a multinational company from establishing a polluting industry on its own territory but does nothing when the same company sets up in another country—generally an economically dependent country—it is acting unethically and producing both environmental contamination and inequity.

The process of work itself and the arrangements for protecting workers differ in a multinational company between the "mother company" and its subsidiaries in the third world. The labor movement has denounced this situation, but governments and international organizations have been much less interested.

Where relations between countries are concerned, it is very clear that economic issues and interests predominate over ethical and humanitarian considerations and international solidarity.

This fundamental issue must be addressed if we are to be able to define the scope of international health, in terms of its content, action, and doctrinal base.

With all its actors engaged in rational economic activities, our world is losing any notion that life on our planet is indivisible and that the possibility of survival depends on explicit collective action among humans, countries and regions. We know very well, for example, that

---

[1] I will mention only some of the many authors who have distinguished themselves in this area of thinking: Breilh and Granda, in Ecuador; Donnangelo, Cordeiro, Fleury, Paim, Nunes, Luz and many others in Brazil; Testa, Bloch, and Belmartino, in Argentina; Laurell, in Mexico, and Franco and Trujillo in Colombia.

environmental damage in one part of the planet has uncontrollable consequences for distant regions apparently unrelated to it.

Joint action is now essential at the international level to preserve a healthy environment which can maintain life on our planet and give communities of human beings the living conditions enabling them to fulfill their potential for a healthy, productive existence.

These notions are either being forgotten or are ridiculed as "purely ideological." We must, then, revive the ideas of *utopia and solidarity* to establish a base on which we can construct a proposal for studies, activities, and political action in international health. Worldwide "political action" is required of those engaged in international health so that they add their voices to those who are fighting for a global reordering of relations between countries and among human beings in which social, environmental, and planetary issues are given priority over the reductionist economic view of development.

The role of international health, as a discipline, is to study and point out to world society and governments the pathogenic social, economic, political, and cultural elements that are identified in the process of relations between countries, even if in their initial formulation they appear to be naive or impracticable positions. One might well ask:

• how in the world could it have been imagined two or three decades ago that there would today be such a high "ecological awareness"?

• who could have imagined two or three decades ago the truce that now exists between the superpowers?

Likewise, it is possible that the enormous increase in information about the links between living conditions, economic and political relations among countries, and health will be reflected in worldwide political pressure from social and political movements for "pro-health" measures of international scope which at present we cannot imagine. Such measures would join economic incentives for the development and international transfer of health-promoting technologies, measures to prevent harmful economic processes and practices, economic incentives to redistribute world food stocks, and differential treatment for such issues as the external debt of countries which increase their investments in health and education, etc.

Meanwhile, the political survival of the current international power structure depends on reorganizing relations among countries. In this process the question of health will certainly be relevant, since it represents an individual and collective good that is almost universally accepted in different cultures and political systems.

In conclusion, I will list a partial and incomplete range of areas and topics that should be incorporated in training programs in international health:

- The various notions of international health and its reconceptualization.
- The major social, political, economic, and cultural issues in the world and their expression in terms of health.
- Political, social, economic, and cultural processes and health in different social contexts.
- International solidarity and bioethics reconceptualized as a paradigm of international health.
- International health as a political issue and its expression in social movements and by political parties and actors within countries and at the international level (the European Parliament, Union of Latin American Parliamentarians, etc.).
- Sectoral health issues and their expression in the discipline of international health.
- Migratory flows between countries and their consequences for the health of populations and international health.
- Hunger and the process of the worldwide production, distribution, and marketing of food.
- The question of the environment as an international health problem: polluting multinational industries; exports of toxic residues; the activities of the health sector in relation to the world environment, and other issues.
- The question of health technology: production, transfer among countries, patents.
- The organization of health services and systems: models.
- Health problems of international scope: parasitic diseases and health surveillance.
- The expression of the main international health issues in international health law and human rights.
- International organizations: their role, past activities, and prospects. Integration as a strategy to realize the potential of activities. The role of the United Nations in defining rules for "healthy" coexistence among countries.

References

1. Adas, M. *A fome: crise ou escândalo.* São Paulo, Moderno, 1991.

2. Cardoso, Sen. Fernando H., rapporteur of the Committee on the External Debt of the Brazilian Congress. Brasília, Anais do Senado Federal.

3. Frenk, J., J. L. Bobadilla, et al. Health transition in middle-income countries: new challenges for health care. *Health Policy and Planning* 4(1):29-39.

4. Godue, Charles. La salud internacional: un concepto en formación. Conference document, 29 pages, presented at the Quebec meeting, 1991.

5. Instituto Brasileiro de Geografia e Estatistica. *Pesquisa nacional por amostragem de domicílios.* Brasília, Instituto Brasileiro de Geografia e Estatistica, 1989.

6. *Jornal do Brasil,* February 3, 1991, p. 13.

7. Laurell, A. C. La Salud-enfermedad como proceso social. *Revista Latinoamericana de Salud* (Mexico City) 2:7-25, 1982.

8. Omran, A. R. The epidemiologic transition: a theory of the epidemiology of population change. *Milbank Memorial Fund Q* 49:509-38, 1971.

9. Possas, C. *Epidemiologia e sociedade: Heterogeneidade estrutural e saúde no Brasil.* São Paulo, Hucitec-ABRASCO, 1989.

10. United Nations Children's Fund. *Situação mundial da infância.* 1989.

11. World Bank. *World Development Report, 1988.*

12. World Bank. *World Development Report, 1990.*

Technology Transfer and the International Health Profession

Paul F. Basch

The World Health Organization's target date for *Health For All* will be reached in the year 2000, less than a decade from now. That year will mark the end of the present decade, century, and millennium, and can serve as a convenient nodal point for projecting our interests to the future. Persons now studying international health will be at an early point in their careers in the year 2000: How can they best be prepared for professional leadership in the increasingly interdependent and interactive world of the future? What will be the major concerns of international health workers? In particular, how will the field be transformed by the development, transfer, and application of technology?

The technology we use in large part determines the pattern of our daily lives and the productivity of our work. Every familiar product, from bread to breadboards, from pencils to penicillin, and every useful procedure and method was once a technological innovation that has since become widespread.

The application of technology helps human beings:
1) To identify, gather, and modify useful resources from their environment;
2) To protect themselves from the many hostile aspects of that same environment;
3) To obtain and transform the materials needed to express their creativity, and
4) To escape from the limitations imposed by their physical strength and their five senses.

Technology does these things in a cumulative way, as each advance builds on those that preceded it. Since the earliest settlements and civilizations the only human activities that have progressed without significant interruption have been science and technology. Considering the broad range of its concerns, our chosen specialty of international health seems particularly sensitive to technologies of all kinds which may impinge on health, on the operation of health services, and on the creation and implementation of policy. So-called "medical technology" is defined by the Office of Technology Assessment (OTA) of the U.S. Congress as "the set of techniques, drugs, equipment, and procedures used by health care professionals in delivering medical care to individuals and the systems within which such are delivered."

The foreseeable future

Not long ago I was in Cairo on an assignment concerning control of schistosomiasis in Egypt. Evidence of this disease is found in mummies from the thirteenth century B.C., and today it is considered the Number One public health problem of Egypt. It seems credible, then, that schistosomiasis will continue to be present at least for the coming few years. The same assumption may be made for other durable issues such as population increase and environmental deterioration. By the same token, the new is likely to be inherently less predictable because it has a briefer record and seems relatively unstable. I am writing these words on a laptop computer: a few years ago I could not have done this, and a few years from now my machine may well be considered a museum piece, to be replaced by something far better. Can we extrapolate the epidemiologic situation for relative novelties such as AIDS to ten or a hundred years hence with the same degree of confidence as for schistosomiasis?

Predictability is not always in accordance with the apparently obvious. For example, smallpox was present in the world from the most ancient times until quite recently, and it disappeared in the blink of an eye, using technology of the Nineties (actually, the 1790s).

Technology forecasting. Although notoriously unreliable, technology forecasting is practiced because planners "have become increasingly aware of the need to anticipate technological change to reduce the risks and uncertainties associated with their decision-taking and planning activities."[11] These authors of this statement point out that "Short term forecasts tend to be overly optimistic about what might be accomplished. Long term projections, covering several decades, tend to be too conservative in their estimations of what technology might achieve and of the social changes deriving from such achievements."

Health-related inputs and outputs

To help us try to predict the decisive international health issues of the future, we can treat the world as if it were a big computer and ask in appropriate microelectronic jargon: what are the health-related inputs, what are the outputs, and what happens in the central processing unit which converts the one to the other?

The inputs

The actual health situation in any place and time is determined by the interplay of many elements, some local, some universal. These factors, mentioned here in briefest outline, must be taken into account if the work of international health professionals is to be truly significant:

Demographic. The human population changes continually, not only in number but in proportionate age structure. The survival to adulthood of 85% or 90% of children born in developing countries, plus increased longevity, is leading to a higher median age of the population, a predictable increase in prevalence of chronic health conditions, and a realignment of priorities.

Ethnic. Local populations vary in their genetic makeup and in culturally determined viewpoints and behaviors (for example, about child rearing) that can affect the incidence of certain conditions.

Epidemiologic. The mix of agents and illnesses is always changing: as smallpox vanished, AIDS appeared. Gastric ulcers decline and cancer of the cervix increases. Despite great efforts, measles refuses to be eradicated in the United States, and epidemics of pertussis, cholera, and kala-azar continue to occur.

Environmental. Climatic conditions vary in place and time. Floods, droughts, earthquakes, typhoons, and other natural disasters occur with some regularity. Resources are bring depleted and pollution of air, water, and soil is becoming more widespread. Industrial accidents induce unknown types and numbers of adverse health effects.

Economic. Disposable incomes drop or rise in different areas. The cost of health services increases everywhere, and officials struggle to develop financing and cost-containment plans. The debt crisis in many developing countries forces cutbacks in health and medical services.

Political. Governments and social policies may change. Medical care systems become reorganized. War and civil strife generate many refugees.

Behavioral. The use of tobacco, alcohol, and narcotic drugs may spread or diminish; family violence and trauma may result.

Technologic. All technologies and their products can have effects—positive or negative—on individual and public health.

The "central processing units" for international health

From the real world in which everything is related to everything else, the health inputs listed above are integrated, interpreted into definable pieces, and denominated as issues. Child Survival. Safe Motherhood. Occupational Health. Health Care Cost Recovery. Equity. Sustainability. How are these subjects identified, defined, and differentiated out of the seamless whole of human existence? How do we know that the tribal customs of the international health community generate a product that really corresponds to objective reality? If the same world were divided into different compartments, would that give us better leverage for improving whatever it is that we call health?

Some international health professionals see the world's major health problems primarily as technical ones, soluble by generous applications of science and technology. To others, ill health is grounded in poverty, injustice, ignorance, and prejudice, and can be improved only by directed changes in the social and economic orders. Some see the best solution in primary health care and argue whether it should be selective or comprehensive; some prefer vertical programs, others like them horizontal. By any strategy, health problems are viewed as resolvable or at least ameliorable; for if they are not, there seems little point in making great efforts in this field.

The particular approach taken is often guided by the outlook of individuals in positions of influence in academia, private voluntary organizations, and bilateral and multilateral official agencies, which influences the directions taken by their organizations. The great American foundations provide many examples: the John D. and Catherine T. MacArthur Foundation of Chicago has decided to support high-technology basic biological research on parasites; the Edna McConnell Clark Foundation of New York has shifted its tropical disease emphasis from schistosomiasis to blindness; the Pew Charitable Trusts support health policy studies and transfer of new technologies for diseases to third-world countries; Pew and the Carnegie Corporation of New York have a binational maternal and child health project with Mexico; and the Rockefeller Foundation supports international epidemiology centers, among other things. There are good and defensible reasons for such decisions: the degree of improvement that can reasonably be expected from applying the resources available (the impact factor); the existence of some realistic means with which to confront the problem (the technology factor), or identification of problems that are not "spoken for" by other groups (the turf factor).

Some persons, primarily in academic, industrial, or government offices and laboratories, see the same input elements as a challenge to their ingenuity and strive to produce a physical product such as a vaccine or device, or an intellectual product such as a computer program, which is intended to alleviate an international health problem. Still others may see new applications for controlling tropical disease vectors in the characteristics of existing materials such as agricultural pesticides. In each case there is some element of technology ripe for transfer from one country to another.

The outputs

In coming decades the attention of international health professionals will be directed to both classical and emerging problems and daily work will be carried out using both conventional and novel tools. The customary issues of maternal and child health, specific disease control programs, health education, nutrition, family planning, equity in distribution of health services, and so on will remain with us.

I believe that in the near future greater attention will be given to the following areas:
1) The health of adults and its relation to national development and economic productivity; and the associated issues of
2) Occupational health;
3) Aging of populations and provision of services to the elderly;
4) Financial aspects of providing health services, particularly their efficiency and effectiveness, and novel financing and cost-recovery schemes;
5) Environmental health, including pollution in various forms; and
6) The application of technology, particularly of developments in genetic engineering and immunology. Innovative methods and products will be promoted to prevent infectious and parasitic diseases, and greater attention will be given to hormonal and immunologic control of fertility.

As with all other fields, international health is being revolutionized by computers for writing and data management, by fax machines and modems for instant communication, by camcorders and VCRs for making field "notes" and providing information to the public, and by other miracles of the microelectronic age. Whether we like it or not, these enabling and facilitating technologies shape the structure, control the functioning, and determine the outcome of our endeavors. As described by the Canadian visionary Marshall McLuhan, the medium is the message.

Understanding what we are doing. The field project, research study, methodology, or physical product that emerges from the mysterious central international health processing unit must be transferred to the receiving country and appropriately implemented before it can have an effect on the target population. A variety of techniques for project assessment, evaluation, and audit have become staples of the profession; indeed, an evaluation component is required *a priori* in the design of most overseas projects. The situation is not so clear with respect to technology, much of which appears to be transferred with little planning and without adequate post-transfer assessment.

A focus on health-related technology. Most observers will probably think first of "medical technology" more or less along the lines of the OTA definition given earlier. Still, it is hard to overestimate the impact on health of other technologies through their role in formal and informal education; communication; information gathering, transmission, and diffusion; record keeping, and data analysis. Similarly, biotechnology provides the promise of better health directly through vaccines against infectious diseases such as malaria and less directly through improved agriculture and animal husbandry.

Technology transfer. All innovations specifically intended to improve health involve the application of technology, often new or newly transferred, with undetermined repercussions within the context in which it is introduced. Technologies such as renal transplantation, CAT scanning, ELISA immunodiagnosis, or the use of synthetic growth hormone, considered routine in one environment, may be novelties in another. The many uncertainties inherent in transfer require some kind of objective analytic methodologies to help support decisions (1) for or against adoption of any particular technology, and (2) about how a technology will be deployed once adopted. Inherent uncertainties must be identified and measured to help anticipate the effects (including economic ones) likely to occur and to help ensure, insofar as possible, that the technology will be beneficial to the communities involved.

The scientific basis for acceptance of technology

The unidirectional transfer of health-related technologies from richer to poorer countries is not merely the exportation and importation of commodities, but demands a transfer of the scientific basis and understanding that underlie the apparatus, methods, and procedures. Sometimes the most appropriate technology for solving a health problem may be an advanced one; in other cases a simple one is called for. Until the transplanted technology takes root, becomes integrated into its new environment, and is viable on its own, it can not really be considered to be transferred—only transported.

The relationship between provider and user countries must be one of collaboration rather than dependence. Full exploitation of an imported technology requires the presence of a scholarly infrastructure sufficiently robust to master the technology and adapt it to local conditions. Absent a scientific basis, the receiving country can apply the technology only in a superficial and mechanical way. In the long term the transfer will not be viable and will result in continued dependence and a feeble indigenous capacity to solve local problems locally.

Building capacity in the receiving country's research environment

Varied projects to transfer technology have included the training of scientists and support staff in relevant methodologies, from the operation and maintenance of diagnostic hardware to the performance of complex techniques such as polymerase chain reactions, cell fusion for monoclonal antibody production, or cDNA library construction. While these abilities may be necessary in particular circumstances, the process of transferring technology must go further and help support the development of underlying scientific capability in user countries.

In one country which I visited, I was told with some derision by a local investigator that if they could, his laboratory staff would "come in at 10 and leave at 11." Such attitudes on the part of technicians are not easy to dispel in an atmosphere that places little value on their work, where chances for advancement are minimal, and where financial and psychological rewards are grossly insufficient. Although local regulations often make it difficult to provide adequate incentives, motivation can be enhanced by encouraging professional work patterns, reinforcing self-confidence, and building pride in fulfilling goals. Achieving objectives can be aided by defining and overcoming obstacles in the scientific environment, clearing bottlenecks to progress, and strengthening local scientific capabilities. An approach to this process is not only to provide appropriate advice and materials, but to facilitate the access of local investigators and students to world scientific literature, teach computer literacy, and stimulate discussion and intellectual curiosity about all sorts of scientific, ethical, and methodologic issues. This capacity building is costly and commonly neglected, but in the long run it is an essential part of technology transfer, and its absence may negate the potential of the most sophisticated science.

Technology assessment and decision making

The subject of technology assessment has developed a literature far too rich and diverse to be reviewed here. There are several generalized discussions of medical technology assessment, such as that of Banta and Behney,[1] the excellent small volume by Brorsson and Wall,[2] and the many publications of the U.S. Office of Technology Assessment (for example, one published in 1982[9]), the U.S. National Academy of Sciences,[4,8] the Pan American Health Organization,[10] and other agencies.

Predicted benefits of new technologies must be balanced against economic and other costs. The international health professional who is competent in this area can contribute to enlightened governmental decision making in the health sector. Developing-country governments must strive to obtain the maximum health benefit for diminishing amounts of money. At the same time, few individuals in Ministries of Health are prepared to deal with the complex issues involved in evaluating emerging health-related technologies. Decisions about applying technology are difficult to make because of their relative novelty, undefined cost-benefit-risk ratios, and unknown economic, environmental, epidemiologic, demographic, and cultural consequences. Related issues involve scientific and political control of the importation, adaptation, and diffusion of technology and the roles of academia, industry, foreign donor agencies, and intergovernmental organizations.

A critical view of technology transfer

Some people see the transfer and spread of technology as a threat rather than a benefit. Authors such as Illich[6] have suggested that most medical technology is uneconomical and counterproductive, even harmful. Such views, clearly out of favor with most national and international health establishments, should nevertheless be considered.

Halfdan Mahler, the former Director-General of WHO, has said that "In too many instances, health technology is selected by individuals whose professional goals bear little resemblance to societies' health needs, or it is accumulated in a fortuitous and haphazard fashion."[7] In contrast to the skeptics, suspicious of and hostile to every innovation, there are those who mistake novelty for progress without demanding evidence of actual utility. According to Mahler, "Technology for the sake of technology is a dangerous addiction-producing drug."[7]

The actual benefits to health of applying a technology may be ambiguous and difficult to assess. Administrators often point to the resources made available (number of physicians, nurses, hospital beds, amount of money, and so forth) or the number of procedures or services provided, but these have little to do with the increase in health provided to a population. Mortality and morbidity indicators may come somewhat closer to demonstrating health impact, but they lack information about any improvement in the *quality* of life resulting from a technology, which after all is the main purpose of the entire enterprise.

Greenwood and coworkers[5] have shown that in the Gambia, West Africa, the proportion of fully immunized infants is actually greater than in the United Kingdom, and infant mortality from the six immunizable diseases covered by the Expanded Program on Immunization (EPI)— diphtheria, pertussis, tetanus, polio, measles, and tuberculosis—is relatively low. Although cause-specific mortality from EPI's immunizable diseases has declined dramatically, the overall infant mortality rate in the Gambia remains about 10 times that in Great Britain, primarily from malaria, acute respiratory infections, chronic diarrhea, and neonatal causes not covered by the immunizations. While EPI officials point to the success of their program, others remain unconvinced.[3]

Each technology must be considered independently for suitability in each application, like a key and a lock. A key that works in one lock may not be in others. Some keys are masters, opening many different doors, while others have highly limited use. The same is true of technologies, depending on the specific goals and objectives of those who implement them. Some technologies, such as childhood immunizations, have received widespread endorsement, but even these must be reviewed periodically in each country. For centuries smallpox vaccine was considered highly beneficial, until transmission diminished to the point that the adverse effects of the vaccine posed a greater risk than the disease itself. That particular technology then became unacceptable.

Relation to training needs in international health

For anyone who will function in the international health sphere of the future, the basic principles of public health will remain the same as they are now. Similarly, the fundamentals of biostatistics and epidemiology are invariant. A solid grounding in these essentials will always be necessary and must be relearned by each generation of scholars. On the other hand, investigational and presentational technology will provide ever greater capabilities as more focused and specific laboratory techniques and statistical software packages appear without let. While this is generally beneficial, there is a danger that individuals may become seduced by their tools and begin to believe that the gel or the computer is the subject of their investigation, rather than control of *Plasmodium* transmission and improving health in the community.

All students of international health utilize various technologies in their own education and research. Many will engage at a casual and perhaps subconscious level in the international transfer of technology while doing their own work, and a few may build a career specifically around this subject.

Those of us engaged in the teaching of international health recognize that science and technology will play an even greater part in the world of the future. The transfer, diffusion, and implementation of health-related technology is highly relevant, is likely to become increasingly prominent, and should find a place in the consciousness of every practitioner of international health. Not only the presumed benefits, but the potential costs, risks, and consequences must be discussed thoroughly and realistically. This does not mean that all international health professionals must be specialists in this area, but that they should have at least a general acquaintance with the subject. It therefore seems reasonable that international health teaching programs should include formal course work on the international transfer and assessment of technologies that affect health.

References

1. Banta, H. D., and C. J. Behney. Technology assessment. *In:* J. M. Last (ed.), *Maxcy-Rosenau Textbook of Public Health and Preventive Medicine.* 12th ed. Norwalk, Connecticut, Appleton-Century-Crofts, 1986. Pp. 1809-1829.

2. Brorsson, B., and S. Wall. *Assessment of medical technology: Problems and methods.* English edition. Stockholm, Swedish Medical Research Council, 1985.

3. Goodfield, J. *A chance to live: The heroic story of the global campaign to immunize the world's children.* New York, Macmillan, 1991.

4. Goodman, C. *Medical technology assessment directory.* Washington, D.C., Council on Health Care Technology, Institute of Medicine, National Academy of Sciences, 1988.

5. Greenwood, B. M., A. M. Greenwood, A. K. Bradley, A. Tulloch, R. Hayes, and F. S. J. Oldfield. Deaths in infancy and early childhood in a well-vaccinated, rural, West African population. *Ann Trop Paed* 7:91-99 (1987).

6. Illich, I. *Medical nemesis.* New York, Pantheon, 1976.

7. Mahler, H. Social policy for health development and health development for social progress. Address to the WHO Regional Committee for the Eastern Mediterranean, Karachi, Pakistan, 1976.

8. National Academy of Sciences. *Assessing medical technologies.* Washington, National Academy Press, 1985.

9. U.S. Congress. Office of Technology Assessment (OTA). *Strategies for medical technology assessment.* OTA Publication OTA-H-181. Washington, OTA, 1982.

10. Panerai, R. B., and J. Peña-Mohr. *Health technology assessment methodologies for developing countries.* Washington, D.C., Pan American Health Organization, 1989.

11. Saren, M. A., and D. T. Brownlie. *A review of technology forecasting techniques and their application.* Bradford, England, MCB University Press, 1983.